Praise for *All Things Must Fight to Live*

"Mealer is a gifted writer who reports his harrowing experiences with humility and humanity." **—Greg Houle, African Update**

"The country's agonies are far from over, but, in Bryan Mealer's new book *All Things Must Fight to Live*, they now at least have their definitive account . . . It is Mealer's gift that even when he is covering what is, journalistically, well-worn territory—the fog of war, the addictive and atrophied life of a combat reporter—his writing is not only fresh but empathetic . . . With the maturity and talent he displays in this book, Mealer could have a dazzling future as a chronicler of distant lands. He has already set a new standard by which all correspondents might approach other forgotten wars."

—*Time*

"Gorgeous, heartbreaking, and redemptive. Bryan Mealer has given us a story of a people and a land nearer to our hearts than we know. An immensely honest job of reporting, wonderfully told by a writer who feels as much as he sees."

—Robert Kurson, author of *Shadow Divers*

"Vivid prose and compelling emotion . . . [Mealer] recalls the feared Cobra commander of boy soldiers who held sway by the belief in magic, and the soldiers, dressed in wigs and prom gowns, committing unbelievable atrocities. He also reports his own 'creeping emotional atrophy' as he is repulsed and then spellbound by the violence and by the courageous people who struggled to make sense of the fighting." **—*Booklist***

"Bryan Mealer has put his life on the line to bring us a story of terror and courage from the heart of Congo. It's already an accomplishment just to go to such a place; to return with such a powerful and important story is rare indeed. Both as a journalist and as a reader, my hat's off to Mealer."

—**Sebastian Junger, author of** *The Perfect Storm*

"Goes a long way toward making the phrase 'dark continent' the anachronism that it should be." —*Minneapolis City Pages*

"Mealer spent three years in this shattered land, and his book is a perceptive, empathetic, stomach-twisting presentation of the human condition during chaos . . . Mealer's book is a quiet paean to the courage he has witnessed, and its final salute to 'the many proud people of Congo' is as much eulogy as affirmation."

—*Publishers Weekly*

"One has to be young and perhaps a touch mad to voluntarily travel, as Bryan Mealer has, by foot, boat, barge, bicycle, rickety airplane, and a train that goes off the rails, through one of the most violent places on earth. But a sane and cautious person would not have been able to bring back the vivid and tragic stories he has, from what is by far the world's bloodiest—and most underreported—zone of conflict."

—**Adam Hochschild, author of** *King Leopold's Ghost*

ALL THINGS MUST FIGHT TO LIVE

Stories of War and Deliverance in Congo

Bryan Mealer

BLOOMSBURY

New York   Berlin   London

For Ann Marie, my parents, and my sisters

Copyright © 2008 by Bryan Mealer
Afterword copyright © 2009 by Bryan Mealer

All rights reserved. No part of this book may be used or reproduced in any manner whatsoever without written permission from the publisher except in the case of brief quotations embodied in critical articles or reviews. For information address Bloomsbury USA, 175 Fifth Avenue, New York, NY 10010.

Published by Bloomsbury USA, New York

All papers used by Bloomsbury USA are natural, recyclable products made from wood grown in well-managed forests. The manufacturing processes conform to the environmental regulations of the country of origin.

Portions of this book have appeared in *Harper's* magazine in slightly different form.

Map on p. viii by Joyce Pendola.

LIBRARY OF CONGRESS CATALOGING–IN–PUBLICATION DATA IS AVAILABLE.

ISBN-10: 1-59691-345-2 (hardcover)
ISBN-13: 978-1-59691-345-5 (hardcover)

First published by Bloomsbury USA in 2008
This paperback edition published in 2009

Paperback ISBN-10: 1-59691-626-5
ISBN-13: 978-1-59691-626-5

1 3 5 7 9 10 8 6 4 2

Typeset by Westchester Book Group
Printed in the United States of America by Quebecor World Fairfield

Suffer, suffer for world. *Amen!*
Enjoy for heaven. *Amen!*

—Fela Kuti, "Suffering and Smiling"

CONTENTS

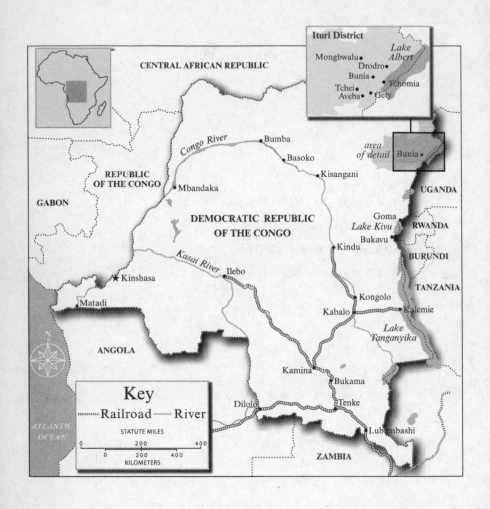

Ituri District

Mongbwalu●
Drodro●
Bunia●
Tchei●
Aveba● ●Gety
●Tchomia
Lake Albert

area of detail Bunia●

CENTRAL AFRICAN REPUBLIC

Congo River
Bumba●
Basoko●
Kisangani●

REPUBLIC OF THE CONGO
Mbandaka●

GABON

DEMOCRATIC REPUBLIC OF THE CONGO

UGANDA

Goma●
Lake Kivu
Bukavu●
Kindu●

RWANDA

BURUNDI

Kasai River
Ilebo●

★ Kinshasa

Matadi●

Kongolo●
Kabalo● ●Kalemie

TANZANIA

Lake Tanganyika

ANGOLA

Kamina●

Bukama●

Dilolo●
●Tenke

Lubumbashi●

Key
·········· Railroad ── River

STATUTE MILES
0   200   400
0   200   400
KILOMETERS

ATLANTIC OCEAN

ZAMBIA

INTRODUCTION

We went in first with soldiers, young and terrified Ugandan kids straight from the villages, whip-thin in their baggy fatigues and wound tight around their triggers even high above the clouds. The Ugandan army flew Antonov-26s into Congo, scrapped by the Soviet bloc and born again for African war, steel Trojan horses loaded with gun-mounted jeeps, barrels of diesel, and crates of banana moonshine. You found a place on the floor and instantly started sweating, nestled between rifles and rocket launchers so close to your eyeballs you could study the paint chips on the grenades. There was little cabin pressure to soothe the landings, and going in fast, you felt like your eyes would pop out of your skull. The soldiers buried their faces in their hats to hide the tears. And all you could do was wince and give a thumbs-up and be thankful the engines were so loud that no one could hear you scream.

Later on it was UN Air, the almighty "move-con," sleek, white 727s that floated in like flying nuns. Inside you were greeted by cordial South African blondes who served Coca-Cola and gave quiet comfort to the malaria evac whose IV drip hung from the overhead compartment. You could read a book or fade out with your headphones or lose yourself in the six hundred shades of green below. Coming in was normal enough, but after returning from the field still plugged into the war, stepping into those planes was like being dunked in pure oxygen, or finding your way to the mother ship after crossing a hostile, unsheltered land.

There were eleventh-hour charter flights and Airbus red-eyes, six-seater Cessnas and the French-army Hercules, where female crew members doled out pizza and left you feeling ashamed by your own filth. There were speedboats across the Congo River, old German warships that ferried you over Lake Tanganyika, and one guy I met rode all the way from Paris on a Honda four-stroke before the border guards rolled him clean.

There were journalists and aid workers, diplomats and diamond dealers, assorted opportunists, and third-world peacekeepers deputized and deployed into hell. You could guess the new guys by the way their eyes never left the window; sitting next to them always made me nervous. There were many ways of going in, and everyone had his own reasons. But when we arrived, there was always the same war. Many came simply to test themselves against the brutal country, and I've learned there is nothing wrong with that. What mattered was what kind of prints you left behind in the red dirt. Five centuries of those bootprints now packed the soil and snaked into the trees, so many they bled into one enormous trail that hid below the camouflage and slowly choked the land.

But get down close and you can see.

One of those trails was mine.

Chapter One

IN THE VALLEY OF THE GUN

I

For me, the war started with the sound of a horn.

On the morning of April 3, 2003, as dawn broke over the green hills of northeastern Congo, several hundred ethnic Lendu warriors gathered along the lip of a narrow valley overlooking the sleeping villages of Drodro, Largu, and Jissa. The villages were mainly occupied by members of the Hema tribe, who'd become archenemies of the Lendu in a macabre conflict hatched amid Congo's larger, ongoing war, which had swept across the vast nation in 1998 and already killed several million people.

The Lendu fighters carried AK-47s held together with duct tape and wire, rocket-propelled grenades, and mortar tubes strapped to their backs. Some had long spears with steel tips whittled to saw teeth, arrows dipped in poison, and broad machetes ground to a razor edge. They'd marched all night from their villages deep in the hills, trailing along their women, children, and elderly, who now gathered in the rear and waited for the signal. Finally it came: the low wail of a horn, of a warrior squeezing his air through the narrow bore of a bull's antler. And at the sound of the horn, the bottom dropped from the hills.

They came in three waves: the first rushed in behind a volley of machine-gun fire, rockets, and mortars. The mud-walled huts of the villages exploded and burst into flame as rocket fire and shrapnel ignited the thatched roofs. Villagers scrambled out of their homes and ran for the trees, only to find that every exit was blocked. Gunmen caught them in the open and cut them down with rifles, while others emptied their guns into the thin walls of homes, then torched the roofs.

The second wave moved through with spears, arrows, and machetes to finish off the wounded. Those found hiding amid the manioc and sugarcane were dragged to the street and their throats cut. The warriors pounced from body to body, their long blades painted with blood, shouting, "Come out, Hema! The Lendu have come!"

Those who managed to hide in the trees lived to watch the massacre unfold. One father watched a group of Lendu boys surround his six children in their yard. The boys carried machetes and AK-47s. One of them took a running kick at the smallest child, a six-month-old infant crawling in the yard. The blow sent the child straight into the air, like a deflated ball, and machete blades caught her tiny body on the way down. The warriors then dismantled the remaining five children in the yard.

Down the road, survivors kept still in their hiding spots while several warriors opened the chest of a dead man, cut out his heart, and ate, blood streaming down their wrists. Other fighters held severed arms over the burning rubble and picked at the charred meat with their fingers. As the warriors dispatched the living, the third wave, the Lendu elderly, women, and children, rounded up cattle in the nearby fields and looted the village food pantries.

Around eight A.M., a second horn sounded and the warriors melted back into the hills. That morning, over a dozen Hema villages and nearby settlements were raided and destroyed. Initial reports estimated nearly one thousand people were murdered in just under three hours.

At the time I was living in Nairobi, eight hundred kilometers to the east and a universe removed. I was two months out of New York

City and still mesmerized every time I stepped outside into all that sunshine. I'd moved to Kenya to find work as a freelance reporter and had been spending my days and nights with detectives patrolling the Nairobi slums, hunting the carjackers and thieves who made that city one of the scariest places I'd ever been. But few editors in the States seemed interested in my African cop saga, and after two months' work, I was going broke with nothing to show for it.

During my first week in town I'd made friends with the bureau chief of the Associated Press. Susan Linnee was a twenty-five-year veteran of the wires who'd seen her share of people like me, guys who rolled in with half a clue about the region and talked as if they were reading from an encyclopedia. But she graciously allowed me to use the bureau to make phone calls and use the computers and never once bristled at my inexperience or naïve comments.

In Congo, the news of the Drodro massacre took two days to travel seventy kilometers south to the small United Nations base in the town of Bunia. Susan received the news flash across the wire, and a few hours later I walked into the office from one of my patrols. She called me into her office.

"Have you ever been to Congo?" she said.

I shook my head.

"Do you know anything about Congo?"

I said no, nothing.

"Well, I'm sending Rodrique and Azim on a flight this afternoon."

"Okay."

"You should go with them, see how they work. It'll be a good experience for you."

She handed me an envelope with a plane ticket inside. I looked up, confused. Rodrique Ngowi and Sayyid Azim were seasoned staff who'd been to Congo many times; I had no connection with AP at all, other than loitering in their office.

"Pay me back when you can," she said. "I'm sure you can sell the story somewhere." I rushed home and packed a bag, then paused at the door before finally walking out. By evening, I was sitting in a hotel bar in Entebbe, Uganda, buzzing with paranoia about the morning departure. I thought of the map of Africa that had hung on the wall of my old apartment in New York. I'd marked the places I'd wanted to work, places in Ethiopia, Eritrea, along the Serengeti for the great migration. But Congo remained this green abyss, stitched by lost-looking rivers that snaked through bad jungle. Guys like me disappeared in places like that, I'd thought. There was a small television in the corner of the bar playing CNN, and while I sipped my beer, American tanks were rolling into Baghdad.

The Ugandan army had occupied Congo since 1998, when Uganda and Rwanda invaded the country to oust the Congolese president, Laurent Kabila. They still ran their flights in and out of Congo from the old Entebbe airport, the one that had been attacked by Israeli warplanes in the hostage rescue in 1976. The white concrete terminal remained chewed and peppered with bullet holes the size of golf balls. We piled into one of the old Antonovs parked on the tarmac, piloted by a ruddy, potbellied Ukrainian wearing white athletic socks and sandals. As we climbed the ladder, I saw he'd dismantled the landing gear and had it scattered across the tarmac like evidence at a crime scene. Inside the plane, the reporters and soldiers were pressed shoulder to shoulder. I found a seat on a stack of paint cans in the corner of the hold, and as we lifted off, the pile collapsed and doused the soldier next to me in thick, blue paint. He didn't even flinch, just clutched his rifle and watched the paint dribble down his leg and pool onto his boot. Forty-five minutes later, the pilot nose-dived into Bunia and we emerged into the white light, tears streaming down our cheeks and deaf from the noise.

Bunia was the regional capital of the Ituri district in the sprawling Oriental province, where seven thousand Ugandan soldiers were based. I'd expected Congo to be thick jungle and sucking humidity. But Bunia sat on the western rise of the Great Rift Valley, over twelve hundred meters above the forest, where the landscape was mostly grass-covered hills. The air was hot, but dry. And in the early mornings when the sun was right, the town's dust-choked boulevard looked as lonesome and lawless as in an old John Ford film.

The Ugandan soldiers were scattered throughout the hills of Ituri and, following the Drodro massacre, had moved several platoons to that village for security. The next morning their jeeps drove us the seventy kilometers north into the hills toward Drodro, a spine-shattering ride that took five hours over switchback roads that were rutted and washed from the rains. The soldiers were based at a redbrick Catholic mission tucked amid the trees, where about one hundred half-naked and hungry survivors had staggered from the bush for protection.

Inside the tiny mission clinic, the wounded were doubled up on beds and foam mattresses that lined the concrete floors. There was a woman who'd lost her leg to a machete, her eyelids fluttering like moth wings as she faded in and out from the pain, and a five-year-old boy with a necklace gash from ear to ear where the raiders had tried to take his head. The clinic had no real medicine, and inside the hot, airless chamber, the sickly-sweet smell of infection hung thick and syrupy. After half an hour my vision began to pixelate and I nearly fainted against the wall. I stumbled out into the fresh air and was sick in a nearby latrine, praying none of my colleagues had seen me run. I managed to go back and finish my interviews and came out with a decent story, one I sold to the *Chicago Tribune* for four hundred dollars—my first.

But I wasn't satisfied with just one story. One story had only lifted the lid, and down inside was this dark, forgotten war that grabbed hold and wouldn't let me go. By the time I flew back to Kenya two days later, all I could think about was going back to Congo.

★   ★   ★

5

In Nairobi, I tapped into AP's archives, borrowed books from friends, and began reading everything I could find. The war in Ituri between the Hema and Lendu was just another front in Congo's years-long war, a devastating conflict entirely orchestrated by outsiders. The war had initially been sparked by the 1994 genocide next door in Rwanda, when Hutu militia had massacred around eight hundred thousand ethnic Tutsi in just one hundred days. When Tutsi-led rebels finally crushed the genocide and took the capital, Kigali, tens of thousands of Hutu killers rushed over the border into the forested mountains of Congo. There they regrouped for further attacks on Rwanda.

Rwanda's new Tutsi-led government began accusing Congo's then dictator, Mobutu Sese Seko, of giving refuge to the rebels. In late 1996, Congolese rebels backed by Rwandan and Ugandan troops seized control of eastern Congo to exterminate the Hutu militia. And once they had a foothold in the east, they marched for seven months across the jungle to Kinshasa in the west and overthrew Mobutu, imposing the rebel leader Laurent Kabila as president. But once in power, Kabila alienated and ousted his Rwandan staff who'd put him in office. So in August 1998, Rwanda and Uganda invaded again with the help of neighboring Burundi, while Kabila mounted a firm defensive with troops from Zimbabwe, Namibia, Angola, Chad, and Burundian rebels.

The country eventually divided into three parts: the regions held by Kabila's government-allied forces; Rwandan-occupied areas shared with their Congolese rebel group Rally for Congolese Democracy (RCD); and the Ugandan-held territories controlled alongside their rebel groups Movement for Congolese Democracy (MLC) and an offshoot of the RCD called RCD-Kisangani. The mercurial allegiances of Rwanda, Uganda, and the government to their various rebel factions caused even greater turmoil and infighting. As a result, these groups splintered throughout the war and produced a dizzying list of acronyms like RCD-G, RCD-K/M, and RCD-N that filled several pages. But civilians were always caught in the middle no matter who was fighting, and over the next nine years, the war claimed over five million lives, most dying from sickness and hunger as they fled the fighting. The death toll from Congo's war would surpass that of any other conflict since World War II.

The armed groups fighting in Congo financed their stay largely by stealing the nation's minerals. The battlefields of eastern and central Congo were full of gold, diamonds, and other minerals such as coltan, which was in great demand to manufacture the cell phones and laptop computers for the dot-com boom of the West. The forests were lush with exotic wood, and the southern plains spilled with copper and cobalt just waiting to be dredged. By 2001, the Rwandan army was estimated to be earning nearly $20 million per month from stealing coltan, and the RCD rebels pulled in $1.5 million a month from diamonds. One rights group estimated Uganda exported over $60 million in Congolese gold in 2003 alone, most of it headed for Switzerland.

To administer their looting of gold, coltan, diamond, timber, and coffee, Uganda and Rwanda used these rebel groups as proxy forces to hold power. They trained them in jungle camps and flooded them with weapons, ultimately creating even more factions when those groups would splinter. And to hold sway over these groups, Rwanda and Uganda exploited the deep well of ethnic tensions that already existed among the tribes. In Ituri, the two foreign armies began salting the wounds between the Hema and the Lendu.

The Hema and the Lendu tribes of northeastern Ituri had lived in strained harmony near the Ugandan border for three hundred years. The Hema had crossed into Congo in the sixteenth century from Rwanda and Burundi, cattle herders who were closely related to the Tutsi of those regions, along with Hema and Banyoro tribes of Uganda. The Lendu were a mix of Nilotic and Bantu peoples, farmers and hunters, and one of the more populous tribes that mostly occupied the vast, remote hill country.

Mobutu had always favored the Hema. Like the Tutsi, they were the educated, landowning, and politically savvy elite. This favoritism had begun with Congo's Belgian colonialists, who'd rewarded Hema with large tracks of grazing land, jobs within the colonial government, and made extra efforts to educate their children—all of which alienated the Lendu, who were regarded as backward stock. During the chaotic last days of Mobutu, a wealthy Hema farmer in the Walendu Pitsu region of Ituri seized a large tract of Lendu land in a backroom deal with government officials and began evicting Lendu residents. The Lendu farmers could do little to stop him, since most of their deeds and documents had disappeared in the crumbling Mobutu empire.

So in 1999, the Lendu assembled their warriors and staged vigilante raids against Hema in the region, killing some ten thousand people in eighteen months. Hema militia then turned to the Ugandan army for help, using them as guns for hire against their enemies. Together, they slaughtered thousands of Lendu. In turn, the Ugandan army began arming the Hema militia to control the region's gold fields and other resources. When that relationship spoiled, the Ugandans backed the Lendu. Over the next several years, the number of slaughtered Hema and Lendu civilians exceeded fifty thousand—the death count spiking as warriors supplemented their spears and arrows with automatic rifles and RPG-7s supplied by their neighbors in the east. Mass killings of civilians like the massacre at Drodro, Largu, and Jissa had been happening in Ituri regularly, yet many were never investigated or even reported.

In July 2002, Rwanda and Congo signed a peace pact in Pretoria, South Africa, that ended the Rwandan army's active role in the conflict. Rwanda pulled its twenty thousand troops from Congo by October 2002, leaving Uganda as the last foreign army still operating in country. Soon after, Ugandan president Yoweri Museveni, under pressure from the international community, gave the orders for Uganda's remaining seven thousand troops to begin their slow exodus home.

The security of Ituri—still angry, factionalized, and armed to the teeth—would now be the job of UN peacekeepers, who'd soon arrive to replace the Ugandan soldiers. Peacekeepers already held positions in North and South Kivu, near the Rwandan border where the war had begun, but the UN had little presence in Ituri. Despite the grisly deaths of over fifty thousand people in the war between the Hema and the Lendu and their sponsors, the UN had only a small contingent of unarmed military observers in the vast area covering over four million people. Because the scale of Rwandan and Ugandan support of Hema and Lendu militias in Ituri was largely unknown until May 2003, many in the UN (and many of us journalists) still considered the conflict merely a "tribal war," with few links to Congo's larger multinational war.

The Ugandan army threw a big parade on April 25, 2003, as they began rolling out of Ituri. All across Bunia, shops closed early, and hundreds of sweaty bodies jammed both sides of the airport road to watch the soldiers march past. A thirty-piece army brass band stumbled through a lethargic rendition of the Ugandan national anthem, followed by a procession of armored personnel carriers, gun-mounted jeeps called "Mambas," and two rattletrap Russian tanks piled with dozens of gaunt, whooping soldiers. The traffic made the dust unbearable, and when the tanks sputtered past, they coated the reeling crowd with an aerosol of hot engine grease.

As several companies of soldiers took up the rear of the parade—weathered Kalashnikovs dangling at their hip, gum boots slapping the yellow dirt—young girls rushed out and loaded them with cigarettes, boiled eggs, and bags of peanuts. Farther up the road, groups of women spit at their feet and shouted for them to just go away. The parade was a colossal event, never mind the size, for it marked the ending of a brutal period of foreign occupation and, much to our collective fear, also kicked off a brand-new era of viciousness and murder.

Anticipating the Ugandan withdrawal, hundreds of fighters, both Hema and Lendu, were gathering in the hills outside Bunia, waiting for the perfect moment to seize the prize. Bunia was already an embattled spoil of war, occupied by several rebel factions over the years who'd vigorously fought to hold it. It was a nexus of trade routes in and out of Uganda, both overland and across Lake Albert, thirty kilometers to the east. Bunia essentially connected the Oriental province to East Africa and Asia, and Lake Albert itself provided a flourishing fish trade. Bunia had a functioning airport, a sprawling and healthy market, and most of all, the hills around Bunia were filled with gold.

Many of the once-nationalized gold mines in the hills north of Bunia, located near the towns of Mongbwalu and Kilo, were seized by Uganda or Rwandan-backed militia when the second war began in 1998, with miners forced to dig for the militia or to pay entry fees in gold or taxes. Alluvial gold is also bountiful in the streambeds of the Shari River on Bunia's outskirts, which provide many local men their living. The tumbledown wooden shacks of gold dealers lined Bunia's main boulevard. Prospectors in mud-crusted clothes filed in with gold dust and nuggets wrapped in cigarette foil and walked out with wads of American dollars. Controlling Bunia went hand in hand with controlling the gold, and whoever controlled the gold carried the better guns.

The Hema militia had taken Bunia in August 2002 and quickly moved to seize Mongbwalu. Earlier that summer, Lendu combatants had killed scores of Hema in the gold-mining town, so the Hema were bent on revenge. They attacked in November, murdering more than two hundred Lendu and ethnic Nande civilians, who they gunned down in the streets or brutally executed by smashing people's heads with hammers and slicing their throats, then burning the bodies.

The Hema militia was led by Thomas Lubanga, a beanpole of a commander, who towered over his militia army, many of them child soldiers whom he'd recruited from villages decimated by Lendu raids. He was charismatic and loved publicity; he would throw marathon press conferences when reporters were in the area, ending his diatribes against his current enemies by dancing atop the tables. (Two years later, he would also be the first war criminal arrested to stand trial in the International Criminal Court in The Hague, charged with conscripting and using child soldiers.)

Uganda's relationship with Lubanga's militia had spoiled in mid-2002, and in March 2003, army commanders had used Lendu fighters to help expel the Hema from Bunia. The Lendu militia itself consisted of two subgroups—one from the north of Bunia, the other from the south. Uganda's relationship with the southern faction—known as the Ngiti—subsequently failed, and the Ugandans had begun trying to push them out in turn.

The Drodro massacre made a puff in the newspapers, but was dead gone the next day. And the UN started saying the death toll was largely exaggerated, even though it hadn't conducted a real investigation. But in reality, the April 3 attacks had been so efficient and macabre that humanitarian workers in Congo were afraid the conflict was spiraling into another Rwanda. I convinced an editor to send me back to chronicle the killings and join a UN forensic team scheduled to uncover the mass graves. I arrived back in Bunia as the Ugandans were pulling out and started trying to arrange rides into Drodro. But once there, it became clear another massacre was unfolding right there in town.

The last Ugandan soldiers were scheduled to leave Bunia on

May 6, two weeks away. When they did, it was almost certain the Lendu Ngiti militia would sweep right in to fill the vacuum. By the time I arrived in Bunia, they were hitting the Ugandans every day, slowly closing in on the town. Bunia's population of Hema took on the mien of the hunted. Everyone feared the raid, it seemed, but the UN.

II

After a few days in Bunia, I quickly fell into the rhythms of the town. I buzzed up and down the broad boulevard on the back of motorcycle taxis and hired a steady driver named Oliver. The 350,000 residents of Bunia were mostly traders and merchants who operated out of the white-stone colonial shops that lined Lumumba Boulevard, the main commercial strip, selling everything from motorbikes imported from China, to radios, jumper cables, and the ubiquitous Blue Band margarine found in every corner of Africa. Along the narrow paths of the town market, plump women sat behind tall mounds of brightly colored beans, manioc root, and spinach, and stacks of salted fish that smelled so strong it stung your throat in the heat. All down the boulevard, little boys walked the road hawking fried chapatis, and women glided in tight lines down the grassy median, balancing bundles of laundry atop their heads and bowls spilling with bananas. Old men rested their tired bones in the awning shade with radios pressed against their ears; chickens scratched in the dirt; moto-taxi drivers waited at the junctions in sunshades and open shirts; and the stoic money changers sat at their stands hovered over cubes of grimy francs.

The Mobutu government had neglected Bunia for decades, leaving the stately colonial buildings along the boulevard to crumble and fade. And numerous battles between armies and militia had left the boulevard scarred with gun pocks and blast wounds. The post office had been locked for three years, and the bank for ten. The water ran cold and brown from the pipes, and electricity was a precious luxury. The roads leading to town were full of sinkholes that reached up to snap the axles of trucks and flatten tires. Gasoline was sold by little boys with jerricans and tin funnels, while down the road, pumps at abandoned filling stations were rusted and stripped for parts. The remnants of better days still whispered in mocking tones: one building along the boulevard bore a faded advertisement from a colonial-era insurance company. OWN YOUR LIFE, the sign suggested.

Just as I arrived, the first cellular tower was being erected, and in the coming days residents would line up at the new office of Celtel for phones and prepay cards that would change how they did business and bring the rest of the massive country much closer. Across the street was the new MONUC headquarters (the French acronym for the UN's Congo mission), where painters were trimming the windows in UN signature blue, a color so mixed up with Congo's blood it would later pinstripe the new national flag.

I had checked into the Hotel Takabeya, just on the edge of the market, where the women wore brassy blonde wigs to serve greasy omelets and tea at six thirty in the morning. During the day I'd stop by the UN to check about rides into Drodro, maybe do some interviews, then have dinner at the Club Hellenique, the only decent bar and restaurant in town, located next door to UN headquarters. At night, it was cold beers on the patio of my room listening to BBC and Voice of America on my shortwave radio.

I'd needed an interpreter for interviews, so the day I arrived at the airport, I'd walked around asking everyone, "Know where I can find a translator?" Only one person had answered in English and said he'd send someone over. It was a dumb rookie move, especially since I didn't know anyone or their delicate tribal affiliations, but it paid off. The next morning I walked out of the dining room at the Takabeya and found Johnny Ngure waiting for me in the courtyard.

Johnny was short and thin with a wispy, boyish mustache and base-ball cap pulled low over his eyes. He was a student at the local teacher-training school and his English was good. I hired him on the spot.

Johnny told me how his father had been murdered by Lendu fighters a year before, shot in the back as he tried to run during a raid north of town. His body lay in the street for three days while Johnny hid in the bush. Johnny had buried him alone in a hand-dug grave. The only story about his father that he seemed to enjoy telling was how he gave Johnny his name. "After Johnnie Walker the whiskey," he said. "I was always walking and running away."

Johnny lived in a dim, mildew-infested dormitory just behind the UN headquarters. His mother had died of illness years before, and after his father was killed, Johnny paid his tuition and rent by pushing wheelbarrows of dried fish from Lake Albert to Bunia, a two-day haul through the mountains.

"I hope that you will be happy with my job," he said that day. "It's important to me. My father was a journalist, too."

I spent my mornings that week having tea with Brigadier General Kale Kayihura, commander of the Ugandan army in Congo. We'd sit under the shade of the small concrete terminal at the airport, from which his men were gradually departing.

What troubled the general most was how the UN was preparing for his withdrawal. The first of 350 Uruguayan peacekeepers had begun trickling in that week, and MONUC was hoping the small force could contain the war slowly creeping toward town. To maintain their international force, the UN was flying in tons of cargo every day, erecting a giant prefab city of good intentions that would soon dwarf the town it'd come to help, a blue-and-white Potemkin village shuttled about in white Toyota SUVs that filled the streets and every parking lot.

The people of Bunia didn't realize it, but the UN had no

intentions of saving them in the event of an attack. The Security Council's mandate for MONUC only allowed soldiers to protect UN staff and property. The mandate worked swell for those areas of the country where fighting had ceased. But in Ituri, the blue flag of the UN only cast a shadow, and not a long one at that.

It was an ugly paradox the Security Council refused to swallow. Everyone agreed the Ugandans desperately needed to leave, but in the same breath they'd acknowledge the troops were preventing further massacres (or helping stage them, depending on whom you asked). The Ugandans were dirty cops, but they were the only law the people had. And during those mornings over tea, the general assured me, over my astonishment, that history would regard the Ugandans as heroes once MONUC dropped the ball and Bunia was awash in blood.

"Does the Security Council think about the security in this region?" he said to me one day. "Their politics seem to be prevailing over human life."

He'd often conclude these rants by squeezing my shoulder and with a long, exhausted look saying, "I'm so glad you're here as a witness."

I mainly spoke with the general because he wasn't afraid of journalists, unlike the UN staff, who seemed to deflect my every approach. The general was good with questions, even if answers were never part of the deal.

"General, some people say your officers are stealing gold."

"*Stealing gold.* Nonsense. You've been here. Have you seen us stealing gold?"

"Personally, no, but—"

"What's with you Americans and Europeans?" He reached out and grabbed my wrist. "I've never understood why you people are so thin in the arms."

On my second day in Bunia, a Friday, the first Lendu warriors appeared on the streets. In an attempt to pacify Bunia before the

Ugandan withdrawal, MONUC had set up talks in town and invited both Lendu and Hema leaders: intellectual types who referred to themselves as "general secretary," along with militia leaders—roguish gangsters who decorated themselves with phony military credentials and carried ivory-tipped staffs. The militia leaders had also brought in dozens of "bodyguards" from the bush, while dozens more combatants had poured into Bunia to join the national army, part of a power-sharing deal recently brokered between the government and the rebels the previous year. But the government disarmament camp wasn't up and running, and none of the boys were asked by MONUC to surrender their weapons. By the end of the week, four different groups patrolled the streets with guns. Thus the fall of Bunia began from within.

I first saw them walking down Lumumba Boulevard with a sickening swagger, drinking beer outside the gates of the Hotel Musafira, and getting stoned in the shade. The Lendu boys carried taped-up Kalashnikovs hiked across their shoulders and slid their fingers across their throats as they passed young Hema girls. Some wore ill-fitting uniforms stripped from dead Ugandan soldiers, while a few younger boys dressed in sequined ball gowns that dragged in the dirt, clear-plastic fright masks and punked-out yellow wigs. Around their biceps were strips of leopard skin and animal teeth tied with vine, and amulets full of strange milky liquid dangled from their bandoliers.

The boys believed the trinkets and dresses protected them from bullets during battle, a belief they seemed eager to test again. The dresses and wigs conjured a magic ruse, a second identity, that confused their enemies and shielded them from harm. Cross-dressing in Ituri wasn't as widespread as in other African wars; later that year in Liberia, stoned gunboys in drag would pack the front lines as government forces battled encroaching rebels. The battle armor was also intended to frighten and intimidate, and that first time I caught eyes with them on the streets of Bunia, I quickly looked away. Those weren't the eyes of boys, not anymore.

Little by little, the gunboys took a piece of Bunia each time the sun went down. For three straight mornings after they appeared, a different moto-taxi driver was found dead, shot or hacked up in a ditch on the outskirts of town. At the same time, I began getting regular visits at my hotel from Jean-Pierre, a boxy troll of a man who claimed to be a local journalist. He'd wear the same black suit and blue, button-down shirt and carried a leather briefcase full of photos of dead bodies. Most were massacre victims from the villages, people emptied of all their organs lying in wooden coffins; people missing heads, arms, testicles, and strips of flesh from their buttocks. He charged twenty dollars for each photo, which he sold to passing journalists, though I never knew anyone who'd actually bought one. One morning I was interested in a shot of a guy sprawled in the road, his pond-water eyes staring blankly at the clouds. There was a gaping, sinewy gash in his neck from a machete blade.

"That is the taxi driver killed this morning," Jean-Pierre said. "Thirty dollars American."

"Thirty? Why thirty?"

"*Monsieur*, he is still lying in the road."

The morning the first taxi driver was killed, Oliver didn't show up at my hotel with his bike. I didn't hear from him all day and soon began to worry. Two days passed and I became scared that Oliver would appear in one of the photos in Jean-Pierre's briefcase. Late that afternoon, Johnny came by and said he'd just seen Oliver by the roundabout.

"So when is he coming?" I said.

"Oliver said he won't be driving you anymore," Johnny said. "He's afraid the Lendu will kill him if he's seen driving a white man, a journalist."

By Tuesday the following week, the taxi drivers would stop working altogether, partly out of protest against their colleagues being killed, but mainly out of fear. Few cars were in Bunia at the time, so without the motorcycles, the streets grew quiet and sinister. Many people took this as a sign and just stayed home.

During my first days in Bunia, I also began hearing rumors about other massacres out in the villages, or in the bush just outside of town. Since it was unwise to travel outside Bunia, I often relied on two UN press officers, Leo and Christophe, to confirm or deny these reports. On Friday, I heard about a Lendu attack on the town of Kasenyi, on the shores of Lake Albert, where many people were reportedly killed. I found Leo in the Hellenique eating lunch.

"Oh, yes, big massacre," Leo said, never turning from his spaghetti. When I pressed him further, he looked up, annoyed, and said, "I don't know, call Kinshasa," referring to UN headquarters in the capital about eighteen hundred kilometers to the west.

But most frightening were the increasing reports by residents of massive numbers of Lendu and Hema militia congregating on the edge of town, preparing for a fight. It was impossible to know when or how this would happen, how many warriors there were, or if it was even true. And asking the UN only confused me more.

"Yes, yes, things are tense," Leo would say.

"Don't worry," said Christophe. "Things are fine."

On Saturday I found the general pacing the airport runway as heavy guns echoed from the northern hills, near Rwampara. "We pulled our men out of there as the UN instructed," he said. "Now these Lendu are shooting civilians." He walked out past the tarmac into the high elephant grass. "You hear that? They're using a fifty-caliber." He ordered two gun-mounted Mambas toward the shooting, and a few minutes later the hills rumbled with mortar blasts and antiaircraft guns as the soldiers made contact.

The day before, he said, one of his soldiers had been shot through the chest while guarding a bridge north of town. "They stole his uniform. And then, those Lendu cut out his tongue!" A voice crackled over the radio saying the Lendu had been pushed from Rwampara. "Did I tell you that we found the head of one of our soldiers?" he continued. "It was lying in the bush. The rest of him had been eaten. I tell you, these Lendu are like animals. They have no remorse!"

Just about then, a cargo plane touched down full of more Uruguayan peacekeepers. They stepped out into the white sun and adjusted their eyes to the blinding light. Each wore a blue flak jacket and clunky helmet. "The UN is sending these people into a trap," the general said. "What business do these men have dying here?"

Later that same day, a UN military observer was killed in Komanda, a little village sixty kilometers southwest of Bunia, when his vehicle ran over a land mine in the road. Another observer traveling with him had his legs blown off.

The unarmed military observers had been the first UN presence in Congo back in 2000, sent in to monitor the cease-fire between warring factions. Like the UN's mandate, they were effective in places where war had ended, but in Ituri, their deployments were often like tossing meat to a cellar of dogs.

I met one observer that week in the Hellenique, a Uruguayan named Juan, who'd recently returned from a long mission in the northern hills. He explained how he'd been dropped with three other soldiers deep in the bush with just their packs and radios. They were given crude maps and little intelligence, and none spoke any of the local languages. They were instructed to find the local chief and ask permission to set up a small command post. If the chief refused, he said, they were to inform him the UN was already sending the rest of their gear in choppers. "And if we were attacked," Juan said, "they told us, 'Just use your radios.'"

The following month, two more observers—Major Safwat Oran from Jordan and Captain Siddon Davis Banda from

Malawi—would be gunned down by Lendu fighters near the gold mines of Mongbwalu. I'd later watch peacekeepers load their black body bags onto planes in Bunia and ship them home. One had been shot in the head, the other in the stomach; the UN had recovered their remains a week after villagers buried them.

As I sat there that night drinking with Juan, I looked down and noticed his hands vibrating against the bar. He told me, "Out on observation, I imagined my own death, and it was more clear than in a dream." He was putting back beers in rapid succession. "Each night I went to bed, I watched it play over again in my mind. Every night I died."

On Saturday night, heavy shooting began on the edge of town. It woke me up at two A.M., sustained burps of machine-gun fire, followed by a series of single rounds. The gunfire came every night afterward; one evening, I lay wide-awake for hours following single shots that popped fifteen minutes apart and, each time, inched a little closer to my window.

On Sunday, Johnny and I were taking a motorbike into Mudzipela, a Hema neighborhood just north of my hotel, where Johnny's father had been killed. He wanted to show me the grave. But on the way there, a group of boys stopped us in the road. "Please, don't travel any farther," one said. "The Lendu are killing people in the streets." A couple of rifle rounds echoed through the trees, but nothing more. Back at the UN base, no one knew anything about it, and I was too afraid to return and check myself.

Steadily, paranoia began working its way into everyone. One night I sat at the Hellenique with two South Africans who claimed to be UN intelligence officers sent to monitor the Ugandan withdrawal. Unlike most other UN military staff, though, they didn't wear uniforms or badges and were always vague about their "mission." They didn't have a vehicle, nor did they stay in rented homes or nicer motels like other UN staff. They stayed at the Takabeya, next door to me, endured the cold bucket baths and blackouts, and frequently invited the brassy, wig-wearing women into their rooms. I liked them a lot.

The three of us sat on sofas in a dark corner of the restaurant, sharing a large bottle of Primus beer. The radio behind the bar crackled with old soukous love ballads, and the lights flickered from Bunia's shaky current. A few tables were filled with the UN's mostly Euro staff in their jeans and T-shirts, barking orders in French to Jean, the long-faced waiter, to bring their brochettes and plates of toasted cheese. The intelligence officers began talking about "the Conflict" in whispers, and I marveled at the things coming out of their mouths. That morning, I'd heard a woman working in the fields had been hacked in the head by a gang of Lendu. When I said the word *Lendu*, one of the officers threw a finger in front of his lips and told me to quiet down.

"Please," he said, and motioned to a table of Congolese, all non-English speakers. "We only use the terms *the H* and *the L* when discussing the Conflict."

He surveyed the bar, then leaned in and whispered, "You never know who is listening. For instance, be careful around Jean the waiter. We're still not sure if he belongs to the H or the L."

Soon it became too dangerous to leave even the main boulevard at night. Hit-and-run gangs of Lendu and Hema teenagers were kicking down doors in the outer neighborhoods, looting homes, raping women, and killing. The UN had banished the remaining Ugandan soldiers from patrolling Bunia's streets and would often be called out to intervene during these violent attacks. One morning after a night of heavy shooting, two UN employees stood outside the Hellenique smoking cigarettes. One said he had been awakened that morning by a little girl pounding on his door.

"She said the Lendu were in her house and were about to kill her parents," the guy said. "What the fuck am I supposed to do? I called security to go check it out."

"We're not here to protect civilians," his friend snapped. "You can't save the world, mate. As far as I'm concerned, let the bastards kill each other."

The other guy looked up and said, "Then what are we doing here?"

Each night the gunfire grew heavier and louder, and residents said they were the shots of execution squads. At first I tried drinking myself to sleep, but it only made matters worse. After a while, I made a habit of packing my bag before going to bed in case I had to run out in a hurry. At the end of my second week in town, I'd started switching hotels every few days and not telling anyone where I was staying: one night at the Takabeya, a couple nights at a guesthouse behind MONUC, and finally I settled in a hotel near the airport called the CAPA. It was the safest hotel in town, Leo told me, because several MONUC officers also stayed there. Therefore, chances of being evacuated in the event of an attack were good.

Then one evening over many beers, one of the South African intelligence officers' local "contacts" said he had information I should hear, something about my translator. "I know this person Johnny," he said. "Johnny works for the Hema. Your friend is a rebel."

Deep down, I didn't believe a word of it, but the idea still nagged me. Johnny was an Alur, a neutral majority tribe, though they sometimes got grouped with the Hema when the Lendu were cutting the cards. Over a Coke at the Hellenique the following day, I grilled him about his allegiances.

"Johnny, this guy says you're a rebel," I said. "I know that's a stupid word, but tell me the truth. It's my safety here."

I watched his body deflate like a balloon as he stared down at his lap. *"Please, no . . . ,"* he said. It was all he had to say. I'd hurt his feelings, and it was then I realized how deeply the fear had soured my own judgment.

Paranoia ruled, it engineered our thoughts and actions, guided our conversations, poked us out of bed in the morning and tucked us in at night. Contingency plans, evacuation rosters ("Who's on the UN's evacuation list? Hey, journalist guy, have you seen the evacuation list? Was my name on it?"), and half-baked theories on when and where the enemy would finally strike—this was the repartee of frightened military men, hardened souls whose nightmares were cast with African boys in prom dresses carving them up in their beds.

During these weeks, there was a theory the UN officers in Bunia followed like gospel: that the gunboys, full of beer and howling for blood, never attacked before eleven in the morning, on weekends, or when it rained. This theory had held true so far, and it certainly eased my mind as I sat in the Internet café on Lumumba Boulevard. *Three for three,* I thought. *In the clear.* It was morning, a Saturday, and the sky was the color of lead and threatening rain.

Over the past ten days in Bunia, my e-mails to friends had grown cryptic and detached, mostly uncensored descriptions of what was taking place. "Twelve shots last night, closer to my hotel than before . . . man found hanging from tree this morning, woman hacked up in a ditch . . . Just another day in Paradise. Funny, huh?"

I was sending my mother a standard "I'm safe, gotta go" note when the manager of the café walked over to my computer, flipped the power, and shouted, "Go now, we're closed!" I got pissed off and reached to turn the machine back on, but saw that I was all alone and stopped. The other customers were in the next room by the tall windows, peeking out at the boulevard, which had suddenly filled with Lendu warriors.

There were hundreds of them, more than I'd ever seen. They carried beat-up Kalashnikovs and rocket-propelled grenades, long spears, and sharpened machetes. One boy had on a 2Pac T-shirt and a different sneaker on each foot. Others wore wigs and were shirtless and wrapped in bullets. Most were barefoot and their toes were dusted in the boulevard's yellow dirt. Their eyes were narrow and catlike from the joints that bounced in their lips as they marched past.

An older man standing next to me looked terrified. From his expression, I guessed he was Hema. He cocked his head to hear the Swahili words the boys chanted in the streets, then turned to me. "They're saying it's time to pay."

After the last fighter passed the window, I ran outside with a few others. We stood together at the edge of the empty boulevard and saw more boys tearing toward us. Someone said they were Hema soldiers coming to fight the Lendu. As they approached, the air around me filled with gunfire. I turned to run as three bullets smacked into the building behind me, kicking out puffs of dust and concrete. I tried to hit the ground, but something propelled my legs forward.

People came running down the street as gunshots popped at their backs. They wore crazy electric smiles on their faces, the same gimme-danger grins worn by people who run from bulls. I was headed back inside the café when a Congolese woman in a yellow dress grabbed my hand and said, "You better hide. It's not safe for you here," and led me to a house off the road.

We ducked into a ground-level apartment just behind the café and she closed the door. The living room was dark, with thin shoots of sunlight cascading through the curtains of a nearby window. Several other women sat on sofas and foldout chairs, whispering soothing words to a few children at their feet. The women were immaculately dressed in bright floral skirts and smelled of strong perfume. Their breezy French mixed with the rolling gunfire and was punctuated by cackling laughter and elaborate hand gestures.

"This happens all the time," said the woman in the yellow dress, in English. She noticed my leg trembling, gave a small laugh, and said, "Are you afraid?" Then she stood up, smoothed the wrinkles in her dress, and disappeared into the kitchen to make tea.

I sat there for twenty minutes while thoughts formed in my head and quickly blew apart, until there was nothing but gunfire and brief lapses into silence. At my feet, two children played like kittens on the floor. Even as the fighting grew more intense and rumbled like a train in the bathroom, they never made a sound.

The front door then suddenly swung open, sucking every bit of wind from my lungs. But when I saw who was there, I jumped from the sofa and nearly kissed him on the mouth. It was Johnny, sent straight down on heaven's rope from the warm kitchens of my mother and grandmother. I'd given him the morning off and now he was standing in the doorway, winded and smiling.

"I have a motorbike," he said. "Let's go."

We waited while the shooting moved down the street, then ran to the back of the house where Johnny'd stashed a Honda he'd borrowed from a striking taxi driver. I got on the back and Johnny kicked the engine.

"Johnny, how'd you know I was there?"

"I just asked someone."

We lit off down a back road, through leafy tea fields, and within seconds we'd moved beyond the shooting. Once we were safe, the panic and fear released their grip and I began to laugh so hard I nearly fell off the bike.

So that's what it's like, I thought. I knew I should be more afraid, but for some reason I felt a calm so sharp it spooked me. It certainly wasn't from bravery, but whatever it was, it left me with the clearest tunnel vision I'd ever experienced. It could've been a lot worse (weeks later, Rodrique Ngowi would be pinned down on the same street as .50-caliber rounds passed inches from his head). I knew that I'd been kissed with luck, saved by a rainy-day reserve of

prayer and a woman I'd never met. But as we drove back to my hotel, the thing that kept running through my mind was *Yes, yes.
That's it exactly.*

I'd made friends the week before with a Swiss doctor from the
aid group Médecins Sans Frontières (MSF—or Doctors Without
Borders) who'd recently arrived at the Bunia hospital to operate
on the war wounded. When I arrived at the hotel that night, I
found the doctor sitting at a table on the front lawn, badly
shaken. He'd had a tough week. On his second day in town, he'd
announced on the radio that there were fifty empty beds, and
those wounded outside town should make an effort to get
treated. One of his first patients was a teenage girl who'd been
shot in the leg and waited ten days to come to the clinic because
the roads weren't safe to travel. Her entire leg had turned black
and crawled with caterpillars. "Who knows how many more are
still out there?" he'd told me. "When they learn about the beds,
you can expect a line out the door." The hospital was terribly un-
derstaffed, and on the day of the gunfight, I'd actually made plans
to assist him while he performed amputations, which had become
common procedures.

He'd been at the hospital performing surgery that afternoon
when the battle along the boulevard shifted right in front of his
door. The local staff had bolted immediately and left him alone
with fifty patients. For three hours he crawled on the floor and radioed the UN for help as mortar rounds and grenades shook the
foundation, but none arrived. The Ugandans had finally swung by
and carried him out. He now sat in the courtyard, his breathing still
labored from the stress. The hotel had no beer because the market
was destroyed, so I went into my bags and brought out a pint of
whiskey I was saving for a rainy day. I gave it to the doctor.

"What's stopping these militia from coming into my hospital
and killing everyone?" he said, draining a full glass with one gulp.

The year before, in nearby Nyakunde, Lendu warriors had entered the large village hospital, searched for Hema patients, then butchered them in their beds. The slaughter continued for ten days until twelve hundred people were dead.

"I promised my wife I'd be safe. We just bought a house." He poured another drink and turned it over, then buried his face in his hands and whispered, "Shit, shit, shit." Two days later they pulled him out.

In the wake of the gunfight, more people began to leave. Most of the Hema who could afford a ticket rushed to the airport and tried to board flights to Beni, Goma, or Kinshasa, anywhere but Bunia. They waited patiently for hours in the sweltering lobby dressed in their best clothes—the women in their colorful *pagne* wraps, clutching little boys in suits that swallowed their shoulders. Once a plane landed, any plane, they rushed the runway, dragging children and suitcases and cardboard boxes bound in tape. One afternoon a group of them mobbed a cargo plane headed for Kinshasa. About six people managed to grab hold of the open doorway as a stocky Ukrainian pulled the ladder and the plane taxied toward the runway. The crewman scrambled to push them off with his feet, kicking several men to the pavement. A woman carrying a baby was pummeled in the face, but managed to squeeze through his arms and steal aboard.

The people who couldn't afford flights still flocked to the airport, which quickly became a massive camp of the displaced as the Ugandans prepared to leave town. People jammed the airport road and massed around the one-story terminal, and from a distance it appeared the airport itself was ablaze from all their cooking fires. Many came from surrounding villages and carried what they could manage: a few pots, some clothes, jugs of water. Several thousand were choosing to march four days to the border with the army, rather than stay behind and risk the odds. In the end, tens of thousands streamed into western Uganda. But while they waited at the airport, most of them ran out of food and water, and sanitation was spiraling into an emergency.

In the early afternoon of May 5, the day before the Ugandans left, a rowdy gang of children assembled by the loading ramp. In the center was a young Ugandan soldier clutching a box of rations he was trying to distribute. As he handed out the first few, the children rushed him and ripped the box from his hands, sending the shiny tins of canned beef rolling across the dirt. The mob seized the scattered loot, then hurried back to their camps with their prizes.

Just then a UN cargo plane thundered onto the runway and taxied toward the ramp. As it swung around, its exhaust jets kicked up a stinging dust storm that sent the children and the soldiers running for cover. A crew of workers rushed over to the plane's rear cargo hatch, but the only thing to unload were a few steel rods. Easy trip. Then the engines fired again and the empty plane took off as quickly as it landed. And with the returning quiet, the gang of children returned for more rations. The soldiers were now giving away their beans.

As Bunia descended into chaos, the UN forensics team finally arrived to investigate the April 3 massacre. The team was made up of two independent Argentine forensic anthropologists who'd unearthed mass graves everywhere from South America to Bosnia. Today they'd travel to the hills of Ituri. Along with seven Uruguayan peacekeepers and a dozen UN staff, we boarded the white UN chopper and traveled thirty minutes over the electric green until we arrived at the redbrick Catholic mission at Drodro. Because of the volatile security in the area, the UN instructed the pilot to drop and leave—don't even stop the engines.

Several hundred people now packed the sandy courtyard of the church, and hundreds more were sleeping in the bush. It was damp and cold, too wet for fires. Our delegation was greeted by a silent mob of children with bloated stomachs, hacking and wheezing from chest infections, sick from the weather and severe diarrhea. The situation had only gotten worse since I'd last been there. One of the priests said there'd been attacks in the surrounding settlements every day since the massacre, despite the unit of Ugandan soldiers stationed there to protect them. He opened a ledger that contained a list of people killed in the past three weeks. I counted forty-seven names. "When the Ugandans leave here," the priest said, "the population is going to disappear. Today they're here, tomorrow they're gone."

In Largu, a few kilometers up the road, the forensics team zeroed in on a grave at the base of a small cliff, surrounded by manioc and banana trees. The wooden cross staked at the head of the grave indicated twenty-six bodies buried underneath. Five local men grabbed shovels and hoes and began digging into the heavy red dirt, while the village chief and a flock of residents stood behind a cordon of white tape and watched in silence. I stood near the edge of the hole, pressing a bandanna soaked in whiskey against my face; the UN had warned the smell of decay would be overwhelming. After an hour of digging, the workers reached a thin layer of banana leaves in the soil. Just beneath lay the body of a woman who'd been hacked with a machete through the skull. In the hook of her arms was the decomposing corpse of an infant.

The forensics team snapped a few photos, and as a steady afternoon rain began to fall, the grave was filled with dirt and our group returned to Drodro to meet the chopper. No exhumation, no examination. According to the UN, they just wanted to confirm dead people were really in the grave.

In Drodro, the village chief called a meeting with the UN officials. "How can you spend so much time and resources examining our dead, while doing nothing to protect the living?" he asked. He explained that once the Ugandans left, everyone would be slaughtered. Was it possible, he asked, to get a small unit of peacekeepers to protect the village when the Ugandans withdrew? The UN told him to write a formal request and take it to Bunia, and later, Kinshasa would be notified of his concerns. "But the rains have washed out the roads," he answered. "Can I have a lift in your chopper?" The UN told him no, but agreed to deliver the request. Before any further discussions could be had, a Uruguayan captain rushed in and demanded we evacuate immediately. Seventy Lendu warriors had just entered Largu, where we'd been only minutes before. Gunshots pattered in the distance. "They're coming to attack us!" the captain said. Seconds later the chopper touched down and we clambered aboard. Then it whisked us away, up and over the hundreds of faces still looking to the sky when they finally disappeared.

On May 6, the day Uganda pulled its last soldiers out of Congo, I arrived at the airport at dawn, determined to get a seat aboard the general's plane back to Entebbe. I didn't like leaving so soon, but I simply didn't trust MONUC to protect me. The night before, the UN had ordered all their officers to vacate their rooms at the CAPA and move to the main headquarters. I'd spent the evening mostly alone in the hotel, then lay there all night fully clothed waiting for the raid. I didn't know if I could handle another night like that.

As I arrived at the airport that morning on the back of Johnny's motorcycle, I wondered what would happen to the people I'd met, the hotel staff, the boy who sold me cigarettes on the street. Most of all, I worried about Johnny. Before we parted at the airport, I gave him a few packs of smokes, my French-English dictionary, a wad of cash, and a firm lecture on staying safe. "I'll be fine here," he said. "I have to stay for my school. And besides, where else can I go?" I gave Johnny a hug and watched him disappear into the crowds, kicking myself for not buying him a cell phone when I had the chance so I could keep in touch.

Just then, someone tapped me on my shoulder. "Hey!" a voice said. "Are you an American?"

I turned around to find a tall man holding a backpack and camera, looking somewhat overwhelmed. Samson Mulugeta was an Ethiopian-born American reporter based in Johannesburg. He'd just stepped off a Ugandan cargo plane from Entebbe, and now he was here. "I'm from *Newsday*," he said, half-yelling over the engine noise. "Hey, are you Mealer? I read your AP story about the gun battle. I'm here to cover the Hema-Lendu thing."

I could hardly make out what he was saying over the roar of machinery; for a minute I just stared at him, convinced he was some kind of hallucination.

"You're here . . . *what*?"

"*The tribal war.* The UN told me a forensics team was coming. When's the forensics team coming?"

"Man, they're gone. That was five days ago."

"They're *what* . . . ?"

"Man, I'm *leaving*, I'm getting out of here. It's not safe here."

"It's *what* . . . ?"

"You need to leave with me, *now*!"

I tried to convince the guy, told him everything I could, even made it sound a whole lot worse than it was. But he wouldn't listen. He'd come a long way already, and with everything I was telling him, he probably smelled a good story. I didn't blame him. The least I could do was try to help. I gave him the telephone number of one of Johnny's friends, who Johnny had told me would be able to get in touch with him, then told him about the Hotel CAPA. "It's the closest hotel to the airport," I said. "You might be safe there." Then I watched him disappear as well.

The general was sitting in the shade nearby, watching his men load the last remaining gear into trucks and a few idle planes waiting on the runway. His face was pinched and exhausted. He'd come down with malaria the night before. "More reason for me to get out of this place!" he said. He stood up and paced awhile, then sat back down. "I just got a call saying these Lendu are on their way. What am I supposed to do? I wash my hands of this place. Let MONUC figure it out."

When the last soldier was ready to leave, we boarded a small twin-engine plane and the general sat alone. As the plane circled up and over Bunia, I looked down and saw the group of Lendu, like a column of ants, marching toward the town.

III

Two hours later, a band of Lendu fighters raided the Catholic mission in Mudzipela and murdered ten people in their rooms. One of them, a priest named Raphael Ngona, was a contact of mine, who'd survived the Drodro massacre only weeks before. Bunia then fell with ease. The Lendu had it by the throat the next afternoon, and by evening it was carrion.

For the next several days the Lendu went house to house looking for Hema. They painted their stomachs and faces coal black and kicked down doors. They pulled families from their beds, from behind furniture, out of closets, then dragged them to the streets and shot them through the head. "Come out if you are Hema!" they screamed as they swept through bedrooms and over back fences. "The Lendu have come!"

One woman who managed to hide witnessed several warriors enter her neighbor's home and drag an old woman to the backyard. The boys lived down the road and everyone knew them well. "Spare me, I've done nothing wrong to you," pleaded the woman. The boys were drunk and informed her she belonged to the wrong tribe, then hacked off her hands and feet. Finally they killed the woman and cut her body into small pieces, which they scattered in the road outside her home. When they were finished, they went inside the woman's kitchen and washed their hands of her blood.

Others saw friends beheaded by young boys amped on liquor,

and one watched a lone warrior crouched in the road, feasting on the open organs of a man he'd just killed. Another looked out from her window as militia apprehended nine people on the streets, including three women holding babies. Militia stripped the children from their mothers' arms, cut the kids' throats, and smashed their heads in the dirt. Then they shot the adults. Around the same time, militia attacked Bunia's Nyakasunza parish, slaughtering two more priests and twenty civilians who'd fled there for refuge.

When the killing was done, the painted gunboys howled and sang as they paraded down the empty boulevard waving the severed hands of their dead. They wore the ears of their victims strung around their necks, and some festooned their bandoliers with kidneys and bladders.

Then, on May 12, the Hema militia broke through the Lendu defenses and pushed them out of town. Over the preceding five days the Hema had vigorously fought from their base north of town and had been hammered back each time. Hundreds of civilians had been killed in their cross fire, but their final assault had proved victorious. But soon as the Hema militia won control of Bunia, they simply looted what was left and began raping and killing Lendu civilians.

The entire week I sat at home in Nairobi and stared at the radio, waiting for some kind of news. Over and over I called the mobile phone of Johnny's friend and tried repeatedly to get through to the number Samson, the reporter, had left me. Nothing. I called the Hotel CAPA, but could never decipher what was happening on the other end. People I didn't know kept answering the phone and hanging up, and at times I heard gunfire like popcorn in the background. A BBC reporter got through to one of the UN press officers at headquarters, who said they were under attack and living on the floor. Finally I saw a *Newsday* story describing a similar scene inside the UN compound and knew that Samson was safe. But the story told me nothing about Johnny.

★ ★ ★

The first real lull in the fighting came on May 15, and it was then I found myself on a flight with American missionaries headed back into Bunia. Ten minutes before landing, our copilot, Dave, a handsome, leather-skinned missionary, walked out of the cockpit and sighed so loudly I could hear it over the engine. More bad news.

"They're sayin it's still pretty rough down there," he shouted. "Lot of shooting this morning."

I pressed my forehead against the cool window glass and watched the clouds part to reveal the green hills of Ituri. I couldn't believe I was going back. All week I'd convinced myself I'd never go there again, repeating it over and over, until I packed my bags and caught a taxi to the airport. Now at ten thousand feet over the border, the notion was slowly becoming real.

The missionaries were running the first available flight back into Bunia: a six-seat, single-engine Cessna that would sit on the ground for ten minutes, then fly out carrying church members waiting to be evacuated. My group of reporters—Helen Vesperini from Agence France-Presse, Rodrique from AP, and a few others—had spent all the previous day in Kigali, Rwanda, waiting on a rumored MONUC plane, but when that fell through, we'd driven thirteen hours back to Entebbe. As the missionary plane began its descent, I saw the familiar mud huts of Bunia and slivers of smoke rising from breakfast fires. Dave then informed us we were going to circle the airport before diving in—he was afraid the plane might get shot. He bowed his head and led us in prayer.

At the airport I grabbed my backpack and jumped out into a throng of UN military hardware and people clamoring to leave. The tarmac was now choked with chalk-white armored personnel carriers, mountains of sandbags, and dozens of Uruguayan peace-keepers wrapped in flak jackets and helmets.

Mahmadou Bah, a UN press officer, ran up and grabbed my

hand, shouting over the din of departing planes, "Don't go any-where. The road's not safe. We'll have to take you in under guard."

I saw another familiar face near the terminal building—it was Juan, the Uruguayan military observer I'd met at the Hellenique a few weeks before, the soldier who'd just returned from the long observation mission in the bush. He was now on his way out, his green duffel resting at his feet. God knows what his week had been like. I flapped my arms and screamed his name.

Juan saw me, hiked his bag over his shoulder, and ran over. Before I could even say hello, he tossed the bag onto the tarmac and grabbed me in a powerful hug. When he pulled back, I looked in his eyes; they were like staring into a river. Without saying a word, he grabbed his bag, ran to a waiting C-130 cargo plane, and disap-peared inside. I walked back to the terminal and watched the mis-sionaries help a few old women and kids board the plane. Then I watched them leave.

I caught a ride into town with a convoy of aid workers tailing a fast-moving UN armored vehicle. Before pulling out of the air-port, the driver told me to prepare myself for what I was about to see. "It's all gone," he said. "They've destroyed it all." The first place we passed was the Hotel CAPA. Through the gates I could see the doors kicked open and trash strewn across the parking lot. Six teenagers sat out front smoking cigarettes, each one cradling a Kalashnikov across his lap. And when we finally turned onto Lu-mumba Boulevard, the lifeline of the city, I sank in my seat.

The shops along the boulevard were gutted shells: doors busted off hinges, windows raked with bullet holes, heaps of garbage spilling out of entrances. The wooden kiosks of gold dealers and cigarette salesmen had been turned on their sides and smashed to splinters. Greasy black circles now stained the roads from burning tires, and everywhere you looked there were empty sandals.

The boulevard now belonged to the young Hema fighters. They wore loose army jackets over scrappy T-shirts and grimy blue jeans.

A small group of them gathered outside a deserted shop, laughing at a joke someone told. Farther down the road, one of them walked out of a shop carrying a looted office chair over his head. As we passed, he cocked his chin in our direction and grinned. I caught his eye and felt my face start to burn.

The UN headquarters now looked like a maximum-security prison. The squat, concrete fence surrounding the building had been crowned with silver mantles of razor wire. Five armored vehicles sat parked outside the gate like stone pillars, set between barricades of more wire and steel. A dozen Uruguayan soldiers stood guard, arms ready.

The Lendu had overrun the peacekeepers almost immediately. As soon as the militia stormed the town, the UN soldiers retreated to protect their base. Three days into the battle for Bunia's streets, one of the two groups (it's not clear exactly who) attacked the UN headquarters with heavy machine guns and mortar rounds that exploded in the yard. The soldiers could do nothing but fire rounds over the heads of militia, even as they watched them attack people in the street with machetes. And there were many reports of Uruguayan soldiers buckling under the strain as bullets flew around them, including one captain who retreated inside the compound to hide. "I don't have my helmet," he screamed. Several logistics officers grabbed his arms and threw him out the door. "You're a fucking soldier," they told him. "Now go do your job!"

During the fighting, people had fled their houses and massed outside the UN gates—only to find they were locked out. To escape the shelling, some attempted to run headlong through the wall of razor wire. A woman desperate to get inside tossed her baby over the wire then barreled through herself. They were both cut to shreds. When the people realized the UN had no intention of protecting them, they rioted. Stones and garbage were hurled at the building. A corpse was tossed over the fence. Tires were set ablaze in the boulevard and roadblocks were erected from rubble and large rocks. This lasted two days until the mob grew big enough and strong enough to finally crash the gates.

Once inside, they left the UN no choice but to distribute the basics of aid: plastic sheeting, medicine, food. Four thousand displaced now lived around the headquarters in a space the size of a city block. Aid groups such as UNICEF, Oxfam, and German Agro Action were feeding them high-protein biscuits and trying desperately to repair the town's water main, which had been cut during the fighting. There was already an outbreak of cholera.

Since the hotels were all destroyed and occupied by gunmen, our group of reporters had to sleep at UN headquarters. But UN staff occupied every inch of floor inside, so the journalists were put outside with the displaced. We set up our tents under a tarp along the side of the building, which had served the previous day as the mission's triage center. Bloody gauze and shattered syringes littered the dirt, and a Canadian UN officer chuckled when he saw me spread my bedroll. "You guys are sleeping on a lot of DNA," he said. A snaking coil of razor wire hemmed us in, and just beyond it the edge of the displaced camp began. Nearest us, several middle-aged women hovered over small charcoal burners cooking pots of rice. A group of kids sat around them pitching bottle caps.

As I unpacked, I looked up and noticed our neighbors staring through the wire. I didn't know how to interpret their gaze, but it wasn't friendly. It was ice-cold and vacant, and I was even getting it from the kids. Not knowing what else to do, I smiled and waved. I then looked down and noticed our collective inventory of junk scattered across the dirt: satellite phones and computers, generators, cases of water, canned meats, imported cheese, whiskey bottles, chocolate bars, cartons of cigarettes, an espresso maker. Embarrassed, I quickly gathered my own things, crammed them back into my bag, and hurried off.

When I stepped out from under the tarp, I saw Johnny walking across the grass. A rush of relief swept over me. "You're okay,"

I shouted, and threw my arms around him. "Things are not so good," he said. "I can't go home. They've stolen everything I had."

Samson had found Johnny soon after leaving the airport and hired him right away. Johnny was still driving the motorbike he'd borrowed from his friend, so he checked the reporter into my old room at the CAPA, and they spent the morning doing interviews. That afternoon, fighting in Mudzipela emptied the town and the two parted ways. The next day, Johnny stayed behind at Hellenique while Samson walked next door to MONUC headquarters. Not long after Johnny entered the bar, the Lendu attacked the town. Johnny ran outside and flagged down a moto taxi and headed toward the CAPA, determined to grab Samson's luggage before the militia sacked the hotel. He'd also stashed his borrowed motorcycle there in the courtyard for safekeeping. But several warriors blocked the road and told them to halt. Terrified, Johnny emptied his pockets and the gunboys turned them loose, but by this time, the fighting had grown so heavy they turned back and returned to the Hellenique. Just outside the bar, Johnny saw a friend's small child running alone and petrified down the street as bullets cut the air around him. Johnny raced outside and grabbed hold of the kid, then sprinted toward the UN base. Finding the gates locked, the two joined several others and squeezed through the razor wire. Hours later, militia reached the CAPA and beat down Samson's door with an ax, stealing his luggage and passport, along with Johnny's bike.

Gunmen had also ransacked Johnny's dorm room and looted what few things he owned. When he finally made it home a week later, a family had invaded his room and taken over. He was now living in the displaced camp with some friends who'd cleared some room in their tarpaulin shelter.

During a brief lapse in fighting, he'd left the camp to investigate, and near the market came upon several Lendu carrying out their killing. Now, as we stood in the grass, Johnny leaned in and rested his hand on my shoulder. His eyes were tired and swollen. "I saw them do it," he said. "I never believed it was true, but when I was hiding, I saw them kill an old man and eat from his heart. I saw them do it." I did what little I could for my friend: gave him some cash and hired him for the week.

An emergency hospital ward was set up in one of the deserted buildings across the street from the UN headquarters. The hospital was a place I returned to every day, sometimes several times, even though I knew what I'd discover each time: that sharp, sickly smell of fluid and infection, the dead glaze over the eyes of a kid coming to terms with the fact he no longer had legs; the way they stared straight through you, so you averted your eyes and still asked questions; the emptiness that crawled through your head as you hurried out the door and stepped back into the sun that was much brighter than you remembered.

In one bed a young woman named Neema rewired whatever ideas I thought I had about that war and what it had done to these people. Neema lay there unconscious, her body sprawled sideways across one of the foam mattresses in the center of the cement floor. Her arms were spread at her sides, and the top of her head was wrapped in a crown of bandages. During the first hours of the Lendu attack, Neema had gone into labor and rushed to a clinic down the road. Just as her baby was being delivered, a mortar round hit the roof and rained shrapnel through the ceiling of her room. The baby survived, but Neema's brains had to be scooped back into her head.

The first time I saw Neema, I stared at her for a long time, trying to process why she was even alive. Then she began to move, at first just her lips, then a twitch in her cheeks. Then her body began to writhe on the bed. Her palms slapped the concrete and she emitted a guttural moan, as if lashing out against a nightmare. I realized she was saying something—it was in Lingala and I couldn't make out the words. "What's this woman saying?" I asked the doctor. He walked over and we watched together. "She's saying, 'I'm dying,' " he said, and turned to see my reaction. "She needs a neurosurgeon desperately. But there's just no way."

Neema's baby had been taken to a house next to Hellenique. One afternoon, Helen Vesperini walked inside and discovered the baby languishing on a sofa, getting fed powdered milk once a day. The incident haunted her for the duration of our trip. Finally she was so mortified she drew up adoption papers on her laptop and told the doctor she was taking the baby home.

Dozens of other people had horrific wounds, but every time I passed the hospital, I only thought of Neema. I made excuses to visit the hospital even more, just to see how she was doing. I'd stand at a distance, pretending to look for someone in her direction, or just lean against the far wall and study her face. Sometimes it had a serene rapture, almost a smile. Other times it was full of spirits. Her eyebrows would lift, as if she were about to sneeze, and from the bottom of her stomach came a low moan that built to a peak, then faded to a heavy pant, leaving her face slack. The sound of her voice leached into my brain like a bad song on a loop, and I heard that voice every time I passed the gunboys in the road.

"I'll tell you what we need," a MONUC officer told me one night. He was former military and had come to Congo with noble intentions, but had quickly become a calloused and bitter man. We'd sit on the front steps of the UN headquarters sipping warm bottles of beer, and he'd often tell me things in strict confidence for fear of his job. During the attack, Lendu fighters had stopped his truck and shoved a gun barrel up his nose. An arrow had even rattled through his driver-side window and stuck in the passenger seat, narrowly missing him. Once, he said, a kid stood in the road with his gun leveled, so he hit the gas and ran over him with his truck. "I'll tell you what we need," he said, drunk, his face as ungiving as stone. "We need an army that can come in here and kill off an entire generation of these fuckers. I mean, what are they gonna grow up to be anyway? These kids are worse than animals."

★ ★ ★

"I'll show you the body," said the young boy, and ran off ahead of me. I heard a corpse was on the road near the UN compound, so I ventured out to investigate. The boy and his two friends, all around ten years old, had raced to see it, as any kid would've done when there was a dead body to look at. I knew we were getting close because the smell hit my throat and hung there. The boys gathered by the side of the road and stared into the ditch, leaning over as if held back by an invisible railing. "It's here," said one of them, pointing down. I saw a black, pulsing mass that erupted in a swarm of flies as I got closer. It was the body of a boy, I think, and the entire lower half of him had been eaten by dogs.

Bunia was full of dogs. I'd never really noticed them before, but now they were everywhere. They scurried in and out of open shops and slept in the awning shade. And wherever there was a pack of dogs, there was usually a body nearby.

I'd first noticed the dogs when a few colleagues and I took a walk one day to Yambi Yaya, a neighborhood south of Bunia, which had been emptied by the fighting. We approached Yambi and were greeted by a man leaning casually on a berm, holding a sandal in one hand as if using it to gesture. But as we drew closer, I could see the man had no head. We reached the village center and found another half dozen bodies sprawled in the dirt. We chased several dogs from the body of a young girl, around fifteen years old, who lay flat on her back in front of a small, concrete house. There were no signs of machete wounds or bullet holes; it was as if she'd walked outside and fallen dead in her steps.

One of the girl's legs twisted out from a pink dress, and the other had been chewed off at the knee. As we got closer, I saw something that turned my marrow cold. Five yellow ducklings were gathered at the base of her knee, picking at the flesh.

That sight spooked us all and became an obsessive topic of conversation for the rest of the trip, most often at night when passing the whiskey bottle on the front lawn of MONUC headquarters. Even weeks later some of the same guys, seasoned correspondents, would stop whatever they were doing, look up, and mutter, "Ducks, man. *Fucking ducks*."

Soon after the trip into Yambi, I started checking out. All week we'd shared the town with the young killers who roamed the streets, puffed and arrogant, while the Red Cross body crews came back each day with their litters full (except the times they were murdered and didn't come back at all). More confusing was that the UN not only tolerated their crimes, but had also invited them into the town for talks. The same men commanding the kids who'd gutted people like fish, strung human kidneys across their bandoliers, and raped old women sat in the Hellenique that week drinking beer on the UN's tab. (Further attempts at "pacification," MONUC had claimed.) Bunia became a world without second thought, a town so lost in its own madness that no one was good anymore.

And trying to work the streets had become more volatile than ever. One day we were touring the empty market and stopped to interview a ten-year-old Hema soldier named Chipe. The other militia said that Chipe had watched his parents massacred in Dro- dro and the trauma had caused him to lose his mind. His eyes now flared and trembled, as if he were bugging on amphetamine, and he'd developed a gasping stutter. Thomas Lubanga, the reedy com- mander of the Hema militia, had taken the orphaned warrior and made him his personal bodyguard. The other gunboys were wary of Chipe and often kept their distance. As we walked through the market, where corpses lay putrid and bloated under the empty stalls, Chipe spotted two women rummaging through a shop and ran after them. He pulled the women from the doorway and began whipping them with the barrel of his gun, swinging it like a trun- cheon, his eyes feral with rage. We threw ourselves to the ground, terrified the boy was about to unload his magazine. Karel Prinsloo, a streetwise AP photographer who'd been standing next to me, summed up our fear perfectly: "Put me in Gaza any day. At least there I know where I fucking stand."

The tipping point came that afternoon while we were visiting the makeshift market near the UN headquarters. (The militia had looted all the stalls and shops, then made the vendors buy their merchandise back at twice the price.) On the way I passed several militia mugging for a knot of news photographers. One of them proudly puffed his chest and displayed an Osama bin Laden T-shirt. Next to him was a teenage girl, tall and gorgeous with a model's smile, wearing a chain of bullets and tossing a grenade in the air like an apple.

Back at the camp, things were tense. A few Lendu had been caught sneaking in, attempting to clear old vendettas. A Hema kid was busted with a grenade and a couple of people had been stabbed. The UN was cutting back its food rations, and people were getting angry. ("We're trying to get the people to return to their homes," a UN staffer told us. "But they'll be killed," we replied.)

I sat down on a milk crate while the others quietly filed their stories. I tried to read a book, but couldn't concentrate. Some woman was screaming into the camp from just over the fence. At first I brushed her off, until I realized she was screaming at us. She was stretched practically through the razor wire, pointing her finger at each of us in turn. The veins bulged from her neck and her eyes danced with hate. What she screamed was in Lingala, so I never knew what she actually said. But her sentences were punctuated with *"Journaliste! Journaliste!"* and I soon got the message.

But I didn't care anymore. I just wanted her gone. I wanted to grab her by the shirt, look her in the eyes, and tell her I was only doing my job, that it wasn't my fault, ask her to please shut up and stop being so *goddamn pitiful*.

I walked out on the grass and found a spot to lie down. It wasn't seeing the suffering Congolese that chipped away at me, but the

way they took their beatings, the way they woke up each day to viciousness and abuse and still sang songs while they walked down
the road. *Suffering and smiling.* I guess the woman in the camp finally got tired of singing.

The tenacity of the Congolese both impressed and confused the
hell out of me. In America we made mourning such a public affair,
pored over the virtues of our dead, and placed great significance on
dates and remembering them. It wasn't like that here. Despite everything that had happened in those weeks, I'd yet to see mothers wail
over their dead in public, or children cry at all for that matter. I'd
certainly see it later, but here the trauma was so malignant it had ravaged everything soft inside and left them numb. I remembered the
way the man from Drodro had described how gunboys kicked his
six-month-old baby in the air and sliced her in half with a machete.
How they rounded up the rest of his kids and butchered them in the
yard. He'd watched it all from his window, yet when he told the story,
you'd think he was recounting something he'd read in a newspaper.

"This happens all the time," the woman in the yellow dress had
told me during the gun battle. Ravage was a disease perched constantly in the corner, and hunger was part of growing up. They endured because it was all they knew. In Congo, people just died, and
over the next five years, the war would kill them at the rate of
twelve hundred per day.

I thought of this as the dozens of white UN Land Cruisers
passed by, as their massive logistics base was being built near the airport, as their staff drank beer all afternoon in the Hellenique, as
cargo planes landed each day loaded with photocopiers, steam-
rollers, forklifts, guns and ammo, lumber and steel beams.

I thought about Johnny and Neema and this town I'd grown attached to, only to see it ransacked and destroyed, and for what?
There'd been no struggle, no uprising against a despot, not even
against those who pillaged their country's wealth and turned their
children into beasts. There was no collective sacrifice for a greater

cause, for anything. There was only poverty and a savage lust for gold and plunder. The point of it all was that there was no point. People just died, and they died for nothing.

For the next hour I lay in the grass, letting the hot sun sting my face. I closed my eyes and drifted off to sleep, hoping to wake up just as a plane landed to take me home, anywhere but Bunia.

The following month, the European Union deployed a rapid-reaction force to Bunia, eleven hundred troops under the command of the French army. The soldiers of Operation Artemis had a fleet of Mi-24 and Mi-17 gunships and a shoot-to-kill mandate. Once the first gunboy took one in the chest from a well-trained French infantryman, the militia realized their game was up. They retreated back to their hillside camps and the violence abated in town.

Over five hundred people had been murdered in Bunia in the week after the Ugandan withdrawal, most of them executed in the streets, and hundreds more were severely wounded or missing. The UN received enormous criticism for failing to anticipate the carnage, and editors and human rights workers pointed to the UN's bumbling in Rwanda as an example of their continuing ineptitude. Even the UN commissioner for human rights, Sérgio Vieira de Mello, expressed outrage and horror at their failure and blamed the war in Iraq for drawing away attention from Congo.

"People are dying there by the hundreds, and that is not happening anywhere else in the world. But who is paying attention?" he told reporters during the siege. "There is an urgent need to demonstrate that the lives of Congolese are as important as the lives of Iraqis or any other life on this planet." (In a sad twist of events, de Mello himself would be assassinated in Iraq three months later when a terrorist bomb ripped through the UN's Baghdad headquarters.)

On June 28, the UN Security Council voted to give its soldiers in Congo a mandate to protect civilians and, by November, had sent in forty-three hundred additional troops. But attacks and massacres continued in the remote villages throughout the summer. Thousands poured into Bunia to escape, collecting at the airport, where the camp had swelled to 14,250 people by August and would remain for years a permanent suburb of grief. But with the town relatively stable, aid workers were able to treat the new arrivals, including hundreds of skeletal, starving children carried in from the bush on the verge of death.

On June 30, 2003, President Joseph Kabila officially announced the beginning of Congo's transitional government, which had been formed following the signing of an ostensibly final cease-fire with rebels in April. The transitional government would be presided over by Kabila and four vice presidents. Two of the men hailed from the political opposition and the former government, while the others had commanded the war's largest rebel groups, the RCD and MLC. The mandate of the transitional government was to integrate the rebels into the national army and hold elections in two years' time.

In the weeks and months following the Ugandan withdrawal, journalists and human rights researchers confirmed that Uganda had left behind tons of weapons for militia. The southern Lendu Ngiti faction had carried out the attacks on Bunia, but their northern compatriots were still being propped up by the Ugandans to control the region's gold. In August, MONUC forces intercepted more shipments of weapons bound for the northern Lendu fighters near the gold mines of Mongbwalu. (In the days before they left, the Ugandans actually turned over Mongbwalu to Lendu commanders in a signing ceremony. Listed as a witness on the signed document was UN military observer Safwat Oran, who would be executed by the same Lendu group the very next week.)

It was a long summer for everyone. Johnny continued living in the camp on a straw mat on the ground, until he was able to return to his dorm. But he was at least getting lots of work. All the violence in May had pulled in the international press, and Johnny soon became everyone's favorite translator. The AP even hired him as the resident stringer, until one afternoon when a militia lieutenant threatened to kill him for helping journalists. Azim, who was in Bunia at the time, quickly put Johnny on a plane to Beni, where he holed up with his sister while the situation calmed.

My colleague Helen Vesperini spent the summer living in Bunia covering the French army for Agence France-Presse. In August she completed the adoption of Neema's baby, named Lea, and took her home to Kigali, Rwanda. The last I heard, Neema was still alive but severely brain-damaged; she slowly recovers. And as for the woman in the yellow dress, I never saw her again.

I returned home to an empty house in Nairobi and too much time to sit around remembering things. I didn't know what to do with any of it, all the bodies and faces. I'd taken rolls of photos in Bunia after the siege—the headless man in Yambi, the teenage girl lying serene in the road, gunboys in hollow-eyed repose—and plastered them across my wall. I locked the doors and didn't leave the house for days, just sitting there in a little room at the end of the hall, staring up at these photos that gave me nothing, told me to either come a little closer or back up for good. It was Susan who finally pulled me out by giving me a job and sending me back to Bunia.

Susan got word that the Hollywood actress Jessica Lange would be touring the airport camp as a UNICEF goodwill ambassador, and since half the Nairobi bureau was in Iraq, Susan sent me to cover it. Lange was flying in to highlight the hunger crisis and that over two hundred women had been raped in Bunia that summer, along with countless others who'd probably never come forward.

The actress arrived at the camp at nine A.M., then made her way to the general hospital, where an emergency therapeutic feeding center had recently opened. Inside the center's dark rooms were three hundred children in various stages of starvation. They lay in cribs shadowed against the light, their temples sunken and disfigured, and skin so tight against their delicate bones they no longer appeared human. Their eyes told you everything, round and filled with terror, or glazed and slipping, but whatever they were suffering, they did it in silence, hardly even a whimper.

The UNICEF officer leading the tour had been caring for them from the beginning. I'd seen her at the airport right after the siege, days since her last sleep, and on the verge of tears or collapse. She now led the actress to each crib and peered inside, and in the depths of her eyes you could see the scabs that had bled and dried somewhere within. They spent the next hour at the giant scale, hoisting the emaciated figures into the slings, while the officer explained in clinical terms the stages in which children slowly died from hunger.

In the afternoon the group came to a cluster of tents in the hospital compound. Passing one, the officer explained it was the temporary ward for patients who'd recovered, children who had just weeks before been hopeless and feared for dead. About thirty children now sat inside the large tent holding cups of juice and biscuits, and out of nowhere they all began to sing. I didn't know the song they were singing, only that every child knew the words, and the sound of their living voices was so hauntingly beautiful, so pure and good in that awful, evil place. The actress and I stood at opposite ends of the tent watching them sing, sitting up on their knees, smiling with bright eyes and juice mustaches, singing the song over and over again, their voices looping and harmonizing, the sound of it like a single flame in a place too dark to see. And as they sang, I looked over and saw the actress weeping behind her tinted shades, and I felt my own throat tighten and the tears come at last. I recorded everything in my tape recorder, and in later months when the depression would find me back in my room looking to the dead for answers, I'd play that song again and again until I could hear it in my dreams. I can summon that music like recall, and even now it plays.

Chapter Two

DAILY BLOOD

In late September, I stepped out of a taxi on Sixth Street in Brooklyn and looked up at the apartment number matching the one in my notebook. I rang the buzzer, and in a minute out stepped this beautiful woman who walked down the stoop and put her arms around me. Our relationship had started the year before as a real whirlwind affair, and after dating only three weeks, we'd decided one night in a bar we were "moving to Africa." Five months later we were on a plane to Nairobi.

But Ann Marie was a playwright, and two months into our African adventure, before Congo, before anything, one of her plays was produced in Manhattan and pulled her back to the States. She'd returned for a brief visit, right after the fall of Bunia, but I'd been so completely out of my head, so wired into what I knew was taking place. I'd stayed up nights sitting by the radio, and since her French was better than mine, I'd open my Bunia notebooks and dial every random number people had given me, then make her talk to the strange, petrified voices who answered. When the taxi had arrived to take her back to the airport, she'd left me in the back room of that big house surrounded by photos of dead Congolese on the walls.

She'd returned to New York and rented this apartment in Brooklyn, hoping soon I'd find whatever it was I was looking for, then come home and share it with her. And now, there I was. I hadn't seen her in nearly five months, and I'm sure we both wondered if I was the same guy who'd once circled the Serengeti on the African map during those fever-pitched months of planning the getaway, who'd plotted epic trips involving long and bumpy

bus rides, the peak of Kilimanjaro, and long weekends in Zanzibar. The ro-
mance had been so thick during those months we'd practically floated all
the way there. In the end, we'd done none of those things, but I'd certainly
found what I was looking for, plus a whole lot more. And now, as I said,
there I was.

I was home, and I was thrilled and grateful to be there. I embraced the
everyday routines and amenities: visiting friends, long dinners at restaurants, autumn in the trees. The newspaper delivered on the stoop each
morning nearly brought me to tears.

In New York, no one seemed to know anything about what had happened in Bunia. I'd meet people in bars or at parties and they'd casually
say, "So I hear you were in Congo. What was that like?" But every time
when I started on the war, the memory slipped out so raw and blood-soaked
I often had to stop. Each moment became another opportunity to explain it
to myself, hoping it would make a little more sense. And since most Americans knew little about Congo ("Now that was Zaire, right? Wasn't there
a movie called Congo?"), they never saw it coming. By the end of the
night I'd be slant-eyed drunk, while some unlucky stranger had gotten
dragged through the blood and gristle at Drodro and Nyakunde and knew
in vivid detail how women were raped and dismembered. After a while I
didn't talk about it at all or would just smile and say, "It was alright, just
glad to be home."

I was glad to be home, for the idea of home, the idea of coming home,
had violently been redefined. But I had no idea what to do with it. All the
gangsterism and murder still remained tangled into a question I couldn't
resolve. So when the AP called and offered me the staff job of West Africa
correspondent, based in Congo, I took it hoping to understand something
I'd missed before. I was going back because Congo was now part of me,
dug in beneath the skin and all I ever thought about. The only way to get
clean was to bring the terrible tale to a conclusion that made some kind of
sense.

Ann Marie and I agreed the job was too good an opportunity to pass by.
She would follow me to Kinshasa in a few months, we decided. Or maybe

she wouldn't. I left New York with my guts in a bag, convinced I'd made some permanent, drastic mistake, yet completely unable to stop myself from getting on the plane.

I

My first assignment in December 2004 was to cover the presidential election in Ghana. When that was done, I flew to AP's funky West Africa bureau in Dakar, which pushes up against the blue-green Atlantic, where I sat at a desk staring at the pounding coastline from a wall of windows, anxious to leave for Kinshasa. I had a hundred questions about living and working in the capital, but no one to ask. Daniel Balint-Kurti, the previous Congo correspondent, had been shipped to Nigeria after only a few months in Kinshasa. The guy he'd replaced had stayed a total of twenty days before being sent to cover the war in Ivory Coast. So no one really knew anything, least of all me.

The only thing I knew about Kinshasa was that Daniel had rented a palace on the edge of town, an old mansion built by Mobutu's former foreign minister that would serve as my new home and office. A driver had also been called to pick me up from the airport. And knowing little more, I boarded a plane. I made it to Kinshasa without incident, walked into the terminal, and was arrested almost immediately.

My eyes must've flashed bright green lights because the police pounced on me as soon as I stepped in the immigration line. At the time, Kinshasa's N'Djili Airport was one of the most lawless and corrupt places on earth, and this was my first go-round, my breaking in. The police and immigration officials were wily professionals at shakedowns and outright theft. Their most successful ploy was enforcing a made-up law that forbade foreigners to leave the country with local (or sometimes any) currency, which they would enforce by pocketing your cash. Once you understood their behavior was motivated by poverty, aggravated by months without pay, you didn't get so upset and soon figured out the local games. But that night, they really put the screws on me good. They dragged my bags across the airport and up a flight of stairs, into a dim office occupied by the chief of airport police.

"Why are you in this country?" he demanded. He wore a light blue uniform and black beret. His eyes were bloodshot and chewing me alive.

"I'm a writer," I said. (Daniel's advice, as saying *journalist* might raise flags.)

"Then why did your driver tell the police you were a journalist?"

"Well, I am a journalist—"

"Aha! So you lied!"

"No, I meant—"

"Perhaps you aren't a journalist or writer at all. Perhaps you're here in the service of someone else, someone like Rwanda."

"You mean a spy?"

"Yes! You are a spy!" And so on. We sat in the room staring at one another for two hours until I finally broke. I handed the chief five dollars and was promptly released.

It was a stupid and minor incident, but the whole ordeal sent me into a spin, which only became worse when we pulled onto the road toward town. The road was a gnashing panorama of gridlock and belching exhaust, screaming taxi touts, cripples hobbling in the dirt in rags, garbage and sewage seeping out of gutters and filling the potholes, and crowds pulsing through it all. The airport road is also one of Kinshasa's major nerve centers, where the trademark *Kinois* bravado is in glorious display along the taxi stands and market stalls. But first-timers rarely see this deep, and I certainly didn't see it then. I made my driver go straight to a grocery store for beer, and when I arrived at the mansion, my new home, I found it was nothing but a shell of a building. The construction had stopped long ago when the foreign minister died, leaving only a sad little kitchen and two upstairs bedrooms. White columns curled up the second-floor balcony like legs of a dead spider, and gaping black holes covered the façade where doors and windows were never installed. It was full of mosquitoes and smelled of mildew. The electricity was also out, making the whole place feel condemned. As the taxi pulled out of the gate, I stood in the dark driveway taking stock of it all, and as I stared at the broken walls and holes in the ceilings, all my luggage lying in a heap in the dirt, not a friend to be found, I suddenly became worried I'd die here, tragically and alone. But I'd asked for it all, and with little else to do, I grabbed my bags, took my flashlight, and climbed the crumbling staircase.

I spent that night sitting on the balcony of my little room, pounding through a six-pack and giving myself a good talking to. And after a couple days, the feeling of doom seemed to lift as I came to appreciate where I'd landed. I'd brought with me the 1951 *Traveler's Guide to the Belgian Congo*, which I'd found in New York before leaving. Flipping through those black-and white photographs and looking out the window, all my previous Congo reporting suddenly took on greater dimension. I'd arrived in the capital, this distant kingdom we'd pondered in theory all those weeks in Bunia. To the people in the east—eighteen hundred kilometers across the great wall of jungle—the capital existed more as an article of faith than heaven itself. But here I was; I breathed deeply and took in the heavy smells of ozone and moist earth, exhaust fumes and garbage fires that burned down the block, and listened to the cackle of women on the road outside my compound. I rented a taxi and spent hours riding through the old boulevards, around immense traffic circles where centerpiece statues no longer stood. The city seemed to have frozen in time and crumbled with the thaw. I realized I'd only glimpsed Congo's tragedy on its surface, but here in the capital, those faded boulevards could take you down deep.

★ ★ ★

Kinshasa, or Leopoldville under the colony, was founded by the British-born American explorer Henry Morton Stanley in 1881 as a trade station for Belgium's King Leopold II. For years, the king had been searching for a colony for Belgium to compete with the rest of Europe's expanding empires.

Stanley was the right guy to find it for him. He had become an international celebrity several years earlier by becoming the first explorer ever to navigate the Congo River, which he did as part of an epic march across the African continent that took nearly three years and killed over half of his expedition. Stanley's bestselling account of the journey had piqued the interest of the king, who arranged a meeting. Stanley passionately explained to Leopold his dream of developing the Congo River and using it to open up central Africa for trade. Congo, the king knew, was full of ivory, and it was just the treasure he wanted. The Belgian government itself had no interest, so Leopold went to work in claiming Congo for himself, his personal empire in the heart of darkness.

To avoid suspicion from his neighbors, Leopold established the International Association of the Congo, whose professed objective was to open the continent to missionary work, free international trade, and eradicate the Afro-Arab slave traders from Zanzibar who were operating in the eastern forests. With his empire-building thus wrapped in altruism, Leopold gave Stanley a five-year contract and sent him back to Congo to lay the groundwork for the new colony, convincing even the explorer of his selfless aims. Stanley arrived at the mouth of the Congo on August 14, 1879, and over the next five years, in two separate trips, established trade agreements with many local chiefs and opened a series of stations along the river, the largest being Leopoldville.

Leopold finally acquired Congo for his own at the Berlin Conference in February 1885. There, he was granted the 2,345,000-square kilometer territory and promptly went to work pumping the forests of ivory, and later rubber, which he did for the next two decades with catastrophic results. Leopold named his new territory the Congo Free State, though it was nothing of the sort, as the king imposed an immediate trade monopoly on two thirds of the colony—his plan all along. The principal trading post and capital was established at Leopoldville, located five hundred kilometers from the Atlantic Ocean up the Congo River, which became the commercial highway for the burgeoning empire.

In 1908, amid controversy over the colony's murderous rubber and ivory gathering practices, the national government of Belgium assumed control over Congo from King Leopold and began transforming the capital from a bustling river post into a modernized metropolis. Throughout the late 1950s, when Belgian Congo was in its prime, Leopoldville was billed as "the city of contrasts" and marketed to thrill-seeking tourists and outdoorsmen as an outpost of luxury hemmed by the darkest wilds. The Belgians built beautiful hotels, museums, and sidewalk cafés, stadiums, cathedrals, and bronze monuments to the king. The boulevards of "European City" were wide and flanked by white colonial buildings like rows of perfect teeth. Africans were prohibited from straying into the Western quarter without a special pass. Yet tourists and the nearly seventeen thousand white residents could walk off their steak au poivre in "Native City," where the blacks would smile for photos with mortar and pestle and bang the tom-tom on cue. "Civilized and savage, Nordic and tropical," said my guidebook, "Leopoldville is the spectacular intersection of two civilizations, which after avoiding each other tend to integrate more and more."

Integration, however, was the farthest thing from reality. Throughout the 1950s, colonized Africans across the continent began demanding their independence, and after anticolonial riots broke in Leopoldville in 1959, Belgium realized it was powerless to resist. On June 30, 1960, Belgium granted Congo its freedom, and five days later, the country fell apart. The colonial army, known as the Force Publique, mutinied outside the capital, and soon the violence spread to several cities. For decades the colonial administration had corralled the Force Publique like attack dogs, keeping them demoralized, uneducated, and hungry. So it was no surprise the soldiers went for the throats of their white masters, targeting first the officers in the Force, then moving into the streets. For the Europeans, their most haunting nightmare was finally manifest as wild African soldiers crashed the forbidden color line into the palm-lined neighborhoods, ransacking homes and gang-raping white women.

Belgian paratroopers immediately swooped into all major cities to protect their citizens, but it mattered little. The whites fled in waves across the river to Brazzaville, down into Rhodesia and Tanzania, and into every empty seat on any airplane they could find. In ten days, around twenty-six thousand whites had vanished, and only a fraction would return, leaving their crops, factories, businesses, and homes for the locals to pick apart, and for the long arms of the viny earth to begin their eternal embrace.

The rioting and collapse of the country was now the problem of Congo's newly appointed prime minister, Patrice Lumumba, and its president, Joseph Kasavubu. Lumumba was a firebrand in the mold of Kwame Nkrumah, the Ghanaian who'd sparked the great independence movement that swept Africa in the 1950s and '60s. A former postal clerk, Lumumba started the first Congolese political party, Mouvement National Congolais (MNC), and ascended rapidly in party politics that gained momentum during the run-up to independence.

Lumumba appealed to the UN to help calm the crisis, and on July 15, UN secretary-general Dag Hammarskjöld sent several thousand peacekeepers into cities throughout Congo to replace Belgian paratroopers and help maintain a semblance of order. It didn't take long for the mutiny to spark other crises across the country. The mineral-rich southern province of Katanga seceded, and Baluba tribesmen in northern Katanga were staging massacres against the army and white settlers. In the central, diamond-mining province of Kasai, a tribal chief announced his territory's secession as well. Lumumba had, meanwhile, given the job of crushing the mutiny and insurrections to a former journalist and army sergeant named Joseph-Désiré Mobutu, who'd been made chief of staff. Amid this chaos, Mobutu was handed an indefinite amount of power, which he used to his advantage.

By September, the mounting chaos finally caused Congo's fledgling government to fracture and split. Kasavubu dismissed Lumumba as prime minister, prompting Lumumba to attempt to start his own rival government. Mobutu had Lumumba, his former boss, arrested in December 1960, and the following month, the former prime minister was executed in Katanga. In November 1965, as chief of the army, Mobutu seized power in a bloodless coup and took Congo for himself.

The capital, Leopoldville, maintained its charm for several years into Mobutu's reign, and the president used it as a showpiece to trumpet his version of the modern African state. In 1971, he changed the country's name to Zaire as part of a wide-sweeping "authenticity" movement meant to reclaim African pride and identity. Leopoldville became Kinshasa; *monsieur* was replaced by *citoyen*; suits and ties were replaced by Mao-ish, high-collar shirts and wool jackets designed by the Big Man himself; and all the Belgian street names and monuments were stripped and taken down.

Yet the Belgian-built mining and forestry industries still poured revenue into the national coffers, and as the Cold War began, Congo was heavily financed by the United States, France, and Belgium, who sought a democratic foothold amid socialist governments in surrounding Tanzania, Angola, and Congo-Brazzaville. During Angola's civil war, the United States funneled aid to UNITA rebels through Congo, which acted as the rebel's rear base.

But the city fell into decline in the 1970s as Mobutu began siphoning off the treasury to hold power. Over a span of years, Mobutu personally sucked dry the nation's operating budget in boondoggle projects, personal luxuries, and kickbacks to political rivals ("Keep your friends close," he liked saying, "but your enemies closer still"). The culture of corruption and extravagance was encouraged at every level of government until the system finally destroyed itself. The flourishing mining sector collapsed along with other industry, loans reared their heads, and with the end of the Cold War, handouts from Western countries and Bretton Woods institutions dried up and vanished.

In the waning years of Mobutu, Kinshasa became almost unlivable. The Big Man's thievery had bankrupted the country many times over. By 1990, the presidency alone accounted for 80 percent of the country's spending. Zaire's national debt was $14 billion at one point, and by 1994, inflation had rocketed to an unheard of 9,800 percent annually. Prices on essential goods soared out of reach, the public sector vanished, and while Mobutu's circle of sycophants and elite businessmen zipped around in Mercedes, drinking champagne in French restaurants, and chatting on their boxy Motorola mobiles, the city's residents suffered the weight of ruin on $120 per year.

When Kabila's rebel army captured Kinshasa in 1997, it was largely without a fight, and a rebel advance during the second Congo war got as close as the eastern outer neighborhoods, but never penetrated the town. The city had never been shelled. There were no bombed-out buildings or craters in the earth, no land mines left in the roads. Kinshasa wasn't flattened like Dresden or Tokyo. But the war and decades of festering neglect had poisoned the city from the inside. It was crippled, as if by a long, drawn-out illness.

When I arrived in December 2004, unemployment was still nearly absolute, with jobs reserved mainly for those with family or government connections. Most people scraped along by selling cheap wares in the markets, or walking the streets hawking whatever random items they were fortunate enough to come across: one pair of shoes polished to window-glass shine, two dog collars, packs of facial tissue, a miniature dollhouse, and a single dishrag. Basic government services were a distant memory: Kinshasa's main post office hadn't received mail in years, but as in every other government office, rank-and-file employees still turned up for work every day hoping to be paid. Most of the city remained without regular water or electricity, and the streets ran with green sewage, an incubator for the malaria that killed countless children in the city.

But as in Bunia, a tough resilience still managed to prevail. The people certainly suffered, but they did it with grace and humor, chins up, stepping out each day with swagger and personal style, which they upheld like a badge of defiance. Kinshasa was still indeed the city of contrasts, civilized and savage, opulent and bleak, so rich with character that my neck nearly snapped every time I drove the streets.

Kinshasa was live music all night long, every night of the week, brash and thumping and spilling down the street at four A M It was legions of street children groping to stay alive in a city that couldn't care if they died, abandoned by parents who believed them witches, devils, and sorcerers, and made to scavenge and hide like rats. It was sirens at midday and government Mercedes racing reckless through the slums; it was a fat man in a French suit mopping sweat with a silk handkerchief; soldiers squeezing out bribes on the intersection; and boys walking through traffic hawking puppies that dangled by their napes, neither dead or alive. It was clouds of exhaust parting on the boulevard to reveal a bombshell in a shiny gown and perfect hair, not a spot of dirt or wrinkle on her. It was families dressed for Sunday services, girls with long copper extensions and boys in boxy suits; the young *sapeur* (one of Kin's mod fashionistas) in the *shawarma* shop with bleached Afro, "Billy Jean" glove, and IRON stenciled on the back of his designer hoodie. And it was thousands of young men standing on corners all over town with no work to do or books to study, so disillusioned and eternally conquered it was a wonder they ever smiled at all.

In a country three times the size of Texas, Bunia and Kinshasa sat on opposite ends, separated by the world's second-largest rain forest. The two cities could've occupied different planets altogether. I'd only experienced the east, and almost everything about Kinshasa was different: the tribal makeup, local languages (they spoke Lingala in the west, Swahili in the east), and attitudes. In the east, people were characteristically mellow (when they weren't being killed), while the *Kinois* could be snobbish and curt. Even the food and music were different. The slow, sad soukous ballads fit right in with Bunia's doomed, frontier vibe, while the capital— wound tight, constantly on edge—demanded as much hipshake per second as possible.

Kinshasa was wholly different from the east, but during my first months living in the capital, the east still dominated my coverage. In Ituri, Hema and Lendu militia were still battling over gold fields and taxation rights to Lake Albert, and in the ongoing conflict hundreds of people were being killed and tens of thousands driven from their homes. Near the border with Rwanda, packs of Hutu rebels were massacring villagers before rounding up the women and gang-raping them while family members were forced to watch. The aid group Global Rights estimated forty-two thousand women and girls were raped over twelve months in South Kivu province alone, and those were just the ones who'd sought treatment.

The already horrific epidemic of rape became worse in May 2004, when renegade soldiers loyal to Laurent Nkunda and Jules Mutebusi had seized the city of Bukavu, provincial capital of South Kivu. Nkunda and Mutebusi were ethnic Tutsi and former commanders in the RCD, the Rwandan-backed rebel group. They'd bucked the government's army-integration program in

2002 and fled to the hills with a cadre of ex-militia. After government soldiers murdered over a dozen Congolese Tutsi in Bukavu in late May, the renegade commanders attacked the town, under the auspices of protecting their people.

Uruguayan peacekeepers, disobeying direct orders, had allowed the invaders to march right into Bukavu rather than fight. For days the renegade soldiers battled the army and raped scores of women across town—including a mother and her three-year-old daughter—and executed people in the streets. The UN's inaction sparked riots in Kinshasa, where residents torched UN vehicles and tried to sack the headquarters. Government soldiers finally drove Nkunda and Mutebusi's men from Bukavu, but not before thousands of residents had fled town and the surrounding villages. And all across the east, the UN estimated over two million people were displaced from the assorted violence, many sick and slowly starving to death in the bush.

In mid-March 2005, UN humanitarian chief Jan Egeland announced Congo had become "the world's worst humanitarian crisis." For the few Western journalists based in the capital, this was fantastic news, meaning we'd somehow edged out the tsunami in Asia and genocide in Sudan in the race for absolute misery. The announcement did wonders in getting my stories printed in American papers, which had previously been like kicking in a hailstorm. If the story involved something exciting such as cannibalism, endangered gorillas, or little girls being raped with machetes, it might have big enough wings to survive its journey across the Atlantic. Everything else left the desk and crashed straight into its watery grave, where a half century of dispatches of bothersome African despair boiled at the bottom.

Following the UN announcement, I'd had a few good weeks of nonstop work, and I was grateful for that. Congo and its grinding troubles seemed to radiate a low-grade depression that settled deep in your lungs like a flu, and I agreed with my new friend Dave

Lewis, the Reuters and *Economist*'s man in Kinshasa, that busy weeks shielded us from this malaise. You got one or two stories in the morning and rode the wave through the afternoon, till it was time for sundowners, or a hearty dinner to put you off to bed. Slow weeks lifted this shield and left you suddenly vulnerable, left you pacing your bedroom with all that murder and mutilation of the past weeks' stories stirring around in the air-conditioning. The depression made you paranoid and suspicious, kept you out at degenerate nightclubs until the sun rose over the palms, and one of these typical weeknights we found ourselves in the VIP Saloon.

The bar was just off Kinshasa's main boulevard and usually filled by midnight with Lebanese diamond dealers, French and Belgian soldiers, and the few Congolese who could afford the five-dollar beers and sodas. The buzz created by the UN's announcement had ended, leaving me and Dave restless and manic. It had been four days since our last story—even the east was quiet that week—and neither of us had really left our apartments.

We ordered two bottles of local Skol at the lamplit bar and watched long-legged prostitutes in red-flame boots dance before the wall of mirrors. The Euro pop on the speakers was loud and monotonous, but punchy enough to lift us from our doldrums. Across the bar at VIP, a group of Belgian businessmen sipped J&B while bar girls sat like smiling mannequins in their laps. Two Germans stood in the far corner, twitchy and bug-eyed, taking turns doing bumps of cocaine in the bathroom.

Dave was one of those far-flung Brits born out in the empire, raised in Kenya and Tanzania and schooled in England. He'd kicked around South America after university, eventually finding his way back to Africa and landing in Kinshasa, where he'd been spellbound by the violent country as much as I was. He was a slick operator, rolling in late for dinner or drinks after greasing one of the government or embassy sources he cultivated like some section-five spook. "Just someone I met somewhere," he'd say, shifting to the menu. "So, what are you having?" I learned a lot by watching Dave Lewis work, and those first couple months he must've scooped me weekly.

He'd just returned from an assignment in Congo-Brazzaville, traveling with UNICEF to gauge the humanitarian situation in the bush. The war in Congo-Brazzaville—just a boat ride across the Congo River from Kinshasa—had ended years before, but rebels known as Ninjas still operated freely in the deep interior. On this last trip, a small wolf pack of Ninjas had ambushed Dave's convoy, guns blazing in the air and lots of shouting. No one had been hurt, but a stoned, crazy Ninja had jumped into Dave's truck, held two grenades to his head, and stolen his cherished jungle boots.

"Two grenades in one hand, and a bloody *joint* between his fingers," he said, demonstrating with a cigarette. We laughed about it now over beers. Sometimes even the most rotten assignments seemed like holidays once back in Kinshasa.

"The UN's saying the Mai Mai are sporting fetuses around their necks," he said.

"Oh, lovely. The Lendu wear human kidneys on their bandoliers. I think I saw it once."

It was our usual blowing-off-steam banter, tasteless and maybe too loud. But something about it must've tapped a nerve in Dave, who went quiet for a minute, then said, "I haven't written one story in six months where someone didn't die."

"Same here," I said. "I'm thinking of counting all the dead people in mine. I wonder how many I'll get."

News of the dead found you in several ways, and often when you wanted it least—two beers into the night after filing all day, or just when you reached the restaurant and put in your order. If Dave was there, and it was something small like a plane crash (those Soviet-era Antonovs fell out of the sky almost weekly), we'd exchange a haggard look and start making deals. "If you wait, I'll wait," we'd say, just to finish our food like normal people. We never waited long; the desk and telephone controlled us like tin men. But while we sat there with a mouthful of food, the dead now among us to sort out, one of us would shoot a glance and repeat our sacred news-grunt mantra: "If we don't file, it doesn't exist."

Many reports of attacks, rapes, and massacres came through confidential sources within the UN, and to them by humanitarian officers, local government officials, or residents—often those who'd escaped attacks, walking several days with children and festering wounds to a military post. One UN contact shuttled information to me through instant message, usually bloody and rancid by the time it flashed on my screen: *Hear about the attack near Tchomia? 18 Hema lost their livers.*

With my contact in the UN, things were never serious, even on those rare occasions when I desperately wanted them to be. Most often the jokes came out of boredom, or those dark recesses where coping mechanisms had terribly malfunctioned after years of being in the bad bush: *Have you thought much about the* Ituri Cookbook? *I have an addition: stewed hearts of Hema in mother's milk. Or perhaps, kidney brochettes with peacekeeper pie?*

One day after one of those unrelenting weeks of sitting in Kinshasa filing daily blood from the east, hardly ever leaving the house, I'd said something that must've sounded naïve, about never having time to write positive, hopeful stories. The reply was quick and barbed: *There aren't any happy stories here, pal,* the message read. *This place is a Viking holiday. It's all blood, rape, and gore.*

II

Even knowing what we were in for, every couple months it was necessary to leave the relative quiet of Kinshasa, the restaurants, nightclubs, and pool parties, and experience the war up close. I'd turn up at MONUC headquarters before dawn and board the white UN bus to the airport, the one with steel grates over the windows for the rocks and garbage often hurled from the road-sides. I'd squeeze in among the Congolese officials in double-breasted suits; the local human rights workers returning wearily to the field. There'd be Indian and Uruguayan peacekeepers laden with boxes of food shipped from home, and UN officers with gelled hair and roller briefcases like software salesmen on the shuttle. We'd all board one of those 727s and leap across the green, sucking carpet.

The personnel planes had become more crowded since I'd last been in Congo. By the time I arrived in Kinshasa, the tiny UN mission that began in 1999 with ninety staff observing the cease-fire was now the largest, most expensive peacekeeping effort in the world, with 16,700 soldiers and an annual budget of over one billion dollars.

Congo's peacekeepers, along with UN agencies, were now saddled with trying to eradicate some twenty thousand militia in the east and assist the two million people displaced by the raids and war. But most important, there was now a massive movement to hold presidential elections.

This was the pinnacle the UN had been building toward. These would be the first elections since Congo's independence from Belgium, and the hopeful vanguard for peace and recovery. Elections were a new beginning, a chance to right all the wrongs, purge the corruption that had plagued the nation since its birth, create accountability in government and state-run enterprises. Elections could make way for a judiciary to prosecute war criminals and corrupt officials, one that wasn't swayed by political payoffs. They would deliver a rightly elected parliament that could function properly and draft laws, and a national army that wasn't as predatory as the militia they were supposed to fight.

Of course, in the vast, forest-covered nation, one empty of roads, electricity, telephones, or local municipal governments, this

also entailed some difficulties. Elections meant taking a largely uneducated population of over fifty million people and explaining
democracy and how to vote. It meant ordering tens of thousands
of ballot boxes and taking them by boat, 4x4, motorcycle, bicycle,
and small plane into the jungles and mountains, along with armies
of election workers who themselves had to be trained. It meant
raising money from wealthy Western nations to finance nearly all
of it, since corruption had left the Congolese government no
money for its own. And most of all, it meant purging the country
of armed groups so people could vote in peace. Battling militia and
planning elections, UN officials said, had unexpectedly become the
single most ambitious project the world body had ever undertaken
in its sixty-year history. And it came at a high price.

As the elections neared, UN soldiers in Ituri were making use of
their robust mandate to hunt and disband militia, ripping down
bases, making arrests, and engaging them whenever resistance was
met. And before long, the strategy took its toll. On February 25,
2005, a gang of Lendu ambushed a foot patrol of Bangladeshi soldiers near a tiny village called Kafe and killed nine. During the
well-coordinated attack, the other peacekeepers fled the scene, and
in their retreat, militia stripped the dead UN soldiers' uniforms and
mutilated their bodies.

The peacekeepers had been sent to Kafe—part of a vast, hill-
swept territory in the northern part of Ituri called Djugu—in late
January to protect more than one hundred thousand people who'd
fled battles between Hema and Lendu militia over taxation rights
to Lake Albert. The villagers, who'd managed harrowing escapes
from these attacks, walked dozens of miles to four separate camps
in the remote hills and, once there, started dying by the hundreds
from cholera, dysentery, and measles. Two weeks after the ambush,
peacekeepers gunned down some sixty Lendu militia using
armored vehicles and Mi-25 attack helicopters. The assault was led

by Pakistani ground troops, hardened from fighting Al Qaeda in the mountains of Pakistan, and assisted by Indian helicopter pilots. Locked in a years-long face-off on their own borders, the two armies now combined to create a rolling killing machine along the bloody hills of Ituri.

In late March, I took one of the twice-weekly UN flights from Kinshasa to Bunia, which had become the headquarters for the five-thousand-strong UN Ituri Brigade. A rush of cold nostalgia hit me as I stepped off the plane and rode into town, which had drastically transformed since the bad days of 2003. The UN mission had tripled in size, and teenage gunboys in wigs and painted fingernails were no longer prowling the streets with rocket launchers. Several new restaurants and hotels had even opened, including an enterprising Indian joint at the Hotel Ituri that catered to Indian and Bangladeshi troops, plus the massive influx of international press and foreign aid workers.

There was a lopsided pool table in the bar of the Indian restaurant, and every night a dozen Italian aid workers would line up to play two hefty Congolese girls who'd established themselves as local sharks. The girls played for bottles of beer, knocking back one after another, yet they never weaved or staggered, and I never saw them lose.

The Italian men wore their hair long and kept it clean and bouncy, even in Bunia's thick dust and heat. They wore tight designer jeans and pointy leather shoes and thundered through town on silver Ducatis, which they had shipped from Italy. The women were young and loud and would fall down drunk in front of tables of staring Congolese.

My first night in town, I had a beer in the restaurant with an old friend, the hardened UN officer whose truck had been shot with arrows during the siege. We watched the aid workers spilling their drinks and running into tables, just another night now in Bunia. "Look what's happened to this town," the officer said, his face twisted in disgust. "These kids don't have a fucking clue what happened here."

Along with the aid workers, Bunia had also become a backwater for cowboy journalists looking for action. You'd see them at dinner, outfitted with GPS systems and dressed in the latest tactical gear, talking about cannibals, gunfights, and child-raping peacekeepers. The ones who rolled in hot from New York were the best, like this American photographer whose business cards were shaped like dog tags, metal and all. I guessed it was only a matter of time before one of them finally walked into the airport camp and shouted, "Anyone here been raped and speaks English?" (It was a classic line passed down as lore among the Africa hacks, only because once in Congo, in 1960, someone had actually said it.)

A few days later I landed a seat on a UN chopper that was taking Ross Mountain, the UN deputy in charge of Congo, on a tour of three of Djugu's camps, where more than seventy-five thousand people now stayed. Before arriving in Kinshasa in December 2004, Mountain had served as Kofi Annan's special representative in Iraq through the elections. He was a straight-talking Kiwi who never tried to sugarcoat the UN's mistakes or bad calls, and there'd been many. Every week Mountain would take trips into the thick of Congo's misery to get a look for himself, and this week he'd asked to see the great catastrophe of Ituri.

Staring down from a chopper over eastern Congo was like glimpsing a prototype of earth during the first days of creation. *Where are all the people?* I always wondered. The camp in Tche was located 161 kilometers north of Bunia in the sweeping, green hills—countryside so stunning it flipped your stomach if you really knew what happened on the ground. About twenty-five thousand people had congregated in the crook of a narrow valley, which quickly became an ideal container for disease. At least twenty kids were dropping every day from measles and drinking dirty water, and groups such as MSF were working days without sleep just to quell the death. About 350 Pakistani peacekeepers were dug into the valley with tons of steel and firepower, but it wasn't enough to stop kids wasting away from diarrhea.

The helicopter landing zone was on a ridgeline overlooking the camp, and as we approached, I could see the Pakistanis had arranged some sort of welcoming ceremony nearby for the guests. The camp had also spread up onto the ridge, and hundreds of its weary residents stood below to watch the helicopter land. But as we touched down, the rotor wash from the chopper blades blew the thatched roofs off several huts and sent a wall of red, stinging sand into the crowd. Children screamed and scattered in all directions. The plastic tables and chairs meant for our ceremony sailed through the air and slammed into people's backs. As the wheels bounced and settled, someone from Mountain's entourage shook his head and yelled, "Jesus Christ, what have we done?"

The people had returned when I stepped out of the chopper. They now crowded together, pressed behind a high wall of razor wire, while others sat perched in trees, watching and waiting. The eyes stopped us cold, even long after the blades had finished spinning. We stood frozen in the awkward silence, waiting for someone to say something. Mountain broke the ice for all of us. "My God," he said, walking forward, "look at all these kids who aren't in school."

A Pakistani colonel escorted Mountain and his staff away, so I headed down into the camp to get my story. And to my surprise, there amid the haze of cooking fires, was Johnny. He'd landed a job as a UN interpreter a few months before and had even sent me an e-mail about the good news. I'd suspected he was kicking around these hills somewhere, but never expected to actually bump into him. I ran over and tackled him with a giant bear hug. I hadn't seen him in nearly two years. He looked healthy and happy, if a little tired and dirty from living in a tent camp with a battalion of Pakistani soldiers, maybe four of whom spoke any English. "I *knew* you'd be back," he said. "I *knew* you couldn't stay away from Congo!"

I immediately enlisted him to translate Swahili for me, and we made our way through the camp, speaking to people who'd escaped the village raids with little but their lives. One man, named Ali Mohammed, had walked outside his hut in Loga just in time to watch Lendu teenagers butcher his mother and two children with machetes. He'd escaped by throwing himself down a mountain and tumbling to the bottom. He was still dressed in the long, torn nightgown he'd been wearing during the first shots of the raid, now his only material possession.

I didn't have time for many interviews. The chopper stayed no longer than thirty minutes in each camp, long enough for Mountain and his staff to speak with aid workers and military, get off some snaps, and declare that, yes, this was indeed the world's worst humanitarian crisis. We then climbed back into the bird, fired up the blades, and sailed off again like a white ghost over the hills.

A week after Mountain's visit, UN peacekeepers pulled out of the camps at Tche, Gina, Tchomia, and Kafe, leaving over one hundred thousand people in the hands of poorly paid, ill-equipped Congolese soldiers, who promptly began looting the tents as soon as the blue helmets were out of sight. A cholera epidemic had already descended on two camps, so when hundreds of people fled the marauding troops, many also carried their deaths with them into the tall grass.

No one understood the delicate dance of warfighting and peacekeeping better than Major General Patrick Cammaert, who was having his own troubles in the mountainous provinces of North and South Kivu, near the Rwandan border. I met Cammaert in early June 2005 in a flower-decked hotel bar in Bukavu, which had become the UN's command post in dealing with the scourge of Rwandan Hutu rebels. The Dutch general was in charge of over twelve thousand peacekeepers in the eastern sector, stretching from the Sudanese border to the southern province of Katanga. And with Ituri alone, there was never a moment when his command wasn't hot.

After peacekeepers had initially allowed Bukavu to fall the previous year, government soldiers had managed to push Nkunda and Mutebusi's men into the hills, where they remained a threat to be watched. But the general wasn't worried about Nkunda or Mutebusi now. He'd just returned from the dense forests west of Bukavu, where Hutu rebels had sliced up the village of Ihembe, hacking off hands and feet of their victims and removing their kidneys. The killings had partly been the work of Rasta militia, an even more macabre group consisting of Rwandan Hutu *genocidaires*, renegade government soldiers, and Mai Mai warriors, regional minutemen who'd formed in the vacuum left by Mobutu's crumbling army. Rastas had kidnapped fifty young girls during the raid and most likely taken them to mountain camps and raped them day after day before abandoning them in the forest to die. During the attack, panicked villagers had fled into the mountains, where many were likely to die from exposure and disease.

The general removed his blue beret and rubbed his temples. He'd toured the scene of the killings, and seeing that kind of evil had really twisted his head. "The brutality, it's beyond comprehension," he said, the words trailing off. "Innocent kids, two years old, just beaten to pulp."

I'd come to Bukavu myself to see the damage from the Hutu raids. The previous day, I'd visited a halfway house for women and girls so brutally raped by Hutu rebels they'd needed reconstructive surgery. I'd entered with a few stock questions and left three hours later, having listened to an entire room full of victims explain precisely how they were ravaged with gun barrels, sticks, and knives and left to die on the forest floor, how insects had entered their bodies, and how they could never bear children or look at their husbands again. They'd lined up to tell their stories, their eyes digging through the walls, and by the time I walked outside I was soaked with sweat and cursing like a scared child.

What was heavy on the general's mind that night was how to send troops into the jungles to protect these people, and how to keep his men from being ambushed in the process. The only way to safeguard the population was to purge the ten thousand Hutu and Rasta fighters from the jungles, which would need to be done before elections could ever take place. With the recent murders of the nine Bangladeshis, Cammaert had already lost twelve peacekeepers in combat in Ituri that year, and the terrain there was mostly treeless and ideal for open-ended assaults. The mountains and jungles near Rwanda were an altogether different war game, where the probability for ambush was extremely high.

But the general had just pulled a brilliant maneuver, convincing the UN brass to bring in units of Guatemalan special forces, trained jungle fighters who could creep through the dense terrain to stage surgical strikes on unsuspecting Hutu. Once the rebels were flushed into open territory, Mi-25 attack helicopters could dispatch them. It was certainly one of the most ingenious tactics the UN had proposed. The general, a decorated soldier who'd just got done serving as Kofi Annan's top military adviser in New York, now found himself a lead player in Congo's confusing nightmare. But the general had his own bad dream, more vivid and horrifying, the one where he was auditioning for the role of UN commander in the world's next Mogadishu.

"I'm losing sleep," he said, staring off into nothing. "I can't stop thinking about those forests."

He was right to be worried. The following January, eight of those Guatemalan special-ops soldiers were killed in action, not in the forests as the general feared, but on the open plains of Haute Uélé district, north of Ituri. In a secret operation entirely unknown to New York headquarters, eighty soldiers were sent to Garamba

National Park to arrest a top lieutenant in the Lord's Resistance Army, a Ugandan rebel group who'd crossed over from neighboring Sudan. Little is known about the actual mission, but most sources conclude the Guatemalans had been tracked early on, then walked right into an ambush. The general was later summoned to New York to explain why eight men were killed and mutilated on the prairie, hundreds of kilometers from their sector. A UN investigation into the operation yielded few results, or certainly none that were shared with the press.

The mystery surrounding the Guatemalan operation would serve as a later example of the difficulty in reporting the UN's military actions in Congo. For instance, the March operation in Loga—when peacekeepers killed around sixty militia—had also resulted in a number of civilian deaths, according to villagers. Peacekeepers had taken small-arms fire as they'd approached a crowded market and responded by pounding the market with mortars, while gunships hovered overhead and emptied their cannons. The militia had used the market vendors as human shields, the UN said, and women and children were also seen firing guns. As with most peacekeeping operations, there was no way to confirm the UN's information.

In fact, most of my reporting days were spent trying to decipher the cryptic bits of information provided by UN headquarters while somehow remaining credible. To sell the world body's new method of peace enforcing to the world press, the UN relied on Kemal Saiki, a tough, chain-smoking Algerian and bona fide Sergeant Slaughter for the struggling blue helmets. Kemal would routinely lay down the law for the gunboys during his weekly press conferences, issuing ultimatums and barbed threats. Dave and I often joked about petitioning MONUC to just give Kemal a rifle and pocketknife and turn him loose in the hills to clean up. He was a former spokesman for OPEC, leagues better than most UN press officers in Congo, and always good for a beer. But still, when it came down to numbers and hard facts, you filed at your own risk.

One Friday night I'd called Kemal to follow up on a raid that had begun that morning south of Bunia. The blue helmets were tearing down another Lendu camp, and we knew they'd made contact.

"How many dead?" I asked.

"Eighteen casualties," he said.

"No, I mean dead. How many militia killed?"

"Yeah, eighteen," he said. "Eighteen fatalities."

I ran with the story. Hours later, Dave called and said he got thirty-eight dead, and Radio France International was reporting ten killed, all from different sources within the UN. At the weekly press conference days later, Dave and I cornered Kemal to get an explanation.

"Look, we're all getting different numbers," I said. "Which is it: eighteen, thirty-eight, or ten?"

"It's eighteen," he said. He then leaned in and whispered, "Look, what really happened was the helicopter fired eighteen shots, and it got mistaken for eighteen *shot*. Get me? We don't really know."

"But you told me eighteen," I said.

"Yeah, or it was eighteen militia standing on the roof of a house when the helicopter released its rockets. The roof collapsed, the people disappeared. Boom. Eighteen."

He pulled out a cigarette and made his way for the door.

"Why are you so obsessed with death counts?" he said. "This isn't Vietnam."

Kemal was right. It wasn't Vietnam. This was worse. And we knew because we had the Number, the count. Every couple of years, the International Rescue Committee, an American aid group, gave us the gift of the official death count. They'd divide the country into health zones and actually send nurses with clipboards into the hills and jungles asking families to count their dead. Their 2005 report estimated 3.9 million killed between 1998 and 2004, about "38,000 excess deaths per month," caused mostly by "easily preventable and treatable illnesses rather than violence." The report went on to suggest that "if the effects of violence were removed, all-cause mortality could fall to almost normal rates."

We recited the official death count at the end of every story, along with a few tight summary sentences of the conflict that I could magically produce without even thinking about it. The death count was the boilerplate, the one thing you dropped into every conversation, lecture, or e-mail to those who didn't know the score. It differentiated Congo from everything else, from Korea, Vietnam, Bosnia, and Iraq. It had killed more than all of them, and every day the count grew bigger and bigger.

Sexed-up homicides came almost daily: death by bullets or machetes or sledgehammers to the head; the steady sequence of plane and train crashes and boats sinking in the rivers. These stories made the papers. But most people passed away in quiet obscurity—of starvation, cholera, diarrhea, malaria, measles, a hacking cough that just wouldn't quit—usually on the muddy floor of the forest where they'd finally run out of strength, or some stranger's home far from their own. Those rarely made the news; they were just the Number. We'd have to get creative with those or sneak them in whenever ten people died of Ebola or plague and the desk went nuts.

Before I could blink, I'd passed six months in Kinshasa and all I seemed to do was file away this ugly depredation. On top of it all, in April my editors had sent me to Togo to cover the presidential election, where the son of the country's dead ex-dictator was sure to win. And when he finally did, the streets exploded in violent riots and army crackdowns. For three weeks I reported that story, and nearly every day I'd get chased through the streets by mobs swinging machetes and nail-studded clubs. One French reporter was doused in gasoline and chased with a lighter. And when it wasn't the mobs, it was jackbooted soldiers pumping the streets with tear gas and wild firing down the alleys. When the desk finally pulled me out, I'd gone straight home to Congo and plugged right back into the war and that foul-smelling machine, mostly telling the stories from my desk in Kinshasa instead of the red-dirt roads themselves, adding color from a box of blood-slaked observations resupplied on those infrequent trips to the east. And after months and months of that work, the mind begged to be released, to find the autopilot and hand over the controls. It was almost too easy to do, shut it down and let the eyes glaze back while you assembled the generic beast from your repertoire of menacing words, drew some teeth and beady eyes, slugged it "CONGO-FIGHT," and flung it on the wires before the ketchup could dry. It was hard as hell to remember that each story deserved the same attention because the people and crimes were real and you were the record. And for those millions who died nameless and afraid, each had a story that would go untold if you didn't tell it, and the very idea would spin you tight if you gave it too much thought. It was the greatest job I'd ever had. But after a while it wore you down, nothing like trauma or shell shock (not from the desk, anyway), but a creeping emotional atrophy, and loneliness so intense on sunbleached mornings it erased every thought in your mind. After a while I began to cultivate a little getaway daydream, of flying to Paris and checking into the nicest hotel I could find, then lying in bed with blackout curtains drawn, just staring into the dark.

But there was no time for Paris, because little by little, the two worlds of east and west gradually began to merge and the violence arrived in the capital. Gradually our cocktail and dinner parties, and then our lives in general, became weighted down by one encompassing subject: June 30, the day many predicted Kinshasa would crumble in a wave of blood and terror.

The date marked the end of the country's transitional government, which had been established in 2003 by government and rebels at the end of the war. The agreement also made clear that June 30, 2005, must be the date of presidential elections, the goal the UN and everyone else were struggling to meet.

But anyone expecting elections in June was living a fantasy, because the UN couldn't plan them alone. They'd need help, and from the one person least able to offer it: Joseph Kabila. President Kabila had come to power after his father, Laurent, was assassinated by his own bodyguard in 2001. He'd immediately made strides in ending the war and coaxed back Western donors and the World Bank, which over the next five years gave Congo $2.3 billion in loans. And doing so, he'd played lip service to the Western diplomats and UN officials who advised him to hold elections.

But Kabila's government was in constant disorder, gutted by corruption, and hamstrung by allegiances within the president's inner circle, and those of his four vice presidents, two of whom were former rebel leaders. Over a quarter of the national budget was still unaccounted for; 80 percent of all taxes and customs revenue disappeared (up to $1.7 billion a year); in the east, that missing revenue directly funded the plague of armed movements. And of the $8 million set aside each month to pay and feed the army, more than half was disappearing before it ever reached the men. The president remained surrounded by people intent on keeping these systems in place, lawmakers and army officers with too much money and power to lose in a transparent, corrupt-free state. As one American diplomat once told me, "Kabila is alone in a lake of piranhas. He knows the second he puts the first toe in, his whole body will follow."

The government promised to contribute $70 million to elections, but by June had produced only $4 million. There was obviously little political will within the establishment to hold elections. So as expected, in late April, the president extended the transitional government and delayed the vote until June 2006. The first hint of a postponement back in January had sparked massive rioting in the capital, which ended when police opened fire into the crowds. I'd only been in town a couple of weeks and didn't venture out into the mobs alone, knowing how easy it would've been for some kid to put a rock in my face and be lost underfoot.

But after the official April declaration, the country's main opposition party, the Union for Democracy and Social Progress (or UDPS, their French acronym), called for protests on June 30, and rumors quickly spread they'd be much worse than the January riots, that mobs would run wild through the streets. It was billed as "Congo's apocalypse," a Y2K in the heart of darkness that would terminate and delete in a rain of bullets and machete blades, and I knew I'd be right at the middle with little place to hide.

I had, however, convinced the AP to let me move apartments. After a few weeks of settling in, the mansion had worked out fine. There was no electricity much of the time, and water worked only two hours per day, but it was livable. The problem was that the house was too close to the Kintambo market, which was a popular staging area for opposition demonstrators. Riots and demonstrations had swept through Kintambo the previous May when UN peacekeepers allowed Bukavu to fall to renegade soldiers. It had been Daniel Balint-Kurti's first month, and gangs of rioters had streamed down our street and mobbed around the compound walls, looking to get inside. Soldiers nearby had to fire rounds over their heads to scare them off. The UN listed Kintambo outside its "safe zone" and forbade its own staff to live there. Worried, I called the U.S. embassy's head of security and asked him what I should do. "Are you kidding?" he said. "Move."

So I'd found a two-bedroom apartment just off the main boulevard in Gombe, the relatively safe commercial and diplomatic quarter. The UN headquarters was a five-minute drive, and the U.S. embassy just a mad dash across the boulevard. Water and electricity were more reliable in Gombe, though never constant. Several times a week I still filed from outside next to my generator, which was like typing while you mowed the lawn. The Indian landlord even provided me with a housekeeper, a shrunken, toothless man named Kasango, who cooked marvelous chicken dinners and prepared hot oatmeal in the mornings, yet insisted on keeping my laundry detergent in the refrigerator.

Gombe was home to most of Kinshasa's expat community, and even with their private security guards, their high walls topped with razor wire and broken glass, and a compound of UN soldiers nearby, the June 30 fear still crept its way inside. Aside from UN and humanitarian staff, Kinshasa had many Belgians who'd stuck around after independence, having invested everything in a falling star. There were also many French, Israelis, and Lebanese, who owned much of the city's commercial center, and Indians who'd returned after Mobutu had booted them out in the 1970s.

The expats' fear was rooted in the city's long history of mass lootings, or *pillage*, mainly carried out by government soldiers. Lootings had marred the capital in the late 1950s in the last days of colonial rule, then again after independence, and twice in the 1990s. In each one of these instances, Belgian or French paratroopers had been dropped in to restore order and evacuate foreigners. The worst of the *pillages* had been in September 1991, when several thousand soldiers rioted in the capital to protest missed wages. Residents quickly joined the melee, barging into homes in the expat quarter and stripping them of everything, including sink fixtures and wallpaper. The mobs picked apart the city like ants— factories, car dealerships, groceries, boutiques—even as French commandos fired bullets over their heads. Mobutu loyalists simply gunned the looters down in the streets. The looting then spread nationwide. Foreigners who'd sank decades into farms and factories lost them in minutes. Fears of famine and epidemic spread since no food or medicines were left anywhere. Hundreds were killed, and from all across the country reports flooded in of foreigners being raped by soldiers.

Kinshasa was rocked by another round of mass lootings in 1997 after Mobutu fled the city in advance of Kabila's rebels. The city still bore the nasty scars of all these events. In government offices, workers sat in darkness since all the fixtures had been ripped from their wires. At the Ministry of Information, for instance, the elevator worked only sporadically, and inquiries into your press credentials often meant climbing sixteen flights of stairs in pitch-darkness since there was no electricity. The walk was best done with a cigarette lighter since many of the steps had crumbled and fallen off. They were slippery, too, since workers used the stairwell as a urinal after the building's restrooms stopped functioning long ago.

We'd sit around and listen to the old hands talk about the *real* crazy days, about watching the city disappear piece by piece in the gunfire and looting while they bravely fought to maintain their small stake. "There were two days between the time Mobutu fled in 1997 and Kabila's rebels advanced onto Kinshasa," my friend Moi would tell us. He was a Congolese businessman married to a beautiful Polish woman, and they'd lived in a large house on the outskirts of town. The city had gone mad after Mobutu's retreat, with ravenous mobs of residents and soldiers looting every quarter. For two days, Moi sat on his roof with a pump shotgun and a case of shells, scattering the crowds that gathered at his gate. Government soldiers would cruise by and listen for the gun blast; the heavier the weapon, the better the chance they'd keep going. Other security forces raced down the block, gunning down looters and lining bodies on the roadside. While Moi blasted away on the roof, his wife, Nesh, kept the NBA play-offs on the television below, poking her head out the window every half hour to announce the score. "I was up there trying to save our house," he'd say, "and there was Nesh yelling, 'Heat 67, Knicks 55' *Boom! Boom!*"

Toward the end of April 2005, Congo's army chief of staff appeared on state television to announce something that had alarmed him. Businesses throughout the city were reporting mass buyouts of machetes, and he suspected the surge in sales had something to do with June 30 plans. Average Congolese were buying the Tramontina blades as fast as shop owners stocked them on the shelves, he said, and someone in power was behind their distribution. The opposition party was vowing to shut down the streets June 30 with thousands of supporters, but even they denied distributing weapons.

The machete scare was made worse by a spate of grotesque murders throughout Kinshasa's Lingwala slum. People started turning up dead with their legs, heads, arms, and even lips missing. Residents started blaming the killings on the mysterious Kata-Kata, which means "cut-cut" in the local Lingala. Kata-Kata was one of several things, or many things all together: Angolan soldiers dressed in Congolese uniforms, Tanzanian and Zambian agents who'd come to overthrow the government, or perhaps members of Kabila's presidential guard, who were killing to make people too afraid to protest on June 30. A few even guessed Kata-Kata was some kind of mutant werewolf who'd crawled out of the forest, an agent of the devil who'd arrived as a harbinger of the end of days.

Rush hour suddenly started two hours earlier because residents didn't want to be caught in the dark. Gas stations also closed earlier, causing a backup of taxis that left throngs of terrified people still stranded at dusk. Ask people what was happening, and they'd tell you, *"C'est Kata-Kata."*

After a pregnant woman was found butchered in the weeds, my housekeeper, Kasango, asked for his entire month's salary to buy a television. I refused again and again, hating the idea of his family not eating for weeks because Kasango wanted to watch TV. I'd say something stupidly paternal like "You can't eat a television!" and he'd reply, *"Patron, c'est Kata-Kata."* I finally gave him the money, only discovering later the TV wasn't for him, but for his daughter, who walked two miles every night to watch television at a friend's house. Buying the television was Kasango's way of keeping her safe at home.

The gas stations were also closing earlier due to a string of violent robberies committed by a gang of rogue policemen (and one woman). They'd zip into the parking lots and rob people at the pumps, then cut them down with machine guns before spraying rounds in every direction, sometimes killing passersby. I'd visited one of these stations to report the story, and as the owner was showing me bullet holes in his walls, a drunken policeman bulled inside and stood leering in the doorway until everyone became afraid and stopped talking to me.

And on May 17, riots broke out in Mbuji-Mayi, the opposition stronghold deep in the central forests. Angry over the election delay, mobs looted the commercial center, burned tires in the streets, and set fire to Kabila's political campaign headquarters. Other mobs then torched the opposition office, finally convincing MONUC to rush in dozens of blue helmets to put down the anarchy. Only two people had been killed, but in the capital the news was received as a chilling omen.

The fear spread through the city, affecting both the rich and the poor, those with everything to lose and those with nothing. The multitude of beggars that plied Kinshasa's traffic suddenly turned more violent in their panhandling, and friends began reporting of mobs of *shegue*—the ubiquitous street kids—jumping onto their cars and pounding the windshields until each one was paid.

I also noticed the change in Kinshasa's roving bands of cripples, who already formed one of the toughest and meanest gangs in the city. Kinshasa was full of cripples: you'd see them every day asking for money in traffic—men with legs corkscrewed behind their backs from polio, war vets missing shoulders, legs, and arms; blind women being led from car to car by ragtag *shegue*. They congregated on street corners and under shade trees with their wheelchairs and hand-peddled carts, a mass of shining steel like freaky Hells Angels. They'd gather in front of businesses, thirty and forty at a time, and demand money. If the owner refused, the mob would hurl bricks through windows and smash cars with steel pipes. Many business owners paid them off, which also gave their stores protection from thieves and miscreants.

I was having breakfast at the Hotel Fontana, next door to my apartment, when they staged an ambush on two police officers. One of the cops had stolen money from a young, legless man at some point earlier in the day, so he'd collected his pals to get some payback. Within ten minutes, about forty people had gathered against a concrete wall across the street. They were screaming and jabbing their fingers toward the cops, really threatening trouble.

Finally the legless man took it alone. With powerful arms, he thrust his torso forward across the dirt road and reached the cop in seconds. The cop saw him coming, threw his AK-47 behind his shoulder, and braced himself, terrified. The legless man lurched forward and wrapped his arms around the officer's shins and held on. The cop tumbled onto his back, reaching up to his buddy with pure animal fear. Once the officer was down, ten more cripples pounced him, pelting him with punches and fistfuls of gravel.

The Indian manager of the hotel ran out and pulled the gate closed, fearing a riot. "Oh, God, not again," he shouted. The restaurant was filled with gruff UN officers and Polish UN civilian cops, who stood with me at the window and watched the poor guy try to save himself. All he had to do was start smashing skulls with his rifle butt or use his boots. But a dozen pairs of UN eyes were on him, and about twenty more wheelchairs were rolling across the street to get a piece.

"Maybe someone should do something," one of the men said.

"Nah," said another, closing the drapes. "These assholes have it coming."

III

While the Congolese waited for some unknown evil to land on June 30, the UN was nailing down contingency plans for an all-out collapse. Warehouses and empty office space, equipped with cots and a week's supply of food, were being prepared to hold over a thousand expats. Secret messages were being encoded into popular UN Radio Okapi broadcasts, giving UN officers instruction on riots and crowd gatherings. The UN also staged an ambitious weekend evacuation drill for hundreds of its staff, only to realize a week later they'd forgotten to inform fifty-five ranking officers.

It was no secret to the Congolese that the *mundele* could leave when things got bad, and they hardly trusted the UN to save them from marauding soldiers. It was true that many Congolese thought the UN was only there to collect their big salaries and thousand-dollar-per-month "hazard pay," and to hell with the rest. And at the end of the day, weren't we all UN? Why else would a *mundele* be in Congo other than to preach or profit?

As June 30 approached, I began buying dozens of cans of tuna and sardines, twenty-gallon jugs for water, and extra fuel for the generator, in the event I was trapped at home while the streets burned outside. I also bought water jugs for Kasango and Eddy Isango, my Congolese colleague, and gave them money for emergencies, but it didn't change the reality of who would stay and who would get ferried away in an armored vehicle. All the expats were stocking up on supplies, or finding ways out, but ask any Congolese on the streets and he'd tell you, "Yeah, I'd love to buy more bread, but who's got the money for that?"

The desperation could only stay pure for so long before it soured and mutated into panic and rage, which was the next logistical step for this place. I'd look at the people on the boulevard and wonder when that last straw would break. In the end, we wondered, what would spark the madness? A soldier shooting someone? Some kind of announcement on the radio? A coup? And how bad would it get? I'd look at the people and wonder quietly, *Will it be you? Or you?* The desperation shined on the faces of the street kids when they suddenly appeared in your open window, tugging at your arm and moaning in that put-on devil voice, *"Boss, boss, j'ai faim, boss, boss."* It was in the policemen who guarded the restaurant when you stumbled out drunk, fumbling for your cigarettes. It was in the eyes of the peanut sellers, the old mamas painting stripes on the road, the countless men lined up under the shade without a job or a pot to piss in, watching you, *le blanc,* walk down the boulevard with your notebook and pen, thinking to themselves, "five thousand dollars a month. *You fucking UN prick."*

I was having a beer with Dave one night at a local Greek restaurant and pool hall. He'd just returned from covering a soccer match at the stadium, where the Simbas had given a sound beating to the Uganda Cranes. Tens of thousands had filled the stadium, already amped by the matchup between one of Congo's former invaders and the uncertainty of June 30. When one of Congo's vice presidents, Zahidi Ngoma, entered to take his seat, the entire stadium bellowed, *"Thief! Thief! Kill him! Kill him!"* And as Dave later drove off in his car, crowds of teenagers pounded on his hood, sliding their fingers across their throats, "We have our Tramontinas waiting for you, *le blanc,*" they shouted. "June thirtieth will be your day!"

About then Nico and Nick, two Greek businessmen we knew, stumbled into the bar already drunk. Nick worked in the steel business and wore a ponytail. He was in his early thirties, kept a loaded .45 in his truck, and was very into his own movie. In his basement he'd already prepared several cases of Molotov cocktails, ready to ignite and hurl at the natives when they climbed his gate. "And if that's not enough," he said with a grin, "I got a dozen gas grenades yesterday from the Belgians."

Nico, the other Greek, owned an Acropolis-themed nightclub in Victoire, an opposition neighborhood we all knew would be among the first to pop. Nico had a crew of muscled bodyguards protecting him at the club and always traveled with a hired Congolese soldier with a Kalashnikov. Days earlier he'd predicted nothing would happen June 30, but tonight the fear had broken him.

"They're saying the government will cut the power, and there won't be water for weeks," he said. "I listen to the staff at the club. They're saying everyone has a machete hidden at home. They're preparing for slaughter."

"Who knows," I said, pretending. "Never trust rumors."

"I hired four more policemen for my apartment," he said. "I can't get enough policemen."

The big Greek took his beer off the bar and walked toward the pool tables. Halfway there, he turned around and pointed to Dave, "If you find my body in the street," he said. "Please send it home to my mama."

As we waited in anticipation for the looting mobs and street violence, I took comfort in knowing I'd had a little preparation. The newswires never sent their grunts into danger without plenty of heavy protection and training. Earlier in the year, the agency sent me through a week of "hazardous environment training," held on a grassy farm outside London, where Royal Marine commandos guided us through the dangers of our trade. The commandos were top-rate special-forces soldiers, steely country boys who quoted poetry and served in both the Falklands and Northern Ireland. They taught us how to dodge bullets and incoming mortars, how to train the eyes to notice land mines, booby traps, and trip wires rigged to grenades. They showed me how to distinguish light-weapons fire from the burp of automatic, long-range assault weapons. I learned how to prod the dirt for bouncing bettys, child-killing butterfly mines, and how to spot a claymore antipersonnel mine, the worst. I learned how to use a compass and determine my bearings, then find my way home with the sun, moon, and stars, and tell north with rocks and sticks and shadows. I learned that brick walls disintegrate under one burst of .50-caliber fire and watched videos of protesters being shot point-blank with shotguns (this to demonstrate how not to challenge third-world riot cops).

Then they taught us how to patch ourselves up in case any of the above weaponry did indeed get us: how to treat a sucking chest wound, how to plug a bullet hole with a tampon, and how to stanch the blood spray from an arterial gash. I learned that when you're being mortared at close range, you must always open your mouth and scream to balance the blast pressure in your body so your innards don't turn to jelly. I learned the best way to dry wet socks is to stick them under your armpits while you sleep, and the best way to treat food poisoning is to drink water laced with iodine.

The first hour we arrived they piled us into a van and sent us through a "make-believe checkpoint" to get a feel for the training. Instead we were ambushed by several men wearing ski masks, who detonated a flash-bang grenade and rushed from the trees firing pistols (blanks, of course). They threw open the doors of the van, yelling, *"Get the fuck out of the car motherfuckers get the fuck out!"* and hurled us violently to the dirt. Our hands were tied and heads covered with flour sacks, the kind you saw in pictures from Guantánamo. It was difficult to breathe, and the fear and adrenaline caused a few people to hyperventilate. They emptied our pockets and marched us in circles through the forest in our hoods to throw off our balance. Occasionally people were led away from the group and farther into the trees, where a marine fired a pistol over their heads to simulate their execution. The marines filmed it all, and later we went to the classroom and watched in wonderment how we reacted to being kidnapped by terrorists.

Other days they sent us down lonely wooded paths and opened

fire on us from the trees and detonated large explosions, just so we could practice hitting the deck. I dove into thorn bushes and sliced up my arms, crab-walked through the mud behind trees and hills and anything that provided cover. The exercises were exciting and terrifying, because the moment you realized you'd messed up (hid behind a thin pile of leaves instead of the ditch three feet away), a great weight swelled in your stomach. I must've died twice, once after stepping on a land mine, and the second time after the guy next to me snapped a trip wire rigged to a claymore buried in the bushes. It was the best money anyone ever spent on me.

Back in Kinshasa, I'd put my driver through a similar course in first aid and kept kits in the car stocked with pressure pads, shock blankets, and syringes for makeshift field IVs. In my room I kept a Kevlar vest with porcelain plates at the front and back, and a helmet to shield my brains from shrapnel. I had all of this gear and training, but doubted it would ever save me from mobs with machetes and nail-studded clubs, or soldiers kicking down my bedroom door.

Over the past six years, my agency had had two staffers killed in West Africa, and two others critically wounded. The region was among the most dangerous in the world, aside from obvious places such as Iraq and Afghanistan. The nerves of New York editors had long been frayed over African wars, and some felt it wasn't even worth the risk at all. When I arrived in Dakar, before I moved to Congo, my boss immediately sat me down, put a gin and tonic in my hand, and told me flatly, "Don't be a cowboy. If you're killed in Congo, they'll shut down this whole operation."

My group of friends dealt with the stress and boredom in different ways. Some of us played squash in the mildewed courts of the Grand Hotel, while others went running along the river road, where brilliant sunsets bounced off the slow current like glass and gave the ugly city an almost wholesome glow. Many lost themselves in the dark, dreary bars or took advantage of cheap dope sold in bushels by nearly every kid who hawked cigarettes on the streets. There were extravagant costume parties with James Bond themes, or where you came dressed as your favorite dictator. Music helped as much as anything, and the Congolese embraced their music as the only national treasure that still belonged to them. We'd stay out all night at the balmy rooftop bars, dancing to live, six-piece soukous bands, or deep in the local clubs where Werrason and Papa Wemba and Koffi Olomide delivered the multitudes each week. Back at home, it was Fela Kuti's "Coffin for Head of State," with its spacey, resonant darkness; Iggy Pop howling, "Baby, wanna take you out with me, come along on my death trip"; or Chan Marshall in the headphones while storms ripped over the river and kicked out the lights, that straight-razor voice like a spirit in the room: "Oh, come, child, in a cross bones style . . . come rescue me."

But during the maximum paranoia of June, our methods of escape began to reflect the violence pressing in. Every Saturday, often after staying out all night, we'd gather in my friend Andy's backyard, strap on gloves and headgear, and fight until we collapsed from pain or exhaustion. It became known as Fight Club Kinshasa.

There were about ten of us, including Dave, some aid workers, and a few guys from the French embassy. Together we had five pairs of boxing gloves, headgear, and leg pads, and usually enough people showed up so you could fight someone your own size, or with the same level of skill. But before any fighting took place, we endured an hour of grueling warm-ups to break the sweat and get us loose, led by Moi and Nico, who'd also been a professional kickboxer in Greece before opening his nightclub in Kinshasa.

Moi got us started with two-minute drills of jump rope, pushups, aerobics, and crunches, often coming by and whacking us in the gut with a foam bat, screaming, "You must feel the pain!" Nico helped us develop our punches and maintain our guard, often in punishing ways. He'd dance around us, his broad chest running with sweat, yelling, "Protect yourself!" The second we dropped our guard, he pounded us in the face. "What ah' you dewing? I said protect yourself!" One week Dave got hit so hard in the forehead he went behind a tree and vomited. After warm-ups, Moi and Nico picked two people to fight while the others watched. The fights were ragged and sloppy, all adrenaline and little skill. Once you got hit in the face the first time, everything you'd just learned flew out of your head. Someone would shout, *"Doucement, douce-ment!"* Gently, gently. But everyone swung his hardest, even when fighting a good friend. We'd back one another into trees with stomach shots or sweep the legs and send them tumbling down. There were few rules, and sometimes people had to be pulled away, those who'd momentarily lost their heads in the violence. It was a fine rush, until all the poison from the previous night raced to your head and turned you green. Each fight lasted only two minutes, but left us so exhausted we didn't speak for long periods afterward. We walked away with bruised ribs, busted lips, and bloody feet since we fought without shoes or socks. It was something few of us would've done back home in Europe or America, but for many reasons it made sense in Kinshasa.

After months of rumors and paranoia, June 30 finally arrived. I set out early that morning with Eddy, my Congolese colleague at the agency, and our driver. The main boulevard was heavily patrolled by UN armored vehicles and trucks of Congolese police, whom the government had finally paid a few days earlier in an attempt to avoid a mutiny. Businesses were shuttered throughout the city, and few cars ventured on the roads, leaving the wide boulevards open for groups of barefoot children to play soccer. It was eerie and silent as the city waited for something to happen.

Once we hit the ramshackle neighborhood of Victoire the quiet was shattered. Large crowds surrounded our car, with young men pounding their fists on the roof and hood, and stuff-

ing the windows with opposition flyers. They were wild-eyed
and wound tight, but at least they were keeping their cool. They
were saving their hatred for the police. The crowd swelled to several thousand and marched toward parliament, so we raced ahead
to meet them. When we arrived, dozens of riot police were already lining up in formation, cutting off the boulevard in a tight
phalanx. These were new units trained by the Europeans for
crowd control; they wore all-black riot gear, including molded
chest plates and helmets and black gas-grenade launchers. Sleek,
disciplined killers filing onto the boulevard like Darth Vader's
storm troopers. Several French policemen with European Union
badges stood quietly behind the formation, filming their minions
with handheld cameras.

We parked the car, and Eddy and I ran toward the police, making sure to stay close to the French. I'd already been arrested a
dozen times in Kinshasa for reporting on the streets, and today I
expected no less. In Kinshasa, you'd get arrested for anything. I'd
be detained by police for simply entering the market, pulling out
my notebook, and asking questions. Crowds would immediately
swarm and begin screaming, "Pay us! Pay us!" and before I could
explain I didn't pay for interviews, someone would get the police,
who smelled a quick buck. Each detainment, like the one at the
airport my first day in town, ended when I passed along some small
cash or threatened to call the minister of information.

Eddy and I found a safe place along the road just as thousands of
demonstrators poured out of the neighborhoods and headed toward the police lines. The lead marchers held long white banners
of the UDPS, and hundreds waved giant palm leaves as a gesture of
peace. They reached the wall of security in minutes, and once
there, all raised their arms with palms to the sky.

"Our brothers, why do you kill for these thieves?" they yelled
at the police. "They give you nothing, and your children are still
dying!"

The police began rapping batons against their shields in a slow, steady rhythm that grew faster and faster, until a blow from a whistle silenced them. The police took four steps back and leveled their gas guns against the crowd. The first round of grenades hit the closest demonstrators directly in the chest, and the second round bounced off their backs as they fled in panic. As the demonstrators scattered in the haze of smoke, the police drew their Kalashnikovs and chased them into the narrow streets of Victoire, spraying rounds into the air. Police later returned dragging prisoners behind them, who were taken to the street and beaten in the stomach with batons.

I'd been shooting photos between the lines, trying to work through the gas. (With tear gas, your eyes locked shut and gushed water, and your throat and lungs contracted and burned, like you'd just inhaled a mouthful of bleach.) And just as I managed to open my eyes, I noticed the French policemen had left and, just then, heard Eddy screaming from the roadside. Eddy was a small man, barely 110 pounds. The police had him by the arms and legs and were carrying him into a vacant field of tall grass. I raced over and threw myself between the police, grabbing Eddy's legs to pull him free. "We're American journalists," I shouted. "Let him go now!"

As I struggled with Eddy, I was swallowed in a crush of police, who threw me to the ground and dragged me through the grass by my shirt. Hands dove into my pockets and ripped out my money and ID. They planted us in the dirt and a policeman stood guard. After we sat there for half an hour, the commander walked over and pulled the memory cards from both our cameras, tore the pages from Eddy's notebooks, and told us to leave. I argued and screamed, but when I noticed Eddy's body shaking from fright, I shut my mouth and walked to the car. Only I was an American and had the luxury of arguing without fear.

Throughout the day, Kinshasa police opened fire into large crowds and beat people with impunity. Demonstrations in Mbuji-Mayi and Tshikapa were put down in similar ways, with police beating people and shooting live rounds into crowds. Aside from Eddy and myself, many Congolese journalists working that day were arrested and jailed, and there was no one to plead for them. But to the United Nations and every foreign embassy in Congo, June 30 was a smashing success. Howling mobs didn't kick down gates to loot and rape white women, and the city—or the area of the city that really mattered, anyway—had been spared the wave of destruction.

"We live in a violent country where there are violent clashes every day," Ross Mountain told me the next day. "The situation ended much better than we'd feared."

Days later at a Fourth of July party at the American ambassador's residence, I spoke to an American security officer who praised the professional conduct of the police, going on about how they did a "fine, fine job" at crushing the demonstrations, and how he wished he could "be there cracking skulls right with 'em." Standing nearby was a Congolese priest from Mbuji-Mayi, who'd been trapped at his church as police shot into crowds outside.

"They fired tear gas into my church," the priest told the official. "I saw people drop from bullets."

"Aw, come on, Father," the American said with a shrug. "It wasn't all that bad."

The American was right, and so was Ross Mountain. Things could've been much worse, and lives were spared by the heavy security presence, which stopped crowds from getting too large and looting the city. What had also helped was a voter-registration drive the government kicked off June 20 in Kinshasa, which had, by June 30, already registered a million people to vote for the first time in their lives. The people finally saw progress, and they spared the city as a result. A rare bit of hope and reprieve had touched the plagued country. Kinshasa had been saved. A week later, militia raided a village in the east and burned forty women and children alive, plunging the whole stinking place back into the cellar of the world.

By then I was already on a plane back to New York. My reason for quitting was mostly personal and had been planned for some time. I was anxious to return to Brooklyn, where Ann Marie was waiting. She'd taken a job and had no plans of moving to Kinshasa. Except for a brief rendezvous in London, we'd been apart for months, and by now there'd been way too many terse exchanges over my scratchy satellite phone. I was worried she'd leave me and all I'd have left was Congo. That scared me more than anything, because I knew I'd stay for years.

But it wasn't just the girlfriend. I also felt I'd failed, not just in my job, but in a much larger sense. I'd failed to trumpet loud enough, been so bogged in the mud I'd never called my editors in London and New York and said, *"This is what we'll do! I have a plan!"* During the 2003 war in Liberia, my bureau chief had become so sick of watching helpless people die that she began an assault of stories built around the central question "Why isn't the U.S. government helping?" And within weeks, marine choppers were landing in Monrovia. It was a different country—a country settled by Americans as a home for freed slaves—and there'd been other reporters there doing the same, but I'd taken away the message. And I'd dreamed of doing that in Congo, really causing a rally (stopping that insanity couldn't be *that* hard, could it?). But my voice had barely cleared the trees.

Earlier that summer, I'd got an e-mail from a friend who'd read some of my stories, wanting to know if there was more to Congo than just people dying. He'd ended the note asking, "Why can't you write more stories we can all relate to?" It was an honest question and one I couldn't answer. It was easy to kick yourself for not writing what you thought should be written. All we really had time to do was make some record of the killing and dying and hope to tell it the right way. I'd been there maybe a year, covered a war and followed it through. It wasn't a long time by any stretch, but long enough to understand that total comprehension was impossible, no matter how long you stayed. No one really understood how twenty-five thousand people could walk twenty kilometers, meet in the same remote valley, and start dying there immediately. No one really understood what drove someone to behead a five-year-old girl with a farm tool, or to wipe out an entire village for the sake of a few dollars in gold or loot. It was all too abstract, even as I think of it now. It was much easier to pretend they didn't exist, and maybe they really don't. Maybe when that white UN bird lifted off the LZ and out of sight, all the dying people simply melted back into rocks and grass. Maybe if one of them pulled out a *People* magazine or said Hollywood kept their hope alive, perhaps that would make them human again, give their misery a song we all know. Maybe then we could relate.

Dave and I had a joke we liked to tell the aid workers and UN flacks after we'd had too much beer, that there wasn't a single person in Congo who had any idea what was really going on. It wasn't a joke where anyone laughed, but one we could both agree on, and that offered a little relief. No one had the slightest clue, top to bottom.

As my plane lifted off and over the river, I looked around at all the people who were leaving, the preachers and profiteers, the doom junkies and cowboys, all the people like me. I imagined we could all use the break, put the death and dying out of sight and out of mind. But I knew what we all knew, that somewhere in that plane the dead were still with us, and no matter who we were, it was still up to us to sort them all out.

Chapter Three

WAITING FOR COBRA

I arrived home to Brooklyn in mid-July, and six weeks later Hurricane Katrina struck New Orleans. In a matter of days I was in Houston, where the city had arranged for over twenty-three thousand evacuees to be housed at the Houston Astrodome. Most were being bused over from the New Orleans Superdome, and off crowded interstate overpasses, where they'd fled after the city's levees had broken and water flooded their neighborhoods.

I'd spent some memorable afternoons in the Dome as a kid, sitting up in the nosebleed seats squinting my eyes to see Nolan Ryan on the mound, or standing to join the rowdy chorus of "C-R-U-U-U-U-U-U-Z" when the legendary outfielder Jose Cruz stepped up to bat. Now I entered the Dome from the second-row stands and was slapped frozen by the image. Down below was this churning sea of black bodies, their faces exhausted and bewildered under the hard stadium lights. Most were dressed in donated, secondhand clothes that hung awkwardly on their bodies. Many lay on cots and covered their faces to sleep, while others sat alone in a trance and grieved without privacy for those who'd died or gone missing in the flood. And weaving through the rows of beds were dozens of nurses and doctors, journalists and camera crews, cops and volunteers, all with a look of gravity in their faces, and all mostly white. My mind seemed to skip for a second. I was suddenly back, staring into the valley of Tche or Tchomia or Bunia after the siege. At first glance, the only thing missing was the haze of cooking fires and the red African mud, and it was the last image I ever thought I'd see at home. And just like in Congo, this misery had spawned its own kind of carnival. In addition to the many preachers and Scientolo-gists and dreadlocked masseuses, there were clowns and magicians who pulled flowers from hats to the delight of children, while parents stood by staring into the walls. And each day the politicians and celebrities net-worked their way inside making promises few could keep.

A few months later I reported from New Orleans itself, where the flattened neighborhoods were full of well-meaning young people bused in for too brief periods of time, and the flooded streets had been reclaimed by contractor pickups with out-of-state plates. At night, gunshots popped in the dark and the law couldn't be trusted. This story occupied me for months after my return because it was so similar to the one I'd left. After-ward, I pitched other stories hoping to point myself in new directions, but those stories never panned out, probably because my heart just wasn't in them. When Congo's election commission announced the presidential vote would take place July 30, 2006, something urged me to go. But there was something I had to do first, and in June, Ann Marie and I threw a big wedding on a farm in Minnesota. We spent a quiet honeymoon in the Sea Islands of South Carolina. And two weeks later, I caught a plane to Bunia.

I

There was little hard information to be had about Commander Cobra, yet in the summer of 2006, his legend seemed to permeate the hills like creeping fog. Villagers, soldiers, and former gunboys who'd come in from the bush, all had different versions of Cobra's history. Everyone agreed Justin Banaloki Matata was a former sol-dier in Mobutu's army who'd lost the job after the Big Man fell. He'd fought with Lendu militia during the war and possessed a penchant for butchery that had earned him respect in battle. Cobra had helped lead one of the most savage attacks to date in Ituri, the sacking of Nyakunde in September 2002. There, Lendu fighters, along with members of the rebel group RCD-Kasangani, entered the Centre Médical Évangélique hospital and hacked to death every Hema they could find (this chilling incident had haunted the Swiss doctor in Bunia). The militia then closed off every exit and trapped the town, and over ten days, methodically butchered twelve hundred people and stuffed them into latrines and wells or left them dismembered in the roads. The leader of the Nyakunde massacre was a commander named Khandro, who many claimed was Cobra's mentor in the field. Not long after the raid, Cobra murdered Khandro and took the crown of the gunboy army, one of the largest and most feared in all of Ituri.

Cobra had something greater than his reputation that he used to drill fear and loyalty into his boys, a weapon as ancient as the red clay itself. The commander had black magic, wielded by an eighty-year-old sorcerer named Kakadu, who many believed could shift his face from old to young and speak through animals and trees. In a country where Christ and Lucifer were merely two flavors in a much larger soup, the gris-gris magic was the spoon that stirred the pot.

Kakadu had found his place among warriors back in 1972, when he led attacks against Ugandan Hema over a border dispute near the Semliki River, just south of Bunia. Then, like now, the sorcerer's gift was a potion that delivered on every gunboy's bullet-proof dream: drink the water, become unkillable, dart through the hail of death like an invisible string. After the Ugandan government complained about the attacks, Mobutu's troops arrested the magic man and threw him in prison for ten years. There, locals say, he honed his craft and stewed in his own powers, walking out virtually a god. He'd lived the past two decades deep in the bush on a farm near Sazi, which became a site of pilgrimage for mystics and those seeking guidance. Payments were taken in livestock, and Kakadu had built himself a veritable kingdom. One of those pilgrims was Cobra Matata, who came seeking power as he seized control of the militia army. In late 2005, government soldiers began sweeps through Lendu villages hunting militia, looting and raping as they went. And to repel this assault, Kakadu joined the gunboy army as prophet and sorcerer and brought with him the black magic of war. Every so often he'd appear in a village market, like a specter in a white robe and wooden staff. His sermons drew hundreds.

"He held a meeting once in Kagaba," said one UN translator from Aveba, seventy kilometers south of Bunia. "He put a microphone in a tree and different voices came through the speakers. That day all militia came seeking their destiny, and the magic leader told each boy his fate in battle."

To the gunboys, especially the younger ones, Kakadu was like a mythic lord who carried death and retribution in his pouch. The boys told how Kakadu planned and sanctioned every battle they fought. Inside a closed hut, the magic man would scrawl a crude map of the hills into the dirt floor, then slice the throat of a white cock. The wounded bird would shudder and bleed across the room, and wherever it fell dead was where the militia would attack. Later, he'd arrange the fighters in formation and prepare them for war, smearing their chests with a putrid ointment made from castor beans, and presenting them with a cloth pouch stuffed with herbs and trinkets, the antibullet.

Together, Cobra and the magic man controlled an army of two thousand militia, many of whom were child soldiers, in a wooded mountain empire known as Tchei, a name that rolled like a tombstone off the tongues of the UN's hardened leaders. The territory of Tchei (not to be confused with *Tche*, the displaced camp north of Bunia) was sixty-five kilometers southwest of town, a sixty-kilometer expanse of dense, tree-covered mountains and deep hollows where the morning mist gathered like cream in a bowl. For the UN, Tchei was a tactical nightmare. The mountaintop base-village offered invaluable views of a huge swath of surrounding land. The base was totally self-sustaining, with nearby streams for water and fields for growing food. The rugged terrain made access by vehicle impossible, and the dense cover hindered air operations. Whoever controlled

Tchei controlled it all. And the UN, under extreme pressure to clean out militia and protect an election, desperately needed control.

At the time, the attention of MONUC, aid groups, and donors was again focused on pulling off elections. The preparation alone had been historic. In a country with only five hundred kilometers of paved roads, no real census for the past forty-five years, and a largely illiterate population with no national IDs, the UN had hired three hundred thousand election workers and sent them into the jungle by boat, dugout canoe, motorcycle, bicycle, and foot to register twenty-five million people. It took some workers weeks to make the journey, and on two occasions, several were kidnapped and taken hostage by local militia bent on derailing the vote. Nevertheless, they'd established 50,045 polling stations throughout the country, an accomplishment every bit as admirable as Stanley's historic trek across the continent.

The list of candidates measured the size of the nation: thirty-three presidential contenders (including Oscar Kashala, a Harvard-educated Congolese oncologist living in the Boston suburbs) and 9,632 parliamentary candidates representing 218 political parties. Five hundred seats in parliament would be chosen. The ballots themselves were as large as broadsheet newspapers and featured photos and symbols of the candidates and their parties for those who couldn't read. Over five thousand tons of election materials were shipped on fifty flights from South Africa at the cost of $50 million. The bill for the election itself, funded almost entirely by the EU, totaled nearly $500 million, around $3 million per day, making it the largest and most expensive ever attempted in Africa.

It was a grand achievement, and precisely the right way forward. But a century of colonialism, war, and despotism had so isolated the Congolese that the aim of elections flew over the heads of most people. Election workers had reached many areas in the forest, but the size of the country made widespread education and training impossible. A common misconception was that elections alone would be the silver bullet into the heart of war and corruption, that once the ballots were cast and winners announced, a new standard of living would suddenly blossom from the ruin. And of the thousands of candidates, few had even been into the jungles and introduced themselves. If candidates had even bothered laying out political platforms (and most hadn't), they were unknown to the people. In the virtual absence of government for so many years, personal politics had evolved around tribe, local alliances, and graft. People would by and large vote for whomever the village chief instructed them to, or for the candidate who passed through with the best hats and T-shirts.

Of the thirty-three presidential candidates, the true contest was between President Kabila and Vice President Jean-Pierre Bemba. Everyone suspected Kabila would sweep the east, and especially Katanga, from where his ancestors hailed. Kabila was a Swahili speaker, and son of the man who'd toppled Mobutu. He'd ended the war and welcomed peacekeepers who had, like them or not, paved the way toward elections and allowed a semblance of normalcy to return in places like Bunia.

His adversary Bemba was the leader of the Ugandan-backed rebel group MLC, which had nearly defeated the government-allied troops of Kabila's father during the war. He was the son of a wealthy businessman whose family was loved in Kinshasa and throughout the central jungles of Equateur province. In the jungles, Bemba was seen as a patriot son battling the outsiders who'd hijacked and derailed the country. The biggest outsider of them all, in their opinion, was Kabila, who they claimed was born in Tanzania to a Rwandan mother (the president was raised in Tanzania, where his father was in exile, but he claimed to have been born in Fizi, South Kivu). It was their explanation for why the president—a foreigner—had auctioned off the country's mineral wealth in shady deals with international conglomerates.

Bemba was loved in the west, but hated in the east, where he was regarded as a megalomaniac and warmonger. In November 2002, his forces had assisted the Hema militia in attacking the gold-mining town of Mongbwalu, where two hundred civilians were murdered. Bemba's gunboy army was so vicious they named their push into Ituri *Effacer le tableau* (Operation Erase the Blackboard) and were grimly referred to by locals as the "Effaceurs." During his recent campaign stop in Bunia, the vice president had even threatened to pick up the gun if he lost the vote.

For the sake of the power-sharing, transitional government, Kabila and his four vice presidents seemed to endure one another in public, but the fact remained that two of the men—Bemba and Azarias Ruberwa, leader of the Rwandan-backed RCD—had once sought to overthrow Kabila's father. And during the war, the president himself had fought against them as a major general in his father's army.

Militia activity and idle threats by war-drumming politicians made protecting the polls on election day the UN's biggest priority. Militia leaders had publicly expressed willingness to support elections, but in private, they knew its mandate was designed to wipe them out. After seven years of hard-earned advances and just as many setbacks, with billions of dollars spent and the stability of all of central Africa hanging on its shoulders, the last thing the UN needed was villagers massacred on their way to vote.

The area was far from serene, though. Various militia still controlled vast swaths of eastern Congo. Mai Mai militia were attacking villages in northern Katanga, Rasta and Rwandan Hutu *genocidaires* continued their rape and pillage in North and South Kivu, and Cobra's men—along with other Lendu factions—still battled Hema (and one another) for resources in Ituri. The combined instability had left over one million displaced and continued to kill over a thousand people each day.

Success depended largely on strengthening the Congo army, a

task even more onerous than planning the elections themselves. The FARDC (Armed Forces of DR Congo) consisted mostly of former militia who'd disarmed—part of the 2003 power-sharing deal between government and rebels at the war's end. By the end of 2005, the UN boasted over twenty thousand militia had surrendered in Ituri, many of them joining the army. The integration of warring factions into Congo's army was crucial in securing the polls, both by removing gunboys from the bush and training and using them to assist MONUC with joint patrols. The government had promised eighteen brigades of newly integrated troops for this task, but by election day, only six brigades were delivered, most of them untrained and malnourished, and many without uniforms or weapons.

In December 2005, a human rights group discovered most of the government money set aside for integration and training had been stolen, with millions embezzled to pay for (among other scams) hundreds of thousands of "ghost soldiers" who never existed. Soldiers received a paltry salary of twelve dollars per month (later raised to twenty-four dollars), which they often never saw. Cholera epidemics killed scores of soldiers across Congo in 2005 and 2006 because of poor sanitation and lack of medicine, and in Katanga, over twenty men starved to death after ration money was repeatedly stolen by their commander. Conditions were significantly worse on the front lines where troops battled militia, as food and clean water rarely reached their positions. As a result, the new recruits fell back on their old militia tactics and lived by the gun.

All across the country, soldiers sacked villages and looted displaced camps they were sent to protect, and crime waves swept through larger towns once soldiers arrived. Congo's Fourth and Sixth Brigades settled into Ituri in early 2006 to prepare for joint operations with the UN to clear militia and immediately went berserk on the local population. Soldiers looted livestock and burned homes, kidnapped and executed young men in the fields, and raped countless women.

Confronted with this mess, the UN threatened to end all support of the local army. But in reality, no matter how great a liability the soldiers were, the UN had no choice but to use them. The militiamen lined up against the elections were just too numerous for the UN forces to face alone, and UN commanders still hoped to instill a modicum of training and discipline into the Congo troops in the event of the UN's eventual withdrawal.

Which perhaps explains why, only months away from the country's first elections, a time that desperately called for peace, the UN and Congo army went ahead with joint offensives, the most robust military operations since the mission began in 1999. Their main target was the massive Lendu force commanded by Cobra Matata.

The first major campaign was in late February 2006, when around 750 Congolese commandos punched the main axis into Tchei as UN forces reinforced them with mortars and Firebird helicopters. On the second day of fighting, the commandos expelled Cobra's militia and took the mountain with ease. But their commanders were late to resupply them, and by the time their ammunition was dropped the following morning, thousands of militia were surging up the mountain. The commandos retreated all at once, taking withering fire and dropping as they ran. Looking back, they could see the gunboys pounce on their fallen comrades like dingoes on the kill, ripping and carving their trophies. When the commandos finally reached the UN-run forward base, bloody and demoralized, they rioted for three days and looted the base clean.

A second push in late May was victorious. Bangladeshi peacekeepers pounded the mountains with mortars and helicopter gunships while UN and Congolese troops walked straight in. But the threadbare army could only hold the position a month. Just ten days after UN forces left the Congolese in control, a small band of Cobra's soldiers approached one of their positions. The gunboys were unarmed and waved a white flag of surrender. When the

Congo troops dropped their guard to investigate, thousands of militia swooped over the mountain and routed them within the hour. The magic man himself had orchestrated the ruse.

The loss of Tchei was an embarrassing blow for the UN; not only had they wasted months of planning and resources and strengthened the militia's resolve, but the combat operations (including several skirmishes with militia between the battles for Tchei) had also killed dozens of villagers and forced thousands more to flee their homes. By the time of elections, the UN found itself with a worsening security situation in Ituri, along with 230,000 displaced people who desperately needed attention.

I flew into Bunia in mid-July hoping to piggyback on the next joint operation before elections. During the May offensive, Dave had embedded with UN and local troops and couldn't believe the things he'd seen: Congolese soldiers looting villages and taking slaves to hump their food and ammo, their Bangladeshi officers watching it all in stunned disbelief.

Hoping to sweeten my chances for a mission, I'd stopped into an Indian grocery in Queens before leaving home and bought a box of sweet rice balls for the UN force commander, Brigadier General Mohammad Mahboob, a very homesick Bangladeshi. He'd taken the gift with a forlorn sigh and asked me where I wanted to go. "Tchei," I said, and heard it echo off the walls. "Very well," he answered. "I'll put you as close as I can. But as you know, we no longer hold the mountain."

It would be several days before the next patrol left Bunia for the hills, so I spent some time getting back into the swing of the country. I rented my old room at the Hotel Ituri and took meals at the Hellenique, happy to see Jean the waiter still scuttling across the floor and forgetting my order. The heavy UN presence had halted nearly all militia activity in Bunia and the immediate neighborhoods. The fighting up north in Djugu had also subsided from the previous year, and the Ugandan trade routes were once again open. Bunia's shops were full and business was strong, and for once people seemed to be contently lost in the routine of everyday living. Despite the problems with Cobra's militia in Tchei, the upcoming elections had struck the town as a jolt of excitement instead of the death sentence it would've been in earlier times.

The UN had even built a massive Rec House on the edge of town, replete with a gym, tennis courts, and wood-fired pizza oven. (The bathrooms also had the only working flush toilets I'd seen in Ituri.) Each night the back lawn was filled with the usual mix of Euro staff and third-world soldiers, ordering gins and eating pizza while waitresses in white vests sauntered across the grass. The lawn doubled as the UN's evacuation landing zone in the event the town was overrun again.

I also used this time to visit the displaced camps near Tchei that had sprung from the fighting. For this I hired Pastor Marrion P'Udongo, a circuit preacher based in Bunia, and the ace fixer for the passing journalists. The pastor was already a legend throughout Ituri, a kind of black Moses who'd served the years of war and displacement as a lighthouse for the broken and scattered. He was a roly-poly man with a megaphone voice and goofy belly laugh, which, when triggered, caused his round eyes to vanish behind thick, black-framed bifocals. The pastor's sermons stirred people into dancing frenzies. Women ran out of houses to kiss his cheek whenever he passed through villages, and men on the roads bowed to him and waved. Militia commanders softened in his presence, and even the most bogey-eyed gunboys dropped the mask when he passed, regarding him like a fun-loving uncle up from the city. That charisma had saved not only the pastor's life, but the lives of many others.

He'd been the assistant pastor at the Pentecostal Chrisco Church in Bunia when the town fell to Lendu warriors in May 2003. Like Johnny, the pastor belonged to the Alur tribe, which the Lendu often pitted alongside the Hema. As Lendu death squads marched from house to house, dragging people out and executing them in the streets, about seventy Hema, many of them members of Chrisco Church, sought refuge at the pastor's house. Among the Hema was the pastor's wife, Julienne.

For four days they huddled inside a large living room with little food and water, praying and singing quietly as gunfire and rockets rumbled through the nights. At one point, the pastor's four-year-old son peeked outside the gates and saw the mutilated bodies of neighbors being eaten by dogs. On the afternoon of the fifth day, a gang of militia finally broke through the gates and discovered them. The gunboys ordered several people into the yard and stripped them naked while others watched in horror. But the execution was halted when a top commander named Pichu entered the house, along with a low-level lieutenant known as Gorilla.

Months earlier, Gorilla had attended one of the pastor's sermons in nearby Mongbwalu, and now he began pleading with Pichu to spare his life. "This pastor can't die," he said. "He is too good a man to be killed like this." After a long debate, Pichu finally ordered the gunboys away and looked at the pastor. "I should kill you and everyone here," he said. "But for some reason I'm not. Something is telling me no."

Instead, Pichu ordered the militia to escort the pastor and his congregants to the UN headquarters, where they'd be safe. And once the group was gone, the militia returned and looted everything in the house.

Two years later, Pichu was arrested for war crimes by UN and Congolese soldiers and placed in Kinshasa's notorious Makala prison. One of his first visitors was Pastor Marrion, who now periodically made the eighteen-hundred-kilometer journey by plane to bring Pichu money and spiritual counsel. "The reason I am alive is because of him. God sent him to rescue us. And you know, Pichu's wife is now a member of my church at Chrisco." He laughed until his eyes disappeared beneath his round cheeks. "My chief, we are living *because of the grace of God!*"

The displaced camps were scattered amid thick-wooded mountains where roads were easy for ambush. It was far beyond the UN-designated "no-man's-land," but the pastor had been running these roads throughout the war. He'd escorted teams of foreign journalists and even traveled here alone with a bullhorn, passing himself off as Lendu to gain trust of the young militia, many of whom he convinced to surrender.

These winding routes had circumscribed the pastor's life, and he'd developed an instinct for their dangers. The pastor had been born and raised in the town of Panyimur, on the Ugandan shores of Lake Albert. When he was fifteen years old, Ugandan soldiers gunned down his father, and three days later, his mother died from illness. "It was high blood pressure," the pastor said. "She died from grief." Like Johnny, he was left alone to his wits to survive in a perilous and rapidly dissolving region. He made money ferrying gasoline back and forth over the Congo border and, for a while, smuggled gold from the fields of Mongbwalu to businessmen in Kampala, traveling at night to avoid soldiers who hunted smugglers and stripped their wares.

In 1990, he'd followed a girl to a church in Bunia run by Swedish missionaries, and there he gave his life to Christ. The call to preach was sudden and strong, and by chance he happened upon a group of Texan evangelists in Uganda who trained him in the gospel. After the Rwandan genocide, he ministered to thousands of refugees who poured over the Ugandan border and helped open churches in their camps. And after several years, he was running those roads again, preaching from village to village and offering a rare hopeful message as war swept the country.

The pastor had a piece of scripture he'd clung to during the days of war, as militia flooded the hills and spread their plague. It was Romans 14:7—"For none of us liveth to himself, and no man dieth to himself . . ." Those words had saved him from execution squads and gunboys in the hills, and they'd given him hope back in 1998, when he'd fallen terribly ill and nearly died. He'd been preaching in Tchomia village on Lake Albert, getting things organized to marry Julienne the following day, when his kidneys and liver suddenly failed. Family rushed him to a hospital in Kampala, where he fell into a coma. Doctors couldn't determine the cause, but the pastor was convinced he was poisoned by fellow preachers in Tchomia. ("They were jealous because people loved me too much," he said.) After eight months in the hospital with no improvement, the pastor was taken back to Bunia to die at home, his body emaciated and weak. And as family and congregants prayed and wailed in the living room outside, the pastor mustered a deathbed prayer, pleading to live. And then came a vision: There he was, standing on a dark stage before a large crowd of people. "And I was *preaching*!" he said. "I was *strong*! I was preaching how God saves us and heals us, and *praise God*, I got out of bed the next week and preached *all the way back to Uganda*!"

The words from Romans continued to guide him as he ministered from camp to camp, connecting with his flock, who'd scattered at the teeth of wolves. And I hoped they'd guide us still as we left the sandbags and razor wire of Bunia and ventured into Cobra's realm. I felt a measure of invincibility when traveling with the pastor, as if his front-seat sermons and warped gospel cassettes supplied a force field as we passed through the valley of gunboys with death in their fingers.

"God promises to bless and protect us coming in and coming out, and I expect him to keep that promise," he said as our Land Rover rattled through the dark forest. "But *oh, my chief*, someone could *really* disappear here! *Oh, yes!*"

The most recent fighting around Tchei had emptied many villages into the pine-covered hills, where they gathered at a village called Gety. Over forty thousand people had collected there by the time we arrived, and hundreds more continued to stagger from the bush barely strong enough to walk. Aid workers had recently arrived and distributed plastic sheeting for shelters, but it did little against the cold mountain air and daily seasonal rain. As we entered the camp, all we saw was a gray, dismal tableau of ragged-looking people, shivering and covered in mud.

A small team of doctors from MSF had set up in an old house at the edge of the camp with no water or electricity. Along with a few aid workers from the French group Solidarités, they were trying to hold back a wave of malnutrition and diarrhea. About forty people were dropping dead each day, most of them children.

The aid workers—fewer than a dozen—had swept in and halted a massive humanitarian fiasco almost by sheer will. In just three weeks' time, they'd already immunized for measles (the first thing you always do in camps, since an outbreak could wipe out everyone), handed out sheeting, blankets, and emergency food rations, and hired one thousand camp residents to help, among other things, dig latrines, purify drinking water, and build bamboo triage centers for the sick.

The person heading the MSF team was my friend Olivier, who'd worked in Bunia with the Swiss doctor trapped in the hospital. I walked in and found him sitting at a wooden table in the dark, sipping cold instant coffee and poring over the latest camp figures. He was exhausted and hadn't showered in days.

The doctors and aid workers had finally stabilized the camp, he said, before the population more than doubled in three days. The death was now overwhelming, and the faces of the doctors who passed through the room were pale and troubled.

"It's been hard on the staff," he said. "They feel they can't save the kids." He sighed heavily and stared off into the chipped and peeling walls. It occurred to me I'd never seen this man at ease. "It's been a tough week for all of us."

Whereas other camps I'd visited were smaller and more

concentrated in a large field or valley, the camp at Gety had swallowed an entire village. A large Catholic mission was the only remaining space (it would later be used for elections); just outside, the camp stretched for several kilometers in every direction. Shelters made from plastic sheeting, clay, and tree branches jammed both sides of the village roads. Once you stepped off the path and into the maze they created, the suffering was outward and unmistakable. Here the morning fog mingled with woodsmoke, and inside the haze, babies wailed and children's lungs seized with wet, bubbling coughs. My steps became instinctively delicate and my voice lowered to a whisper, as if to respect the soft exit of life around me.

The pastor found several people to interview, and one by one we took them back to the truck to speak in private. The tales of rape and murder actually lined up at my notebook. First came Adjove Anyotsi, a preacher from nearby Tchekele. Militia had captured his family and shot his young daughter in the neck while she stood beside him. The following day they raped his other daughter, who I interviewed next. Next came a farmer named Kandro, who spent two months hiding in the forest with his wife and seven-month-old son, until his wife died of hunger. He'd held her in the seconds before she passed and said, "I have nothing to give you." Days later, his son died, too. He'd buried their naked bodies in shallow holes in the forest, but now couldn't remember where.

After Kandro left the truck, I spoke to a seventeen-year-old girl, who'd been gang-raped by four army soldiers on the road near Tchei. "I couldn't stand up when they left," she said, her eyes wounded and wild. "It was my first time to be with a man." She was in such obvious physical pain that we stopped the interview and the pastor guided her to the clinic.

Afterward, the pastor and I walked through the camp and passed the funeral of an old woman who'd died in the night of diabetes. Her body had been wrapped in grass mats and hoisted on the shoulders of men, who led a long procession of women singing and waving palm branches. Just beyond the funeral, a young boy came running up and spoke to the pastor. "His brother just died," the pastor said. "Just now, twenty minutes ago." The boy led us to a nearby hut, where a young woman sat rocking a bundle of blankets in her arms, slack-eyed from shock. The infant's name was Zapatista, and for days he'd withered from diarrhea and vomiting. That morning he'd developed a violent cough, then stopped breathing. His temples were sunken from starvation and his skin was taut and sickly bronze. The mother looked up and lifted the dead boy like an offering. "Take a picture," she said. I snapped the death portrait and backed away, capturing probably the only image of the child in its entire short life. Standing in the doorway, we were told another boy had just died. But it was getting late and we needed to head back to Bunia, and I didn't think I could handle seeing any more dead children.

But about twenty kilometers outside Gety we noticed another cluster of tents at the bottom of a rippled valley. We were making good time, so I told the driver to pull in. Once we reached the camp itself, I begin to wonder if anyone was left living at all. Little by little, though, the people began to emerge from the tumbledown grass huts at the sound of our engine. Their squinted faces gave them the look of survivors who'd been plucked from the guts of a mine shaft.

The chief of Manji-Sona told us about two thousand people were living there, all area residents who'd fled during fights between the government and Cobra's militia. They'd been there six months; aid workers had managed to visit only once. With no food or medicine, they'd survived by collecting firewood and selling it in nearby Kasenyi. The old people who couldn't work were left to starve and were easy targets of the cholera that spread with the rains.

"There are two dead children today," said the chief, whose name was Kanombe. "Would you like to see them?" The children had both died that morning of diarrhea and now lay rigid in the hook of their mothers' arms. The father of the second child, two-year-old Guillaume, was making plans for a funeral. Where will you bury him? I asked. He hadn't thought of it. He pointed to a nearby scrub field. "Just here, I guess," he said, and went to look for a spade. On the edge of the tent, the dead boy's brother was catching termites in the mud because there was nothing else to eat.

Several tents down, a mother's voice called for the pastor. She sat inside the darkness clutching her three-year-old son, who was slowly withering away from diarrhea. The boy's eyes barely registered any signs of life, and his arms and legs trembled under a blanket from fever. I stood there scribbling notes, then stopped because it felt so absurd. For a second I froze, then realized, *I can save this kid's life.*

I ran back to the truck and grabbed my big medical kit and turned it upside down in the backseat. Sifting through, I found half a dozen packets of rehydration salts, antidiarrheal tabs, and some ibuprofen for fever. Simple things. I gave the mother two packets of salts and a bottle of clean water. The rest I gave the chief to distribute, then we climbed into the truck to leave. Our driver was restless to get back to Bunia; only bad things happened on these roads at night. (When I returned to Manji-Sona two days later, the boy was still alive, but his grandmother was unconscious from dysentery and not expected to live. There was nothing I could do; all my medicine was gone.)

During our visit to the MSF compound in Gety, Olivier had pulled the pastor aside and offered him a job. The team of doctors desperately needed a local person to translate and organize the staff, someone they could trust. The request had touched the pastor deeply, and now on the road back to Bunia, he stared ahead in silence.

The aid group couldn't pay as much as journalists—the pastor's sole source of income since the church gave no salary—but he saw their work as morally superior and guided by the hand of God. They'd treated the pastor's children during the war and given him medicine when his kidneys became reinfected, a problem that still caused him constant pain. It touched him that MSF doctors left six-figure salaries in Europe and America to be frontline medics in places most people didn't even bother pronouncing right; that in places where all hope and sanity were lost, these people were always first to arrive, blood up to their elbows and never asking thanks. And in Congo, their staff had been kidnapped and held hostage for doing it.

As we drove, the pastor's eyes darted around behind his thick glasses, and drops of sweat pooled on his bald head as he discerned his message. The Swahili praise music warbled like a warped record as we bucked over the mud-slicked roads. Finally, the pastor turned:

"God put us here on this earth *to live*, to have a successful life, *and to be healthy!* We are not here by accident. We should not just preach that people who believe in God go to heaven. We should know how to spare their lives when they're still on *earth!*

"If it is God's will for us to live a healthy life, to escape the bondage of death and poverty, then MSF is doing the work of God. They are doing a kind of sacrifice. I respect you journalists because you give me money, but I respect MSF because they are saving the lives of us, they are *doing great work, God's work!* In the name of God I will join MSF, *even if they will pay me nothing!*"

Sacrifice in this period of struggle meant a great deal to the pastor, and he clearly believed it measured a person's place in heaven. The peacekeepers who came to Congo and gave their lives for another man's country, for another man's tribe, that was sacrifice. The aid workers who left their blessed homes and families and sank themselves in the mud and excrement of a place that would never appear on a map, to hold a frightened child as it died because the government couldn't be bothered, that was sacrifice.

I sensed that working for MSF would certainly ease the pastor's mind, both in deepening his own sense of duty and safeguarding his dignity. Because on this scale, journalists existed somewhere further down, and that his children depended on them to eat probably cost him many a night's sleep. He'd had some bad experiences recently with foreign reporters, real Hemingway types who'd cursed him in front of locals and bullied the village chiefs. Some had caught their UN flights home without paying, others had embarrassed him by getting too drunk or bringing prostitutes into their hotels. There were also many dedicated, kindhearted guys who passed through to balance that weight, but still, our lot was a gamble.

I never felt I was sacrificing anything other than a few comforts and luxuries I'd grown accustomed to, and whether our stories did any good was a question I still couldn't answer. We'd been sending the reports out of Congo for years now, but how much had really changed? How much did the millions in food aid flown in every year actually change, or the legions of small foreign NGOs committed to their myriad contraceptive programs, mosquito-net drives, and hygiene seminars?

The war was so big and had a hundred different answers to the same few questions. The food aid filled stomachs, but didn't create economies. For every child saved in a camp, three hundred died in the forest. Journalists wrote the truth, but they also lied and took advantage and distorted. And all of us made by Congolese standards a fortune in pay.

It seemed the longer you stayed, the stranger the questions became. And the next day, two of my photographer colleagues, Lionel Healing and John Moore, saw just how strange it had all become. They were driving back from shooting in Gety when they passed a smaller displaced camp near a place called Kotoni. And rising from the heart of the squalid camp was a manifestation of all those questions that had no answers, a freak totem of the savior-destroyers. There, in the middle of the forest was, impossibly, a bright blue neon sign. The two looked at one another, then looked back again. Its message was written in English, in bold letters that read:

PLEASE ENJOY POVERTY

A tall white man in his early thirties sat at the base of the sign, clutching a video camera while preaching to a gathered crowd. His white shirt was yellowed with sweat and tucked into a pair of khakis, and his long hair was greased against his head. He was Renzo Martens, a Dutch artist and filmmaker. He'd spent the year traveling the country and filming the crisis—the UN press conferences, committee meetings, sorrow and hunger in the camps—and the neon sign was a blazing billboard for his message of deliverance, one meant to expose the grand conspiracy behind this deceitful humanitarian front: that misery was Africa's largest export, more than diamonds and gold, and the millions of dollars it generated each year for aid groups and news organizations was too great a boon for them to work toward its end. The system was entrenched and there to stay, so Africans should embrace their poverty and learn to enjoy it, and through this acceptance, be set free.

The film was a montage of Renzo lecturing impoverished villagers on the value of their suffering, throwing drunken parties in the camps at night, where hundreds whooped and danced in frantic drum circles around the blinking totem. His previous film was set in the bleak refugee camps of Chechnya, where he'd interviewed war victims at ration stations—frail old women and a man who'd been mangled by fire—and asked them, "What do you think of me? Do you think I'm handsome?"

As Lionel and John pulled in and stepped out of the truck, Renzo swung his camera toward them and announced, "Ah, the journalists have arrived. Tell me, guys, how much money do you earn from your photos in Africa?" As with the sign, Renzo spoke in English when the camera rolled, never mind that French was the official language. "This exhibit is a resource for the local people," he said. "You might call it an emancipation."

He worked the crowd like a sideshow tout and goaded the photographers toward rage. And when John and Lionel finally left, Renzo chased after the truck with his camera, screaming, "Typical journalists, just take the photos and leave!"

The UN had escorted Renzo to Kotoni in one of their vehicles, and everyone knew he traveled on UN flights. They'd issued him press credentials, probably never asking what in hell he was actually doing, and even flown his neon sign across the country from Kinshasa. And now there he was, crucifying the UN and aid workers in front of hundreds of people who desperately needed them to survive. The UN escort had stood there dumbstruck.

The next afternoon, the pastor and I traveled together to the camp in Tchomia. I'd visited the previous year and wanted to see if there'd been any progress. The camp had survived numerous outbreaks of cholera, and once UN peacekeepers had turned it over to government soldiers, the local troops had raped women and looted the camp. Tchomia was the pastor's old turf, where he'd preached in the village church (and perhaps been poisoned). He'd visited the camp many times over the past year and was well-known and loved. But when we arrived this time, the crowd rose up against him, waving their arms, shouting, and demanding to be paid. Renzo, it seemed, had visited a few days before and given one of his sermons.

"Journalists and aid workers are no longer welcome in this camp," said the chief. "Not unless they pay!" The pastor explained how the children needed the aid workers to eat and help them go to school. And journalists only helped to expose their story.

The pastor told him, "The journalists are not getting rich and they cannot pay."

The old chief just waved him off. "That's not what Renzo told us. And he paid us well."

II

After several days of waiting, the UN informed me I could join one of their units in the hills. General Mahboob explained there were no planned "operations" this close to elections, mainly for fear of further destabilizing the population. But if anything happened, I would have a front-row seat.

Sensing I was headed into a classic "hurry up and wait" situation, I invited Lionel along to keep me company. As it turned out, he'd arrived in Kinshasa just a couple of months after I left. I'd met him over beers my second night in Bunia and liked him immediately. He was a tall, even-keeled Londoner with a rank sense of humor, the kind of guy who'd hand you a gin and tonic and, ten minutes later, casually tell you he'd spiked it with noxious Congo tap. He'd been a shooter for the local news when his wife quit her teaching job to join Save the Children, and they'd assigned her to Congo. Lionel was picked up by AFP shortly after arriving and hurled himself into the story, learning quickly how to operate in the lawless hills.

In Ituri, several weeks had passed without any militia attacks, and the relative quiet had boosted confidence among the residents. Already thousands of people who'd been scattered in camps began walking home to vote where they'd registered. But the calm worried some of the UN commanders. While high voter turnout was the dream, it could also play into the perfect trap.

A rumor had started circulating about a massive election-day assault by Cobra's boys on the Gety camp, coinciding with another attack north of Bunia by another Lendu group. The Catholic mission at the Gety camp was a major polling station, and as the rumor went, the gunboys would wait until the voting lines were long, then sweep down from the hills.

The camp at Gety wasn't regularly guarded by UN or government troops, and the Congolese soldiers nearby had pillaged the area so much that residents felt safer alone. Unable to trust anyone for security, the doctors at MSF were ordered to temporarily evacuate their Gety base, leaving behind only a skeleton crew of local staff. The pastor had hoped to work on election day, and he took the news hard. He'd steeled himself for his heavenly call, but in the end, Cobra and the magic man had been closer to the earth.

The morning after receiving the green light from General Mahboob, after six days in Bunia, Lionel and I hired a Land Rover and were driven to a secluded mountain camp occupied by a company of South African peacekeepers. The camp was a no-frills crash pad for the worked and weary, nothing but a few canvas mess tents and lean-to shelters scattered across the muddy hills. The only adornments were two 82 mm mortar positions and a half dozen minesweeping Casspir APCs parked in the back lot.

The South Africans were a scrappy and salty bunch. Most all had grown up poor in South Africa's dire slums, where violence and early death were always in the wings. A few of the older commanders had been soldiers with the African National Congress (ANC) armed wing, who'd fought against apartheid and survived the horrific township wars of the mid-1990s. But even the younger guys had been touched in some way by the country's turmoil.

"You see that vehicle?" a young captain said to me that first day. He was pointing to one of the tall Casspirs, once an iron horse of the apartheid government and the Angola campaigns. "When I was a boy, they used to chase me through the streets. Now I'm the one chasing people!" He took a drag of his cigarette and just laughed.

The South Africans had seized and occupied Tchei back in May, only to watch their position later disintegrate in the hands of the Congolese troops. They'd fought hard for that mountain, slogged through the mud and rain, and losing it pissed them off. But not long after the operation, they'd engaged Cobra's militia again. The gunboys had tried to cut the supply road from the peacekeepers' base to Bunia, then march into town. But the South Africans had stopped their advance and, after two weeks of daily fighting, had driven them back to Tchei.

When I arrived, the troops were exhausted and still buzzing from the fight. But it was evident they saw beyond the rush of combat and viewed the mission in broader, historical terms. Many of these young grunts saw their mission as a way to uplift the troubled continent by taking on the insurgent rogues, brother against brother, killing as a kind of vital surgery. "It is our responsibility as Africans to help our people here," they'd say in casual conversation. They saw liberating Congo as a necessary humanitarian duty, and their idealism seemed to come directly from their solemn commander, a headstrong man who'd proved himself to be one of the UN's most effective military leaders.

Colonel Joseph Tyhalisi had come to Congo from the UN's mission in Burundi, where his South African unit had assisted in brokering peace talks between rebels and the government. The colonel had a natural gift of speaking on the level to rebels and insurgents in the bush, gaining their trust and bringing them around, since, for much of his life, he'd been one himself.

He'd grown up in Cape Town during the oppressive days of Afrikaner rule, when race laws were brutally enforced and the only education offered to black children prepared them for servitude. In 1985, at the age of eighteen, he'd joined the ANC's military wing, Umkhonto we Sizwe (or MK), which had been staging guerrilla attacks against the apartheid government since 1961. Throughout the eighties, the guerrilla fighters bombed police stations, assassinated officials, and, near Cape Town, attacked a nuclear power plant. Soon after joining, Tyhalisi was arrested by the police and severely tortured, and upon his release, he went into exile in Tanzania and Uganda. There, squads of MK guerrillas received military training for covert attacks inside South Africa, often slipping across the border for two days at a time. Tyhalisi spent the next decade in exile, often living rough in the bush. In 1996, two years after Nelson Mandela won the presidency on the ANC ticket, ending apartheid, Tyhalisi returned as an officer in the national army.

The period spent living in exile in the bush had not only given the colonel an insight into the minds of the boys he now fought, but also a firm command of Swahili. That combo gave him a decided edge over other UN commanders when dealing with Congo's militia. He was also handsome and extremely fit, a model soldier with level-straight posture and eyes that always caught you looking.

He'd scared the hell out of me the first time I met him. He was standing at the gates when I first arrived, so I handed him my credentials and rattled off my big important mission. He'd taken the documents and just stared at me, those eyes digging around inside until I ran out of things to say. Then he turned and walked off. A captain standing nearby just laughed and started giving me the tour. Later, I'd turn around to find the colonel just watching me like some predatory bird, lines of confusion or disgust drawn across his brow, I never could tell which, and I'd have to make some gesture of excuse and leave.

If anyone else felt those eyes on them, it was Cobra. Over the past two weeks, it seemed, whenever Cobra turned around, the colonel was right behind him, humping his weapon and gear through the cold rain with his men. He'd foiled the militia attack, secured the supply road to Bunia, and trapped the gunboys in the hills and, over the past two weeks, had never allowed them to rest.

"Every time I heard they were somewhere, I'd hit them," the colonel said. "Then I'd hit them again and again, until they could feel me in their blood. This Cobra, he's like a fever around me."

The heaviest fighting had occurred on the grassy highlands near the village of Bavi, a militia stronghold where the gunboys operated a gold mine and kept a base. With the colonel in the lead, the two platoons of South Africans had reached the top of the rise and were attacked by gunmen. There was no cover besides the tall grass, leaving the soldiers pinned down as bullets zipped just inches above their heads. With no other options, the colonel switched his weapon to automatic, lifted it above his head, and fired blindly at the enemy, praying his hands wouldn't get blown off.

The South Africans thwarted the attack and pushed the militia back to Tchei. And in the following days, the colonel dropped leaflets from a high-flying chopper with his mobile number listed and a warning: "If you don't surrender, I'm coming after you." He'd also worked diplomatic angles by organizing Lendu elders from Bunia and the vicinity to venture into Tchei and convince Cobra to disarm.

When Lionel and I arrived in Kagaba, the elders had been inside Cobra's mountain camp for several days discussing the deal and were scheduled to come out that afternoon. As soon as we put our bags down, the colonel called his men together. He was organizing a patrol to meet the elders at a rendezvous point six kilometers outside Tchei, then transport them to Bunia to speak with government and UN officials. The mission seemed fairly routine, and the South Africans expected little to happen. But just for assurances, a unit of Bangladeshi peacekeepers stationed in nearby Aveba would join us for reinforcement.

The rendezvous point was near the village of Kamatsi, which was the highest and nearest vantage point to Tchei. After two hours of driving, our convoy was finally called to a halt along a broad, grassy hill where the wind blew heavy and warm. Down below, the soldiers could see the road to Tchei leading into the trees, dissolving against jagged hills and streams where vehicles could no longer pass.

The APCs parked in a half circle and the platoon jumped out and readied their weapons: automatic rifles, rocket and grenade launchers, and two mounted fifty-caliber guns. The colonel shouted, "Get into position!" and his men fanned into a perimeter along the hill. They disappeared inside the neck-high elephant grass, their bodies concealed except for their UN-issued body armor that left them glowing like blue gas flames in the reeds.

There was a rumbling of diesel engines down the road. Seconds

later, several white Bangladeshi APCs barreled through the brambles and stopped on the hill. Sitting atop the first vehicle was
Johnny, my old translator. It seemed like everywhere I went he was
there, like some Forrest Gump in the *Charge of the Blue Helmets.* He
wore a grimy, well-worn flak vest over his parka and an oversized
helmet that slid over one eye.

Johnny was now translating for the Bangladeshi officers in Aveba
and had seen a lot of fighting in the past six months. But each de-
ployment lasted five weeks, and when there were no operations, the
days were long and painfully boring. The comfort of the translators also depended on the base officer in charge, and he'd had some
real assholes. A Pakistani commander once locked him outside the
APC during a firefight, and in Aveba, the commanders were actually charging him room and board. "We eat MREs and live in
tents, man, where it rains through the floor. And they charge me
ten dollars a day! To eat MREs! I hired an old woman from the village to cook *pondu* because my stomach couldn't take it."

But he'd managed to save enough money to buy a small house
in Bunia. He'd also found a girlfriend named Aline and paid a marriage dowry to her father, who'd given his blessing to marry. "Four
goats and three cows," he said, "and a suit for her father. Even socks
and shoes!" But with all the fighting, he'd had little time to think
about marriage, much less a wedding. "Oh, man, and she wants a
big wedding."

The colonel had given the tribal elders two-way radios before
sending them into the bush, and now his handset squawked with
voices. "Where is this translator?" the colonel shouted, and
motioned Johnny over. The elders were close, the colonel said, and
handed Johnny a radio and megaphone and sent him down the hill
to greet the delegation.

After a few moments, Johnny radioed back saying the elders were
coming but were surrounded by militia: "There are many of them,
and they're heavily armed!" The Bangladeshi soldiers rushed behind

their armored vehicles for cover. We could see nothing from where we stood, only the road directly in front of us. "Tell them to come slowly," the colonel said. "I want their hands in the air."

"They say Cobra is with them," said Johnny. "And he wants to greet you."

The Bangladeshi commanders protested, fearful of an ambush. They shouted at Johnny, "Tell them to stay back!" But the colonel waved them off and marched toward the road. "Johnny, tell them to come," he said. "If Cobra has come himself, then I must trust him."

As the colonel marched toward the road to meet Cobra, he knew he had the advantage. In the end, even if the colonel couldn't bring Cobra down from the mountain, at least he'd broken his magic. During the militia attack at Bavi, after the colonel had lifted his weapon and fired through the grass, something strange had happened. The incoming rounds suddenly stopped, and the gunboys turned around and fled. The following day, through one of the Lendu elders, the colonel learned one of his rounds had struck and killed the militia's top lieutenant, Cobra's second-in-command. The lieutenant, it turned out, was Kakadu's son.

When the militia had seen the magic leader's son dead with a bullet through his chest, they'd panicked. Their antibullet magic had failed. They dragged the lieutenant's body back to Tchei and revolted against Cobra, shouting for an explanation of how their commander had died, how their magic shield had been breached. Panic spread through the camp, and as they buried the lieutenant, some distraught boy opened fire and kicked off a barrage. When the shooting finally stopped, fifteen of them were dead.

As the peacekeepers braced themselves for the meeting, a forward party of young militia emerged from the bush and lined both sides of the road. They carried their rust-eaten AK-47s slung over their shoulders with shoestring and vines, and long wooden spears tipped with jagged blades. Many wore the uniforms and berets of dead Congolese and Ugandan soldiers. Their very presence now was enough to quicken the pulse of every UN soldier, for the enemy had rarely been this close. Seeing them was like glimpsing something wild, something rare and nimble that had strayed into the open. Their eyes now locked on the South African soldiers, who, with their jacked bodies and heavy steel, must've seemed like Minotaurs in the reeds.

Johnny pointed the group toward the colonel, who was fast approaching. But as the gunboys crossed our perimeter, the jittery Bangladeshi soldiers chambered their weapons. The unmistakable sound of live rounds locking into place was like a hole being punched in the sky. For a second everything went still. Gunmen from both sides froze in the tall grass, weapons clutched tightly, fingers stroking the triggers. One nervous bullet could spark a wild slaughter.

"So where is Cobra?" the colonel finally said, speaking to one of the elders. The man appeared unable to move. "He's at the end of the road waiting," he said, then waffled. "But maybe he should meet you next time."

"Nonsense," the colonel said. "Take me there now."

The two men led the rabble of militia and peacekeepers down the road and through the tall grass. There at the end, a group of militia parted and Commander Cobra stepped forward. He was a short, dark-skinned man dressed in camouflage fatigues and an olive-green beret. His chest and arms were surprisingly thin, with barely enough meat to hold a silver watch that hung on his wrist. But his eyes were like dead coal, and when they caught me, they told something different. The colonel stepped to Cobra and stared into those eyes. The two men embraced.

"I wanted to meet the South African I'd thought so much about," said Cobra.

"I'm glad you came," the colonel said, "because I've been thinking a lot about you."

The meeting lasted only a few minutes. The two men discussed the militia's surrender, and for the first time Cobra said he was open to negotiations. "You will hear from me," Cobra said, and squeezed the colonel's hand. And for the next half hour, the two armies who'd battled one another across the green hills stood arm in arm and posed for photos.

Walking back to the vehicles, a Bangladeshi captain could hardly contain his joy. "This is the greatest thing to happen in a year," he said. "You were just a witness to UN history."

For the next two nights, the South African soldiers unwound with a deep freeze of Nile Special beer and hard *kwaito* beats pumped from boom boxes. They watched American movies on portable DVD players and cleared pallets of bottled water and onions in the supply tent to make a crude dance floor. On the second night, a lashing storm sent flash floods through the camp and shredded most of their tents. Everything they owned was soaked and scattered in the bush. So the soldiers crowded into the supply tent and kept on drinking, wrapping themselves in ponchos and soggy sleeping bags to fend off the mountain chill. A well-oiled captain stood atop a stack of pallets and raised a bottle. There wasn't a dry stitch of clothing on him. "Remember troops," he said, and the chorus of soggy soldiers chimed in, "there is no reign in the army, only army in the rain!"

"Hey," one of them said to us, "how come you guys are so dry?" It was true, we hadn't left the tent for hours. Still, I was freezing through three layers of clothes. A group of soldiers crowded around Lionel, with his golden beard and blue eyes, and started calling him Chuck Norris. "Mr. Chuck," they said, "you missed the battle, man, we done cut the head off the Cobra."

One of the commanders had instructed the men not to speak to the journalists, so I didn't expect any war stories. Sure enough it came up. "We can't be talking to no reporters, man," they said, just to get it out of the way. Because when the beer finally ran dry, the men started to talk. They huddled around a fire of C-ration heat tabs, boiled pots of instant coffee, and reflected on their days in the violent east.

There was a white soldier named Smith who manned the big .50-caliber guns. When the South Africans had marched into Tchei, he said, one of the first things that greeted them were the boneyards along the roads, the bleached skeletons of dead militia lying in the open grass where they'd fallen. But the shallow graves in Tchei stayed with him the most. "The arms and legs stuck up from the ground," said Smith. "And the dogs stripped them to the bone." He couldn't sleep the whole time he was there, he said, those graves seemed to make their own restless noise.

The soldiers spoke of their colonel with both loathing and supreme love. He was like a god who revealed himself only through pain and sacrifice. "The colonel is hard," said one soldier. "When you speak to him, he just stares at you like a jackal. *I think I will be eaten.*"

"Yes," said another. "But he's always there with us. When he says fight, he is the man who leads the way."

They would follow their colonel anywhere, they said. And the next morning, as the soldiers awoke in puddles of cold rainwater, the colonel arrived to inform them they were going back to Tchei.

In the early-morning chill, the South African soldiers filed into formation and the colonel stood before them. He wore a knit cap pulled low over his head and a grenade clipped to his flak vest. He explained the latest developments to his men, speaking loudly and clearly and without any expression. After lengthy negotiations via satellite phone and radio, Cobra Matata had agreed to surrender with two thousand soldiers. He'd demanded amnesty for his boys and a smooth integration into the national army. Cobra also wanted legitimacy himself, demanding the government admit him into the army with the rank of general.

Cobra would surrender with his boys, the colonel explained, but one last condition was to be met. The South Africans would have to enter Tchei and get them. They would drive until they couldn't drive anymore, then walk into Cobra's boneyard.

The risks were so clear. Everyone knew it was six hard kilometers into Tchei, through mud banks, steep hills, and swollen streams. Much of the journey was under a thick canopy of trees, making support or rescue by chopper impossible. Once inside, your flesh and bone took on cartoonish expendability, worth only as much as a stoned twelve-year-old saw fit.

"We're going to walk inside and bring him out," the colonel said. He'd taken the grenade off his vest and now held it behind his back, fingering the smooth steel like a rope of prayer beads.

"If I tell you to do something, you don't analyze, don't attach any emotions to it. You just do it." The soldiers stared firmly ahead, beyond the colonel to where the green hilltops touched the lead-colored sky.

"What's important is not to panic. Don't think about what's going to happen to you, think only about what you have to do." Beyond the hills were the slopes of Tchei, and along the scarp they saw their bodies lying dead in the tall grass, a still life as innocent as if they'd walked past it in a museum.

"And if something happens while we're there, give each other your backs, you hear me? Give each other your backs and shoot everything in front of you."

The colonel paused. A pair of magpies screeched overhead and swooped to the ground. "Just trust me," he said. "But if you walk with me, make sure you're not very close."

When the colonel dismissed his men, we quietly loaded the vehicles and pulled the convoy onto the road. Sitting in the back of the Land Rover was a sweet-faced soldier who clutched his rifle and stared calmly out the window. I asked if he was afraid, and his lips parted into a smile. "Everything will be just fine," he said. "I believe in Jesus Christ."

The overnight rains had washed out the roads, slowing the convoy to a maddening crawl that only heightened the anxiety. The dense forest reached in and clawed at the windows, and somehow I was certain we were being watched from the trees. I focused on the headlights of the APC a hundred meters behind us, barely visible through the sheen of dirt and mud. I must've zoned out for a while, because when I came to, the first thing I realized was the headlights were gone. I turned to Lionel. "Where's that last APC?"

The major in the front seat must've realized it, too, because he told the driver to stop. The convoy ahead of us continued moving, and soon we were alone on the trail. The major called into his radio for the missing vehicle, but got no reply. *It's an ambush*, I thought, *they've split the convoy*.

The driver whipped the vehicle around and sped back the opposite direction looking for the missing APC, slamming into sinkholes that smashed our heads into the roof. We drove faster and faster. Around each bend we craned our heads and saw only red mud and trees. *Christ, how long ago did we lose them?* The colonel called from the lead vehicle, saying he was also turning back. Nobody in the truck said a word.

Finally, after a half hour of driving, we found the APC turned over in a ditch. Everyone was okay; the driver had taken a hard turn and spun the wheels off the road. We all just kind of laughed and cursed his skills, and no one acknowledged a thing.

When the other vehicles joined us at the wreck, we cracked open the MREs and ate breakfast on the trail. The colonel sat in the lead Land Rover, his boots propped up on the dash. He dug into a can of lentils with a pocketknife and ate from the blade. Loud Swahili hip-hop thumped from the speakers, but the colonel seemed to ignore it. Instead he appeared deep in thought and utterly alone.

We stood watching the colonel from the road, then Lionel leaned in and whispered, "That's my knife, mate, he borrowed it." He was proud as a boy and knew that I was jealous.

★ ★ ★

At the rendezvous point in Kamatsi, the soldiers fanned out once again in a broad perimeter. They carried heavier weapons this time, grenade launchers shaped like oversized tommy guns with multiple rounds strapped to their chests; spare RPG rockets sticking out of backpacks like deadly wands; and you knew the Casspir's guns were live and ready. The colonel sat atop one of the APCs and gazed across the valley with a pair of binoculars. The militia had promised to send escorts to meet the colonel and his men, so we waited for them to show. The wind whipped through the tall grass where the soldiers stood, and the morning sun was already strong overhead.

We waited for an hour, and then another, until every muscle became sore from standing so still. Silver clouds of cigarette smoke rose from the tall grass as soldiers crouched and waited. Otherwise no one moved. A few soldiers talked near the road, and I could see the colonel pointing to the hills and mouthing something to the major. But something about that hilltop and all its empty space sucked away all sound, leaving only wind. And silence like that only left you with yourself. Since I had no flak vest, I spent most of my time behind the APC, leaning against it, sitting in its shade, always within arm's reach.

Somewhere along that wind, around ten A.M., the first militia arrived. I never heard their approach, just looked up and saw them standing there on the road, a dozen of them, maybe twenty. Then within minutes there were hundreds, so many they filled the road and grassy field where we stood. They walked in small squads with four boys leading each pack. Two boys held the ends of a belt-fed machine gun while the others draped chains of bullets across their shoulders like ropes of brass garland. Fetishes were now tied to each boy's biceps, some with glass amulets and bits of herb protruding from their cloth bundles. The air was thick with dope, as rows of gunboys tugged off joints that turned their eyes yellow against their coal black skin. The battle armor and magic were all in place, suggesting a display of power or a readiness to fight—certainly not to give up. I'd seen militia disarm over their years, and no one had dressed up for that.

At news of the impending surrender, the UN brass in Kinshasa had organized a formal signing ceremony with Cobra as he emerged from Tchei. It would be attended by a delegation of senior UN civilian and military officials, plus FARDC generals and representatives from the Ministry of Defense. The UN and government needed every victory they could squeeze out before the elections, and a major warlord surrendering with two thousand militia was the stuff of dreamy PR. Earlier that morning, Bangladeshi soldiers had arrived and erected two giant canopies along the hill with tables and rows of chairs, along with urns of cold water, hot tea, and biscuits.

Around noon, several APCs thundered up the road with the delegation huddled inside. The vehicles stopped along the hill, and when the hatch opened, a UN cameraman scurried out and rolled the film. Delegates emerged dressed in sharp clothes and carrying clipboards under their arms. They were half-blinded by the sun and smiling, but once their eyes focused, their faces seemed to drop at the sight of the young killers glaring back from the high grass, smoking joints and polishing their gun barrels with dirty T-shirts.

The head of the UN office in Bunia, a dapper Ivorian named Charles Providence Gomis, made his way through the soldiers and militia and found the colonel. He was impeccably dressed in a tailored suit and smelled of expensive cologne. "Colonel," he said with burning sincerity, "you've showed a lot of courage and determination and the delegation is proud of you. Without you, we'd have no mission."

The colonel beamed and dug his boot into the dirt, and for the first time I saw his expression break. As the colonel briefed Gomis, other members of the delegation mingled and chatted with the peacekeepers and officers, with the delegates throwing wary glances at the militia in the perimeter. Several approached the militia and attempted conversation, but the gunboys only muttered a few nervous words, a childlike coyness I found almost encouraging. Up the hill, a small crowd gathered under the canopies as Bangladeshi soldiers served tea and biscuits and offered to light cigarettes. The UN cameraman weaved through the crowd shooting it all, his Palestinian *kaffiyeh* flapping in the wind. Lionel and I stood back in the grass just taking in the scene. "This has got to be the strangest party I've ever attended," he said, and there was no denying that.

An hour after the delegation arrived, the colonel reached Cobra by satellite phone. Cobra explained he was having second thoughts about meeting the delegation. He didn't trust the government's promise of amnesty and felt the UN was planning to betray him. He was afraid he would be arrested. "Cobra, you must trust me," the colonel pleaded. Cobra suggested he was still willing to talk, but only if the colonel came into Tchei alone.

Again, the Bangladeshi commanders balked. "It's a trap," they said. "You can't go in there alone. They're setting you up to die." The colonel looked up the hill at the delegates, who were guzzling water and starting to wilt in the heat. "We have only two days before elections," he said. "There are people in these houses that need to vote, and if we ruin a day, then it's over."

The colonel turned to his major. "I'll park the vehicle and walk in," he said. "If I'm not out in three hours, send everyone to get me."

The colonel climbed into the Land Rover with his driver and we watched them disappear around the bend and into the dense bush. Sometime later, the colonel's radio went dead. We waited two hours without word, sending call after unanswered call. The sun was brutal and the breeze had given way to sucking heat. The delegates slumped under canopies, fanning themselves and looking faint. Finally, embarrassed and a little more than worried, they announced they were returning to Bunia. It would be dark in an hour, and no one wanted to be stranded in the dark. With no word from the colonel, everyone started imagining the worst.

"We can't dwell on these options," said the South African major, rubbing his hands along his face as he stared at a silent radio. "For now we must trust him. Just wait for now."

The Bangladeshi commander suggested they go find him. "We'll just go in and stay the night. If someone shoots at us, we'll have plenty of our own to answer back."

"But we don't even know where he is," said the major. "Look, we just have to take it easy." The major walked away still staring at the dead radio, which had by now started to tremble in his hands.

The setting sun threw an auburn glow across the hills of Tchei, and the cool wind returned to chase off the heat. In the orange haze of dusk, the major looked up the road and noticed most of the militia had vanished. Something had happened, it suggested, something was complete. Still, we waited.

At near dark, the major's radio rumbled to life: "Ten-nine, ten-nine, do you read, over?" It was the colonel, alive, and instructing the major to send Land Rovers to the end of the road. "I have the package," he said, meaning Cobra was with him. The major sent the vehicles, and half an hour later, they emerged with the colonel walking briskly in between. He carried his service pistol in one hand at his side. When he reached the hill, his body was shaking so violently he could hardly speak.

"They have two brigades up there, almost a division of people," the colonel said, breathing heavily. "The man himself has like three hundred bodyguards."

The Bangladeshi commander ran over. "We thought you were dead."

The colonel had switched off his radio. "If I communicated at all, I would've taken a bullet."

The colonel explained how, after traveling two kilometers, his driver had parked the vehicle at the end of the road and stayed behind, while the colonel began walking the four kilometers into Tchei. He was soon greeted by twenty bodyguards sent to escort him to the militia base, where Cobra waited. The colonel gave them his rifle, pistol, and grenade, but kept a spare grenade tucked inside his underwear. "If anything happened," he said, "I wasn't going down alone." As he walked in, hundreds of gunboys packed both sides of the road. The militia were unaware the colonel himself had killed Kakadu's son, yet they saw him as the leader of warriors who'd beaten their magic. Most were drunk on corn liquor and their eyes danced crazy. "Here is the meat!" they shouted. "Give us your heart, colonel, it will make us strong!" The boys leveled their rifles at his head, while others reached through the bodyguards with clubs and knives, hoping to throw off their balance and take the colonel down. The colonel refused to look at them and continued walking.

They passed through thick forest, an open field, and finally reached the base itself. It was a village of mud and clay houses, busy with children and families of the militia. Many of the women were also drinking in their courtyards and cried out, "Here he comes!" The bodyguards led the colonel to a thatched hut and told him to wait. After fifteen minutes, Cobra and Kakadu emerged. The magic man had white hair and wore a white robe. He turned to Cobra and said, "Here is the son of the soil I spoke of. He is one of us. He comes in peace." Kakadu turned to the colonel and said, "I'm happy to see you made it," then assured the colonel he wouldn't be harmed.

Cobra took the colonel aside and said he was now willing to speak with the delegation. The colonel's lone march into Tchei had been a test to see if the UN and government were serious. No strangers had ever entered Tchei before and lived, Cobra said. After retrieving his weapons from Cobra's bodyguards, the colonel radioed his major at Kamatsi and ordered the extra vehicles to transport the party of militia to the rendezvous point. The group reached the vehicles and Cobra and one of his lieutenants climbed inside with the colonel. The driver started back toward Kamatsi, but before they got far, the bodyguards rushed forward and blocked the road with their rifles raised. They were afraid Cobra would be arrested and couldn't allow him to continue. Cobra grabbed a weapon from his lieutenant, jumped out of the truck, and aimed it at the boys. "I'll kill you if you don't move," he screamed. The colonel pulled him aside and told him it wasn't worth it. It was getting late, he said, and while they'd been walking toward the vehicles, he'd received word over the radio that the delegation had gone home.

"There's really no point now," said the colonel. "We'll have to talk next time."

The colonel left Cobra on the trail with his boys and a gun in his hand and drove toward Kamatsi. When we'd spotted the colonel approaching on foot, it was because he'd stepped out of the vehicle to speak to some of Cobra's guys on the road, to tell them the meeting was canceled. And after he explained everything to us, he lined the boys up and doled out his rations, then sent them back to Tchei.

III

With Cobra's militia still at large, we entered elections with the specter of violence still heavy in the hills. The UN responded by sending Bangladeshi APCs to Gety to guard the camp and the Catholic mission, where polling would be held. If there was an attack, the Bengali soldiers would be the first responders. Knowing this, Lionel and I grabbed our gear and moved to their base in Aveba. There I could sit and wait for Cobra, whether he surrendered or made his stand. I took comfort in knowing the wait, however long, would be conducted in luxury; the Bangladeshis ran one of the finest camps in all of Congo, a lavish pleasure dome (by UN military standards) that had generated its own lore among the Kinshasa-based correspondents.

Even the South Africans who'd dropped us off in one of the big Casspirs had said farewell with a longing sigh, for this was no mud-slicked bivouac. The Bengali soldiers lived in spacious, World War II–era center-pole tents rigged with electricity and set on prim rows of packed earth, which several soldiers were scouring with brooms when we arrived. A smiling captain greeted us at the door of a converted schoolhouse, which served as the officers' quarters and recreation hall. He handed our bags off and told someone to arrange our tents, then led us inside. "You're just in time for breakfast," he said.

The South Africans had given us MREs to eat, many of them so waterlogged the heat tabs just exploded when put to flame. Lionel and I had resorted to eating cold cans of lentils, pulled from soggy green ration boxes labeled HINDU. After days of this food, our stomachs were caving in, and we'd begun trading food fantasies like castaways.

At Aveba, the table inside the rec hall was spilling with food: omelets, stewed meats and vegetables, and fried parathas smeared with jam. About four officers sat digging in, while an army of cooks rotated out the empty plates for more heaps of steaming food. Each officer had his own personal servant—called a battle man or batman and traditionally taken into combat—who stood patiently behind him while he ate. When the meal was finished, the officer would flick his wrist and shout something in Bengali, and the batman would fetch him tea, fresh fruit, or cigarettes. Outside, two officers sat in the sun while their batmen shaved them with razors and boiled water for their bath.

Lionel and I ate like dogs, looking up every so often to exchange a nod of victory. The hot food and spices warmed our stomachs and lapsed us into a narcotic trance, abetted by the odd Bengali music videos playing on a nearby television, streamed in from a satellite dish outside. At night the officers watched westerns on DVD, such as *Quigley Down Under* and *Silverado*, plus episodes of *The Three Stooges* and *Tom & Jerry*. Their favorite cartoon had Tom and Jerry in combat with egg mortars and carpet bombs made of lightbulbs. The men howled with delight at every stunt and narrow escape, shouting, "I can't believe he did that!" and applauding madly.

After two gluttonous days of eating and napping, I'd almost forgotten about Cobra, the colonel, and the elections. I suddenly remembered the night before, while watching cartoons and sipping tea, the importance of the event, and how everything I'd reported since Bunia had led up to this day. Tomorrow the Congolese would come one step closer to reclaiming their nation from the cesspool of corruption and violence. But across the country in Kinshasa, the dawn of better times still looked a lot like the punishing days of old.

The EU had flown in a thousand French, German, and Spanish soldiers to secure the capital, with another thousand on standby in Gabon. Yet despite the extra manpower, violence had still plagued the city in the last days of campaigning. Vice President Bemba threw a campaign rally at the stadium that drew forty thousand people and ended with his supporters clashing with police outside. Six people had been killed, including two policemen who were shot and stoned to death by mobs. The next day, one of President Kabila's bodyguards shot and killed the bodyguard of Vice President Azarias Ruberwa, himself a presidential candidate, as the two politicians' details crossed paths on the road. And a mysterious Belgian army drone crashed into a crowded Kinshasa neighborhood, injuring five people and burning homes. The drone was intended to fly around the city taking photographs on election day. The army blamed the crash on software error.

As election morning arrived in Aveba, I left my tent and walked to the metal gates of the UN camp and saw hundreds of people streaming down the road. They carried their bundles of belongings on their heads—pots and pans, buckets and blankets—or pushed them on bicycles and oxcarts. Any other time such a procession would suggest something terrible, a militia raid or massacre that would empty the villages and fill the camps again. But now the exodus was reversed, as the camps and villages around us emptied and people hit the roads to vote.

We traveled twenty kilometers down the road to Gety camp and pulled into the Catholic mission. The compound was already crowded and thrumming with eagerness as residents poured in. It was like a different place from the camp I'd seen only days before. The sun was high and warm and had dried away the mud that choked the roads. Women wrapped in bright-colored *pagnes* stood in the voting lines, holding their children and chatting to the crowds that passed. The suffering and sickness no doubt remained in the narrow corridors of the camp, but here, now, something more powerful and hopeful had gained a foothold.

I stood and watched the voters enter the Catholic mission and drop their ballots, and when they emerged into the bright morning sunshine, each had the strangest look on their face, one of deep abatement, as if every muscle had relaxed for the first time in years. It was then, while staring across this place so overrun with death only days before, that the significance of the day finally set in.

In Gety we were joined by Pastor Marrion, who arrived to help us with interviews. For the past week he'd worked with the crush of correspondents in Bunia, hopefully making a good chunk of pay. That morning in Bunia he'd awoken before dawn to stand in line to vote, finally getting to experience the moment he'd anticipated and spoken about for months. By the time he pulled up to Gety in the Land Rover, his face was dancing. "Hello, my chief," he said, his arms opened wide and hands in a fist. "Today is a *great* day for Congo, one of our *greatest* days, praise *God!*"

All around the Catholic mission in Gety, families spread blankets in the grass and shared food. A mother and son carried trays of peanuts and cigarettes atop their heads for sale. Children played soccer with Bangladeshi peacekeepers, who snapped photos and chased them around the pitch with video cameras. The Congolese soldiers even kept to themselves, smoking cigarettes and dozing in the shade.

The pastor and I sat in the courtyard eating peanuts and watching the children play, and from his silence I could only guess the cathartic journey that had to be taking place in his mind as he revisited all the tragic milestones of his life—the death of his father; gunboys kicking down his door—a journey that accounted for all the pain, but eventually led here, to a sunny day in July, watching his nation vote. All across that courtyard those same sorrowful paths were remembered and relived, and I imagined them all fusing together into a splendid arch that spanned the blue sky and allowed those four million souls to finally cross over.

Across the giant country, election day was a peaceful and celebrated event. Even in Kinshasa, all the bleak predictions fell away as polls closed without incident. And despite the setbacks with Cobra's surrender, it appeared that all the UN's hard work and investment had finally paid off.

Negotiations with Cobra were ongoing in the following days, and while Lionel returned to Kinshasa, I stayed behind in Aveba with hopes of entering Tchei with the colonel. Each morning I'd walk down the road from the UN base to a space the size of a pitcher's mound we called Telephone Hill—the only place within twenty kilometers with cellular reception. Each morning I'd call the colonel at his base in Beni, and he'd guarantee that we'd soon be bringing out Cobra. "Just one more day," he'd say. "Tomorrow is looking very good. And when it happens, we'll go in together."

But after three full weeks of waiting, Cobra never came down from the mountain, and I began to doubt if he'd ever come down at all. Three weeks was a long time to wait, but it wasn't all bad. I'd gotten a good dose of rest and mountain air and ridden on patrols deep into the hills, past lush, green hollows where the floor of the world had dropped into an expanse of vines and trees. Johnny had been on duty the first week of my stay, so the two of us hung out in his tent, reading Stephen King novels and watching kung fu DVDs on his portable player. A few more militia managed to escape from Tchei and find their way to the base, and Johnny and I would sit with them and see how much they'd talk. One kid, nineteen years old, explained the cannibal ritual without hesitation: "We eat the livers of the dead Congo soldiers. We eat it fresh and raw, and after the first time, you're never afraid again. You no longer see fear. It's like your eyes are covered with blood. And the taste, I find, is very good."

With election results scheduled to be announced soon in Kinshasa, and absolutely nothing moving in Tchei, I made plans to leave Aveba and travel to the capital. I spent the morning saying good-bye to new friends, trading e-mails and numbers, then caught a ride back to Bunia with a French aid group. Once there, I boarded a UN Boeing and returned to my old home.

The politics surrounding the election told me Kinshasa would be the best place to cover the winner, no matter who it was. It didn't take a creative leap to guess Kabila would win it all. It was just the consequences that were interesting. Kabila may have controlled the east and majority vote, but Bemba was still king in the Lingala-speaking west, where the vice president had pulled thousands to his rallies.

My trip to Kinshasa was also my own little homecoming, my first time back since I'd left the previous year. I was looking forward to seeing the old gang and working the streets together. And a steak and several bottles of wine at Château Margaux would restore my sense of taste after three weeks of Bengali chili peppers.

At one point during dinner in the officers' mess, my throat had actually seized up and refused to swallow. For the past several days, I'd eaten only rice, bananas, and parathas with jam.

I was leaving Aveba a bit disappointed, having waited for something that never materialized. But for the first time, I was leaving eastern Congo feeling something other than dread and fatigue. The election had made me optimistic, elated, as if the sun had finally broken through after a long, brutal winter.

My UN jet landed at Kinshasa's N'Djili airport on a Friday night, and within an hour I was on Lionel's balcony mixing gin and tonics with Lionel and Dave Lewis. After five weeks of living clean in the mountain air, the dirty tropical heat now leeched into my blood and made me thirsty and took me back to some dark days I sure didn't miss. And Kinshasa never disappointed. The mood in town was as peaked as ever, and the vine was full of festering rumors of how the boulevard would soon run with blood.

Once again, Dave had been left to sort through this slush pile of doomsday predictions and report back to London, hoping his tone of voice hadn't taken on the ring of a believer. "Like I've always said, not a single person in this place has a bloody clue what's going on," he said. "Myself included."

Of course, all the scenarios ended with Congo spiraling back to war. If Kabila won, Bemba would declare war in the west, have the president assassinated, and stage a coup; if Bemba won, the rebellion would flame in the east, with Europe and America backing Kabila's troops to salvage deals they'd brokered with the president. After all, the former political-affairs officer at the U.S. embassy in Kinshasa had just become an executive at Phelps Dodge, which had recently been granted a $900 million mineral concession in Congo. Those were just a few scenarios, and with four vice presidents on the verge of unemployment, two of whom were former rebel leaders with standing armies on call, anything was likely.

All the rumors had ratcheted up the antiforeigner sentiment

considerably, and several times Dave had been caught alone at Bemba's rallies after the fat man had spewed his xenophobic poison. Mobs had smashed Dave's windows, tipped his vehicle, and nearly taken his head with a club. He laughed it off in typical fashion, but I could tell he was bone-tired. "My career could probably use a long vacation from Congo," he told me.

But knowing how rumors in Kinshasa thrived like kudzu, I blew them off and focused on having fun. "Nothing's gonna happen," I said. "And if it does, I'll probably miss it."

We ate steak dinners under the shaded veranda of Margaux and listened to the fistfights of *shegue* outside the gates and copped ten-dollar bags of grass from taxi drivers that rolled your head until you swore it would come right off. One of Dave's college friends, Henry Burnand, was a med student in Britain who was doing an internship at the Kinshasa General Hospital. My second night in town, he invited all of his fellow Congolese intern pals out for beers, and we had a big night. We hit the rooftop clubs of Bandal, drinking tall bottles of Skol and dancing with the plump mamas, who pressed us into their bosoms and incited roars of laughter from the tables.

The election results were scheduled to be announced Sunday night, and all of us had agreed to just listen on the radio and skip the drive over to election HQ. But half an hour before the announcement, my cell phone lit up. "Hurry, mate," Dave said, "we've got shots fired on the boulevard."

A UN vehicle had been en route to election headquarters when bullets strafed its side; steel plates in the door panel had saved the passengers. It was unclear who'd fired the shots, but everyone suspected they'd come from the jittery troops of Jean-Pierre Bemba, who were garrisoned in the center of town near the vice president's sprawling riverside mansion. If you included armed loyalists living within a day's drive from town, Bemba had about a thousand men at the ready. It was beginning to feel like the east all over again.

Everything was silent as Lionel and I drove the boulevard toward the election headquarters. It was dark now and the streets were windblown and empty. Lionel floored the jeep and we raced through the eerie stillness, forgetting to breathe until we saw the lights of the election commission office. We whipped around to the side of the building and were stopped by a roadblock. Out stepped a white guy dressed in T-shirt and jeans, strapped with full body armor, night-vision goggles, and a short-barreled Israeli machine gun. "Get the *fuck out of here!*" he screamed. He was American, most likely UN private security. A single gunshot echoed a block away, sending the soldier's eyes skipping off the street corners and rooftops, then finally back to us. "Did you fucking hear me? I said get the fuck out of here *now!*"

The guards at the election commission wouldn't allow us to park inside the compound and motioned for us to turn back. But before we could argue, the air around us rippled with machine-gun fire. A crowd outside the gate panicked and mobbed the entrance. *"Get out of the way!"* Lionel screamed. *"Get out of the way!"* He gunned the motor, nearly crushing people under the wheels. We plowed inside before the steel gates rattled shut.

The election commission was housed inside a local Catholic parish, just across the boulevard from my old apartment. Once inside the gates, we found ourselves in a large courtyard hemmed by the parish buildings. A white UN APC was parked with its cannon facing the gate and manned by a couple of Tunisian peacekeepers, who'd jumped inside their armored vehicle. They now stood halfway inside the hatch, clenching their rifles and lighting one cigarette off the other.

We weren't inside five minutes before the boulevard exploded in heavy gunfire, a metallic caterwaul like an avalanche of rocks over a tin roof. Kabila's Presidential Guard were now fighting Bemba's men right outside the parish. Artillery shook the gates as Congolese tanks fired their cannons, and mortar and rocket rounds rumbled from the riverbank behind us. Soon the whole courtyard was one frantic war room as UN, EU, and Congolese officers tried to determine how to keep the whole capital from splitting apart.

A Uruguayan officer in soccer shorts (he'd probably run straight from his barracks) had a map spread on a wooden table in the grass. "Bring the reinforcements around this way," said the officer, pounding a pencil onto the map.

"That will never fool them," a Congolese officer chimed in. "I know these rebels!" Cell phones and radios chirped incessantly, causing a sonic wall of babble as they were answered in twenty different languages.

From the courtyard, a French officer shouted, *"Attention! Attention!"* and pointed to the roof of the parish. "There's someone with a gun!"

We all dove behind vehicles, as officers fumbled for their helmets and scanned the black sky with their pistols. One female Congolese soldier jumped behind a pickup with our group. I heard Henry Burnand say, "It's gonna be okay," and turned to find the soldier tugging his shirt like a blanky in the night. As every pair of eyes searched the rooftops for the alleged sniper, the tense silence was interrupted by ringtones of "Lambada" and "Scotland the Brave."

The gunfire and cannons continued until early morning, but the Congolese journalists handled it with aplomb. They'd somehow brought in sandwiches, fried chicken, and beer, and when I walked inside headquarters to investigate the aroma, I found them gyrating to heavy soukous.

In the midst of all this chaos, the chairman of the election commission was rushed into the compound inside an APC. The shooting seemed to stop long enough for him to announce that the election was too close to call, and a runoff between Kabila and Bemba would have to decide who would lead the Congo. We were oddly relieved, for a decisive victory in either direction, we feared, would usher in even greater violence than what we were hearing now.

Most of the gunfire had come from the direction of Lionel's apartment, making it too dangerous to go home. So around three A.M., we deemed it safe enough to make a dash across the boulevard to the Memling Hotel, where the nervous guards whisked us inside the gates. The surly desk clerk, keenly appreciating the extraordinary circumstances, charged us three hundred dollars for several hours in a dingy room.

The fighting had eventually shifted toward Bemba's residence, which was four blocks from Lionel's apartment. All night Lionel had been calling to check on his wife, Nathalie, who'd been stuck at home alone while explosions rocked their windows.

So as the morning came without incident, Lionel was anxious to get home. Back in the car, we passed streets littered with shell casings, cars with windshields blown out from gunfire, and discarded uniforms of soldiers who'd stripped and fled. We rolled past the first roundabout at a crawl, too afraid to stop and photograph the lone policeman lying with his head against the curb. If not for the blossoms of dried blood across his chest, you'd think he'd lain down to sleep.

Nathalie was awake when we got home. She was a short, fiery Portuguese woman who wasn't easily rattled. If anything, the night of constant gunfire had left her cranky about missing her sleep.

"Ay, those men kept shooting all bloody night!" she said. "Nothing but *pa-pa-pa-pa-pa*! I could not sleep one *minute*." She was especially pissed about having taken down the curtains from their windows the day before, which had left her exposed during the barrage. "I didn't even need to take them down, why did I take them down?"

The morning remained quiet so we ventured out again. Lionel kissed his wife before walking out the door, telling her, "Going for a quick look around, be back in a couple hours." People were slowly returning to the boulevard, which was reassuring, but as we got downtown, a menacing wind came up, as if to announce more trouble was on the way. Men and women dashed across the side streets and hid in buildings, people poked their heads out of doorframes, and shoes lay abandoned in the road. My ears began to ring and I tasted metal.

"This is bad," I said. "We need to find somewhere now." Trucks full of black-clad Presidential Guard rumbled past, belching fumes out the back. We hit the backstreets and raced toward Dave's apartment at the Grand Hotel, the closest place where we knew it was safe.

Dave and Henry were already outside, along with Jean-Philippe Remy from *Le Monde*. They were about to leave, but we told them what we'd seen on the boulevard. "Come on, just a little spin," they said, and we reluctantly agreed. Dave and Jean-Philippe pulled out first in one car, while we followed behind with Henry at the wheel. ("Make yourself useful with the journalists," Lionel had told him, and thrown him the keys.)

But even before we could leave the compound, a dozen different machine guns erupted a block away. Dave had jumped out to speak with someone on the street just as it had happened and now sprinted through the gates at a full clip, not stopping until he was safe inside. Jean-Philippe followed in the jeep, jumping the driveway ramp as he screeched past. "Never leave the hotel," we said, and whipped the car back around.

The wraparound windows of Dave's ninth-floor suite offered a sweeping view of the city. Many nights I'd sat on his balcony drinking beers and watching the sunset sparkle off the Congo River. The green tops of palm and mango trees seemed to cover the poverty and crumbling neglect, and if you scissored the reel of history in your mind and let your eyes wander, Kinshasa from above was actually a beautiful place.

The Reuters office at the Grand Hotel was as hardwired into the history as anything else. Legend had it that George Foreman had lived there the summer of 1974 while training to fight Muhammad Ali. Whether or not it was true (and we didn't check that hard), the great Rumble in the Jungle still sparkled like a clean space on the country's sordid time line. It was probably the last time Congo wasn't seen through a prism of violence, and even that fight went eight rounds.

From Big George's room we watched the time line extend along the treads of government tanks that rolled down below, wondering when it would finally grow so tangled it hung the country in its own noose. And that afternoon, as tanks and rockets pushed inky plumes across the skyline, I thought it finally had.

Earlier that morning, the head of the UN's mission in Congo, William Lacy Swing, along with the American and British ambassadors and ten other diplomatic envoys and UN officials, had met with Bemba at his riverside mansion. The delegation had come to convince the vice president to call down his men and hopefully meet with Kabila to negotiate a truce. Halfway through their meeting, government tanks had rolled up and surrounded the house.

We'd seen the black columns of smoke from the river and started calling around. One UN officer on the phone with Dave confirmed what we'd feared: "The tanks opened fire with the delegation inside. Swing and the ambassadors are trapped."

Over the next several hours, a fierce and chaotic gun battle unfolded outside Bemba's home while the UN scrambled to rescue the diplomats. Everything at that moment seemed to twist in the heavy air: the seven years of work and planning, billions of dollars, two dozen dead peacekeepers, and the patience of the Security Council, which had already begun to evaporate. If anything happened to any of those men, the whole show was over. So when a chalk white APC finally made it to the door to evacuate the team, you could almost hear the collective sigh whistle through the razor wire at HQ.

But the anxiety seemed to dissipate from one place only to settle in another. Soon Lionel's phone rang, and when he answered, I watched the color bleed from his face. The gun battle around Bemba's residence had again spilled into the surrounding streets, and this time the front lines were just below his bedroom where Nathalie lay cowering on the floor. The gunfire and explosions were so loud I could hear them through the phone across the room.

He screamed over the noise, "Darling, please move away from the windows. Pull the mattress into the corridor and stay there. *Do you hear me? Hello?*" The line was shaky. Their conversation slipped in and out.

"She says she's fine," he said, hanging up. "She's only worried about running out of cigarettes if this keeps up." He laughed, but he was thinking what we were all thinking. Tonight the gunboys would get drunk and go marauding through the neighborhood, just as we knew they would, just as we'd always written about. But we said nothing.

"We'll get her as soon as this shit dies down," we told him, then all agreed it was best to go downstairs for a meal and some fresh air.

Downstairs, dozens of tanned, leather-skinned foreigners lounged around the pool in the late-afternoon sun. Children splashed in the water and leaped off the diving board. Two Chinese businessmen played tennis nearby, and American hip-hop pulsed over the raucous bar, stifling the sound of cannons outside.

It was as if the battle for Kinshasa were only happening within the walls of our upstairs suite, and our nerves were a little raw as a result. (Earlier that morning, we'd mistaken the *sssssp* of blue jeans brushing a potted plant for a stray bullet through the open window. We'd all hit the floor, hearts in our throats.) When our waitress dropped a beer tray and sent Dave two feet off his chair, we finished our drinks and hurried back to our chamber. In the elevator up, we'd stared nervously at one another while "Strangers in the Night" piped softly through the speakers.

I awoke on the sofa before dawn the next morning and saw Henry standing at the wall of windows. Red tracer rounds arched from one side to the next, followed by the staccato reports of gunfire. Ten minutes later, Nathalie called to say the fighting hadn't stopped all night again. Lionel hung up the phone, then joined us by the windows. "She ran out of cigarettes," he said.

The shooting cleared enough that afternoon to attempt a short drive outside the gates, but nothing farther. We found three soldiers lying in the roundabout near the hotel, killed in the morning fight. A poisoned silence seemed to radiate from their open arms. Families from the neighborhood were using the momentary reprieve to leave town. One family walked up holding suitcases and bundles, and as they passed, the mother shielded the eyes of her young daughter as they stepped over the corpses.

Half an hour passed and we were still among the dead, until the strangest moment, when all of us looked up together and said, "We should go." Seconds later, a pair of machine guns popped down the block and sent us sprinting to the truck.

As darkness fell again that night, we sat together on the balcony and watched tracer rounds arc against the sky like red Roman candles. The gunboys were firing wildly.

Lionel's phone kept ringing. You could hear the bullets hitting walls over Nathalie's strained voice. "Just hold on, darling," he'd say. "Please just hold on." After the last call, his body seemed to collapse. "What am I supposed to do?" he whispered, then looked at each of us. *"What the fuck am I supposed to do!?"*

We sat in silence for a long period of time, listening to the battle, until someone asked the inevitable question: "I wonder if it'll kick off again tomorrow. You guys think it'll kick off?"

I'd always loved that question, so pregnant with possibility. It was the reason I'd come to Congo and kept on coming back, and for the past two days I'd seen some of the heaviest fighting yet. I'd come looking for war and found it, and here it was again in its purest and most savage form. But it wasn't the sexy tracer rounds against the night, or the pulse-quickening whoosh of rockets—but a cell phone that sent waves of nausea through my guts every time it rang. The war was ours now, and I felt truly sorry for ever wishing it at all.

"I hope not," I said finally. "I really hope not."

That night I decided I never wanted to see it again, not there anyway, and if I continued to pursue this death and decay, then death and decay would forever be my memory of Congo. A folder of blood-soaked pages would be the only thing I left behind in that place, and that bothered me even more. As a reporter in Congo, I'd always bristled at the nagging question "Why do you only focus on death and never the positive?" It usually came from Africans themselves and struck me as naïve. And working for the wires, there was no time for that anyway. You wrote about the death because if you didn't, who would?

But it was true that in three years I'd rarely ventured beyond the massacres and displaced camps. And now, despite what was happening below in Kinshasa, or in small pockets of the east, the war had ended inside the vast country, and I wanted to see those places that weren't bleeding or blown to hell. I wanted to find the recovery I'd momentarily glimpsed that afternoon in Gety, to meet people whose lives were moving a little ways forward. I needed to see this for my own conscience, and it was the least I could do for the Congolese, who only seemed to suffer and bleed in the news.

As I sat there on the balcony, four new tracers hooked across the darkness without a sound, then disappeared just before the broad river. There was no moon, and the sparse city lights shimmered off the water. My journey would begin there.

Chapter Four

THE RIVER IS A ROAD

There is, despite the myriad difficulties it presents at every hand, an element of fascination about a tropical forest unlike anything else, though the chief pleasure lies in looking forward to getting out of it.

—Captain S. L. Hinde, *The Fall of the Congo Arabs* (1897)

I

The early Kongo people called it *nzere*—"the river that swallows all rivers," and the Congo River is indeed massive; in all the world, only the Amazon carries more water. It stretches forty-seven hundred kilometers from Congo's southern highlands, slicing upward through the second-largest rain forest on earth and hooking twice over the equator before barreling out to sea, emptying into the Atlantic at a rate of over one million cubic feet of water per second. The sheer ferocity of that union has created grooves in the ocean floor a mile deep.

The 1,734-kilometer voyage upriver from Kinshasa to Kisangani—the river's longest navigable route—was one of the great journeys of the world. This stretch of water had brought acclaim and glory to explorers like Henry Morton Stanley, who became the first European to breach its uncharted waters, and it delivered King Leopold a fortune in ivory and rubber that fueled the industrial revolution. But to the Congolese, who were hunted, enslaved, raped, and murdered in this quest for empire, it delivered only oppression and terror, an African holocaust that by the early twentieth century had wiped out roughly half the country's population. A journey upriver was like breaching the very vine-choked memory of the land.

I'd glimpsed its far reaches once before. In August 2003, just after my trip to Bunia to follow up on the fighting, I was on a UN flight to southern Congo for another story when the plane made a scheduled stop in Kisangani, the country's third-largest city along the Congo River. After deboarding and eating an egg sandwich at the airport snack counter, I was told my continuing flight had been canceled. It was typical, especially back in MONUC's chaotic early days. But since there wasn't another flight going south for four more days, it meant I was stranded in Kisangani.

Kisangani had been crippled by the war, both physically and economically. Soldiers, rebels, and bandits had overrun the river and choked all commercial traffic from Kinshasa. The roads in and out of town had crumbled years before, and the airport was now a rebel trophy. With all routes sealed, the city slowly began to starve.

In June that year, President Kabila had announced the official beginning of the postwar transitional government. In July, given this hopeful occasion, six river barges loaded with much needed food and merchandise set out from Kinshasa and landed in Kisangani the day before I arrived. Except for a lone barge in February, they were the first commercial vessels anyone had seen in over five years. As the first boats appeared in the morning fog, hundreds of people rushed into the river and started dancing in the shallows. When I showed up the following day, many were still packed along the banks, helping unload boxes or simply staring at the long, rust-eaten flotillas with laundry drying along their rails. The barges brought not only precious sugar and salt and bags of cement, but two thousand river traders and Kisangani residents who'd been stranded since the war, caught on the wrong side of the jungle and unable to get home. And when the boats appeared from the mist, it was as if they'd traveled from another time, figments of that good dream where the country was at peace and the family was whole, except this time the flesh was alive and the voices real.

Not many barges followed in the years after. Congo's economy remained a wreck throughout the fitful period of transitional government; imports and exports slowed to a drip, and the river captains remained gun-shy and jittery. But that day in August, after five years of war, the divided country had finally come together.

I'd always wanted to make that same journey when I lived in Kinshasa, but never had the time. I'd heard it could take six weeks by barge, possibly longer, but I didn't know anyone who'd actually done it. Plenty of reporters and travelers had made the trip before the war, but after that it became pure suicide, and you wouldn't have found a local guide to take you up anyway, not for any amount of money. But the river after the war, after the nation's first elections, that was now uncharted territory.

The election commission had announced the runoff between Kabila and Bemba would take place on October 29, 2006, and I planned my trip so I could cover the polls deep within the trees. Where exactly, I wasn't sure yet. There were a few towns far up-river where polling stations had been established, places like Bumba and Lisala, but everything else was forest and villages that hadn't changed in centuries. But after the elections, I sensed that change was inevitable and coming soon, or perhaps I just told myself this and believed it true.

In early October, with that plan in mind, I boarded a KLM flight to Entebbe, Uganda, where I caught a UN Boeing to Kinshasa. Once there, I immediately went to work searching for a boat. I was prepared to catch one of the commercial barges I'd seen in

Kisangani that were like the great Freightliners of the river, hauling hundreds of tons of goods within their steel hulls and atop their flat, rust-covered decks. Passengers and river traders squeezed amid the topside cargo, often as many as five hundred on one vessel, living and doing business as the barge crawled up the river. These barges had no timetables and were often plagued by disaster. Sandbars marooned some boats for weeks, others sank from collisions in the night or overcrowding. It was an often dangerous way to trade and travel in a country without roads, and airfare out of reach. But the resilient Congolese sucked it up and endured. I would, too.

I'd done some preliminary work before leaving the States. Through a colleague, I got the name of a local fixer in Kinshasa, whom I e-mailed and asked to ply the river ports in my advance. Séverin Mpiana was a trained electrical engineer with a university degree, but like many Congolese professionals in a city with absolute unemployment, he'd found work in other places, in his case with foreign journalists.

I'd already decided that if he found a boat before I arrived, I'd offer him a job as my translator and fixer on the river. Unlike in the cities, the people upriver spoke mainly Lingala and local, tribal dialects. Séverin was fluent in Lingala, French, and English and had a firm command of Swahili, which would prove useful as we made our way eastward.

I found him in the busy Lebanese *shawarma* shop on the main boulevard, where we'd agreed to meet. He was immaculately dressed in a crisp white shirt, pressed jeans, and designer leather sandals. His features were soft, almost fawnlike, and his speech was quiet and contemplative. I tried to imagine him on the river and couldn't. After a brief introduction, he skipped the small talk and pulled out a notebook.

"I found you a boat," he said. "It leaves in two days."

Perfect, I said, and offered him the job.

★ ★ ★

We caught a taxi to the public docks where the big barges came in, and where Séverin had been the previous day. On the ride over, he said he was eager to travel upriver and revisit Kisangani, where he'd lived as a child and still had family. His father had worked for the Belgian-run Commercial Bank of Zaire during the Mobutu years and had been posted all over the country, including Lubum-bashi, where Séverin was born, then later Kisangani, where Séverin had picked up his Swahili. They'd moved back to Kin-shasa in 1988 when he was twelve years old, just in time for the collapse and everything that followed. His father managed to find a job with Rawbank, owned by an Indian family, where he was now an officer.

His father's position meant Séverin's family was solidly middle class, a rarity in Congo. Two of Séverin's other brothers and sisters had completed college, and his youngest brother was now studying to be a lawyer. The family wasn't wealthy by any means, but they were free of the desperation that plagued so many others in Kin-shasa. And while Séverin had lived elsewhere, he'd never traveled through the interior of his own country, so the trip would be as much an adventure for him as it was for me.

The sun was already brutal when we arrived at the port, cooking off the expanse of concrete and rusting steel tied up to the docks, much of which hadn't moved in decades. About a hundred people—mainly market women going upriver to trade—were camped on straw mats in the dirt, where they'd been for over a week, just waiting for barges to be loaded. They sat under bright-colored umbrellas, fanning themselves, all their belongings wrapped in cloth bundles at their sides and children running in every direction.

We asked one of the dockworkers about our boat, the *Eben Ezer*, and he shouted something in Lingala to a man nearby, who called to another man, who then conferred with several workers unloading a pallet of hair tonic. That way, he pointed, and led us to the water's edge. He motioned toward a white tugboat at the far end of the port.

Two crewmen lay dozing in the shade of a paint-chipped lower deck. They said that, yes, this was the boat to Kisangani, but there'd been a small holdup. The remaining merchandise hadn't yet arrived, and even when it did, it could take days to finish loading, or as long as two weeks. I asked when they expected the merchandise. "Two days," he said. "But maybe four." I was also told there were no cabins to store my bags and computer, only space on the deck, which I'd have to wrestle from the gang of women waiting in the sun. From the tomcat look in their eyes, I didn't like my chances. "But we do have a deep freeze," he added. "If you wish to carry any large quantities of meat."

No, I said, but supposing I do get aboard, how long was the trip to Kisangani?

He looked at his friend and they laughed. "Who knows," he said. "After all, it's the river."

For the next three days, Séverin and I returned to make inquiries, also checking other ports and finding nothing. And after all this time spent in the sun with no prospects, I began feeling a bit hopeless. But on the fourth afternoon, Séverin called saying he'd found another boat: "A much better boat, so *beautiful* you won't believe it. And we'll ride in luxury! No sleeping on the dirty ground."

The boat was housed at a private commercial dock, where several armed security guards opened the gates and led us inside. At the end of the dock sat a giant, barrel-chested river tug called the *Ma'ungano*. She was ninety feet long with three decks, which included the engine room, the wheelhouse, and what appeared to be first-class cabins. The boat looked sturdy, almost new, and sparkled bone white in the sun. The national flag was hoisted atop the wheelhouse, unfaded and fluttering in the breeze.

The captain of the *Ma'ungano* was a stout Frenchman named Albert-Henri Buisine, an old soldier who'd been raised in Congo and served two decades in the service of Mobutu, whom he'd considered his closest friend and a genius the world was cruel to dismiss. After the Big Man's kingdom finally collapsed, sending its minions scattering to Europe and elsewhere, Buisine had turned to the river.

The captain, now in his late fifties, owned six commercial tugboats that plied the country's many rivers, all thirteen thousand kilometers of which snaked and splintered across weathered maps along his office walls. He'd been one of the few captains to brave the river over the past couple of years, and sitting behind his desk, he explained just how much the war had taken from the people in the forest. After fighting closed the rivers and tributaries, freezing all movement of merchandise that sustained the jungle economy, gunmen moved into the villages. They pillaged, raped, and murdered, so people fled deep into the forests like hunted animals, living in the rough so long their clothing simply rotted off their bodies. Several million had escaped to the capital, abandoning a way of life they'd nurtured for centuries. They'd walked hundreds of kilometers through the jungle to get there, leaving a wake of dead along the trail, and doubling Kinshasa's population. "And you should see them all now," the captain said. "Starving in the slums while still dreaming of the forest. *C'est catastrophique!* And those in the forest . . . well, if you go deep enough, you might still find them naked, hiding behind the trees."

But there was good news, he said. The recent elections had been a vanguard for hope and recovery along the river. For the first time in a century, the potential for prosperity had been introduced to the Congolese. Boat captains were braving the river again, people were returning home, and money was changing hands. As for the captain, he'd be pushing twenty-six hundred tons of freight on two barges all the way to Kisangani, which is where I wanted to go.

After spending days at the docks looking for a boat, sucking in the dust and exhaust and finding no luck, I was so relieved to have ended this task that I began to gush, explaining how anxious I was to finally pierce the interior and be with the people, see the ways they really live—"Live instead of die!" I said, regrettably.

"*Bon.*" The captain smiled and walked around the desk. "But tell me something. Will you prefer local or European cuisine? It's important I give the chef plenty of notice."

In addition to Séverin, I'd invited an old friend to travel up the river. Riccardo Gangale was based in Kigali, Rwanda, part of a free-bird fraternity of photographers who toured the sub-Saharan on motorcycles with girlfriends perched on the back, selling photos to whoever would take them. He was AP's man in eastern Congo, since it was easy for him to catch a bus in Kigali and be in Goma in two hours. We'd worked together a couple times in Ituri, where he'd first introduced me to Pastor Marrion, and I trusted him as a solid operator on the road. He was an Italian with a hot streak a mile long and a gung ho love for Deep Purple and testing his limits, sometimes to calamitous ends.

Six months earlier, Riccardo had taken the same voyage from Kinshasa to Kisangani by himself, jumping commercial barges, hiring dugout pirogues, and biking through the jungle. Halfway upriver he'd contracted malaria and run out of food. And jungle-fly bites he'd received then became infected, only compounding the malarial fevers and hallucinations. He'd stopped at a small town and holed up in a house, where he lay shivering and slipping out of consciousness. He was saved only after a pirogue full of diamond dealers passed by and paddled him two days to an MSF camp near Kisangani. When he heard about my plans to travel the river, he'd written me straightaway. He couldn't wait to do it again.

Our plan was to ride with Buisine as far as Mbandaka, about a week's journey upriver, then jump to the public barges that carried hundreds of traders on their decks. Riccardo was certain there'd be barges in Mbandaka headed upriver when we arrived, just as there'd been when he'd passed through six months before. "Yes, there were boats," he said, his Roman accent richly melodic. "Still, I wait five days for the crew to load this *focking* boat. You will see. Five days Mbandaka is five days too long."

With the *Ma'ungano* leaving in two days, we set to work preparing for our journey. We spent a sweltering afternoon in Kinshasa's central market purchasing the necessary gear, like a durable orange tarp for slapdash shelters, nylon rope, foam mattresses, pots and pans, plastic cups and buckets, pills for pain, malaria, and worms, and dozens of cans of sardines, beans, and corned-beef hash. For days, Riccardo and I had already dedicated ourselves to our own rigorous Get Fat Diet, gorging on steaks, doughnuts, and lots of cold beer, trying to gain weight we'd inevitably lose through sweat and diarrhea.

I also brought along my *Traveler's Guide to the Belgian Congo* from 1951, a year when the Belgian Congo was a gem of the African colonies. For seventy years, the colonial masters had ruled the Congolese with barbarism and oppression behind the curtains. But they'd also built sleek European cities connected by packed-gravel highways, luxury trains, and river steamers. How quickly all of that vanished in the forty-six years since independence.

The *Ma'ungano* (which meant "unity" in Swahili) was the last vestige of the era, and it was only fitting I begin my journey along its decks. So far my collective experience in Congo had been looking down, from UN choppers and APCs, from balcony apartments shielded by razor wire and guards, from the Land Rovers and press cards we used to escape the misery and smell of disease when it all became too much. Oddly, I thought, it would take a journey by river to finally plant my feet on the ground.

The evening before departure we stayed aboard the *Ma'ungano* drinking cans of Castle beer on the decks, gloating over our good fortune. Not only did we have a personal chef, but also a private cabin equipped with soft beds, a hot shower, and an air conditioner more efficient than most I'd owned in the States. I went to bed wired tight from anticipation and awoke to the rumble of engines in the pink haze of dawn. Running outside, I saw the river bubbling from the rudders the color of clean motor oil. We were moving seconds later, but so slowly that landmarks stayed in view for hours. By late afternoon, we could still see Kinshasa.

The capital sits along the tail of a wide, oval-shaped expanse in the river known as Malebo (or Stanley) Pool. In 1877, Stanley reached this lakelike area after his journey across the entire width of the African continent, having started from Zanzibar nearly two and a half years before. The core of Stanley's mission had been to discover the source of the Nile River, which several European explorers had claimed lay somewhere along the Great Lakes of central Africa and eastern Congo. One theory was the Congo River was the Nile's source, but the waterway had yet to be fully navigated. Ever since Portuguese mariners had discovered the Atlantic mouth of the Congo in 1482, the river was traveled by explorers and merchants and combed heavily by slave ships working the jungles of western Congo. But because of disease, starvation, hostile tribes, and about 350 kilometers of impenetrable cataracts between Stanley Pool and the sea, none of these ships ever breached the heart of the country. And from the east, no European had ever sailed west toward the sea. As a result, much of central Africa remained a vacuous hole on the map even four centuries after the river's initial discovery.

Born John Rowlands in 1841 in Wales, Stanley was abandoned by his single mother as a young boy and made to live in a workhouse. He fled to the United States in 1859 and worked as a store clerk in New Orleans. Stanley later joined the Confederate army during the Civil War and fought in the Battle of Shiloh before being captured by Union soldiers and thrown into a prison camp. To ensure his release, Stanley then defected to the Union army.

All along this journey he'd changed his name and much of his life story to better fit his intrepid alter ego. Claiming to be American, he became a newspaper reporter and covered the Indian wars on the western frontier. In 1868, the *New York Herald* sent him to cover the British military campaign against Emperor Theodore in Abyssinia. Before Theodore's capital Magdala fell to the Brits, Stanley managed to bribe a telegraph clerk to send his stories first, a journalistic coup that ensured news of the event reached New York before London. A year later, he convinced James Gordon Bennett, editor of the *Herald*, to send him to Africa after the vanished Scottish explorer David Livingstone, possibly the greatest story a journalist could ever hope for. Stanley's book about the journey was a bestseller that made him one of the most famous men on the planet.

Stanley's voyage across Africa began in November 1874 in Bagomoyo on the East African coast with a caravan of 228 people (including thirty-six women), mainly picked up in Zanzibar two months prior. The caravan carried eight tons of food, supply, and weaponry, and a forty-foot cedar boat they portaged in five sections weighing 280 pounds each.

After circumnavigating both Lakes Victoria and Tanganyika—the largest lake in Africa and the longest freshwater lake in the world, respectively—Stanley headed west into the forests toward the Lualaba River (the Upper Congo), which Livingstone once suspected to be the source of the Nile. For days the caravan slogged through soupy mud and quicksand, swarms of biting flies and malaria-carrying mosquitoes that dropped the men on the trail. After finally reaching the Lualaba near Nyangwe, the convoy was attacked by hundreds of warriors who suspected them of being slavers. In his best-selling book about the voyage, Stanley claimed to have fought legions of hostile tribes for the remainder of his journey, many of them cannibals who launched attacks from the riverbanks chanting, "Meat! Meat! Meat!" By the time his convoy reached the sea—exactly 999 days after leaving Zanzibar—disease, starvation, desertion, and skirmishes with natives had wiped out 132 of his original 228 crew members, including three of his British companions. Stanley's heavily armed convoy had themselves left behind a bloody trail of warriors and villagers, killed in berserk defensives that often spun into slaughter.

Stanley's successful navigation of the Congo River was a grand achievement, one that would forever change the African continent. First, it resolved one of its most puzzling questions: the source of the Nile River. His exploration of Lake Victoria confirmed an earlier theory by British explorer John Hanning Speke that the lake was the true source of the Nile. Stanley also debunked the theory by explorer Richard Burton that Lake Tanganyika actually fed the Nile from a northern outlet, which it did not. Livingstone had suggested the Lualaba eventually became the Nile, but as Stanley proved, the Lualaba was in fact the Congo and emptied into the sea. The origin of the Nile was one of Africa's last remaining geographical pursuits, and by solving the riddle Stanley closed the book on four centuries of exploration. But by illuminating the dark spaces, he in turn made room for King Leopold.

The *Ma'ungano* cleared Stanley Pool by nightfall and entered a chain of islands so immense that I often mistook them for shoreline. The first night was moonless and dark, so the *Ma'ungano* tied to shore rather than risk the sandbars. We were still in the open, low-lying scrub near the capital, nothing like the jungle we'd soon enter, yet the still, pitch-black night was like standing in a torrential downpour where every raindrop was a chirp or buzzing of wings. One of the crewmen stood in the wheelhouse and shone the powerful spotlight onto shore, sweeping the dark vegetation and drawing a thick tube of bugs that crawled in sheets across our window screen. Opening the door for even a second allowed in swarms of mosquitoes.

I woke up before dawn the next morning and climbed to the wheelhouse to watch the sunrise, kicking away the thousands of silver-winged moths that had perished in the searchlight. A large breakfast of omelets, bread, and avocado was served on the terrace, and afterward Séverin and I walked to the tip of the first barge to take in the view. The two barges stretched nearly the length of a football field and were fully loaded—both inside the airless holds and atop their rust-covered decks—with sacks of flour and sugar, cheap rubber flip-flops stuffed in bundles the size of hay bales, lawn chairs, crates of Italian tomato paste, Crème Top Claire hair cream, Tiger Head batteries, and two Indian-built Tata passenger vans bound for a customs station deep in the trees. The merchandise was piled up in rounded humps covered with brightly covered tarps. We tiptoed delicately over the ropes and tie-downs that crisscrossed our path, the water just inches from our feet. It was at this moment Séverin informed me he couldn't swim.

Once we reached the end of the barge, the rumble from the engines faded, leaving only the bright splash of water against the slow-moving steel. The river stretched several kilometers across in front of us. Patches of puffy green hyacinth floated past, along with colossal hunks of grassy earth ripped from the shore by the fierce current. The best seat in the house, I thought, but I wasn't the only one. One of the crewmen already occupied a chair at the edge of the barge. He was fast asleep, with one hand tucked lazily down his pants.

His name was Kalu, and for the past two years he'd worked as a loader and deckhand, traveling the river with Buisine about five times a year. His true field of expertise was botany, which he'd studied as a forestry student at the University of Kisangani.

He pointed to the floating chunks of vegetation in the water, which in Lingala were known as *Congo ya sika*, meaning "new Congo." They were a product of the rainy season, he explained, which rejuvenated the land, but also caused the water to rise and shear off the banks. The floating pieces of land were sometimes so large, he said, that antelope were spotted thrashing around on them.

While at university, Kalu had sung lead vocals in a band that gigged the dark and sweaty nightclubs of the city. "My friend and I played all the time. We loved to sing," Kalu said. "I wrote songs about everything: love, disappointment, the slave trade."

Singing was Kalu's first love, but the pressures of a career and family had forced him to postpone the dream. "For four years I worked in the forest studying, involving my mind with science," he said. "And now I'm on the river. I don't have much time for music."

He felt the muse slipping away, so he often spent time on the tip of the boat, waiting for inspiration to strike. "Maybe the view will make me want to write a song," he sighed. And after two minutes of absolute silence, he sat up with a jolt of revelation and calmly proclaimed, "The Congo River is a road. And I am only a witness on this road."

One of his old bandmates, Papi, also took a job with Buisine and worked aboard the *Ma'ungano*. And although they saw one another every day on the river, they never reminisced about old times. Kalu hadn't even sung a note in two years. But this was just a rough patch, a thirty-two-year-old man going through one of life's transitions.

"My music is still in my blood," he said, pausing to gather his thoughts off the soft river sheen. "Maybe it's not over. I figure all I need to do is record two songs, really big songs, and then my voice will become immortal."

The "grand highway" of trade that Stanley had extolled to the king had opened following the Berlin Conference of 1885, allowing Leopold to begin turning a profit on the exportation of ivory from the interior. To maximize the quantity of ivory taken from the forest, Congo Free State officials began paying their agents a profit percentage, which spurred the men to collect more. The gathering parties relied on caravans of local porters to carry equipment and tusks, and to guide agents around the rapids. Soon the crushing demand for porters led to wholesale village raids, where people were enslaved and made to work, often chained by the neck and force-marched down forest trails. Anyone stepping out of line or refusing orders would be beaten with the *chicotte*, a long whip made of dried hippo hide that cut the skin like jagged glass. The weak and the dead were simply kicked off the path and left to rot in the jungle, and reports from that period describe piles of skeletons in the grass and a permanent stench of decay.

The bulk of atrocities were committed by the Force Publique, whose elite soldiers were largely from the Bangala tribe that dominated the inner jungles along the equator. Many were slaves themselves, and many were also children, as Leopold pushed for trained columns of young boys, who were often kidnapped from their villages and made to serve, which they would do through all of Congo's wars. By the late 1890s, the Force Publique numbered nearly twenty thousand soldiers, who were being used heavily in eastern Congo to battle Afro-Arab slave traders for control of the forests. During the First World War, they'd also fight German colonial forces in Rwanda, Burundi, and Tanzania, while other units fought Italians in Ethiopia.

If the wealth of ivory in the forests didn't bring enough foreign interest to the Congo and misery to the Congolese, a worldwide rubber boom soon did. By the 1890s, with the second industrial revolution in full flush, rubber was in demand for everything from automobile tires to telegraph wires. To Leopold's delight, the Congo forests were carpeted in wild rubber vines, which, unlike rubber trees, required no maintenance or expensive cultivation. By the turn of the century, the Congo Free State produced more rubber than anywhere else in Africa and, by 1904, had increased its rubber profits ninety-six-fold since the boom had begun in 1890.

As with ivory, colonial agents were given a share of rubber profits, which encouraged the same brutal means of collecting it. Villagers were enslaved and sent into the forests to tap the wild rubber vines that snaked hundreds of feet up the towering trees, requiring them to climb to the top with buckets. Each person was given a quota, and failure to meet one resulted in whippings or death. But money being made from rubber far surpassed the proceeds from ivory, and soon the vast majority of Congo's forest population were conscripted to collect rubber. To ensure participation, Force Publique soldiers kidnapped women and children and held them in stockades until the village men delivered their required amounts of raw rubber. Many of the women died while in custody or were raped by soldiers, even as their men toiled in the forests. Settlements and villages that categorically refused to collect were simply massacred by the Force Publique. To guarantee the guards were carrying out their orders, soldiers were instructed to sever the right hands of their corpses, and sometimes those of living people. The hands were then smoked and delivered in baskets to regional headquarters as proof of death.

Swept away by such power, the white colonial officers would often order massacres for smaller infractions. One officer whose troops were denied fish and manioc in one village described his reaction: "I made war against them. One example was enough: a hundred heads cut off, and there have been plenty of supplies at the station ever since."

When one of the crewmen on the *Ma'ungano* told me they still hauled raw rubber on the barges, I launched into a long speech about the atrocities along *these very banks*, the amputations, the village raids, heads on pikes. But when Séverin finished translating, the crew stared at me as if I'd just asked how to buy a MetroCard.

"No," the guy said, looking at his friends for reactions. "We don't know about this stuff. You might want to ask the old people."

Walking back, Séverin shook his head and gasped. "So many people here, they have no idea of their own history."

To Buisine, history was everything, and it all connected right here. "To understand Congo," he'd say, "you must first understand the river."

During the afternoons when the heat would drive us indoors, the captain would stand at the wheel and mix the bad lessons with the good. His eyes would break focus on the channel and he'd explain the things he knew, like how the water silver-plated at dusk and hid the sandbars, or how the bank appeared dangerously close in the cool morning air. He'd point out whirlpools roiling in the deep spots or crocodiles camouflaged in the mud. On afternoons after the rains, we trained our eyes upriver and watched ghost ships hover above the water. Low pressure from the storm can play tricks on your eyes, the captain explained, and through a pair of binoculars, the boats returned to earth as the rust-eaten barges they were.

Other times he'd point to the distant bank where a brick building stood shrouded in vines and decay, a remnant of the old empire, and tell the story of the hospital or timber mill the locals allowed the forest to reclaim. He told how during the grand days of the colony there was lots of traffic on the river, with rivermen pushing hundreds of thousands of tons of product a year up and down Congo's rivers and tributaries; now they're lucky if they move a fraction of that. And because there were more boats, the river was dredged regularly, and a well-trained captain was easy to find. Signs were posted along the banks indicating sandbars and snags, depth and direction of tributaries, signs telling the rivermen they weren't alone on the black water at night. The captain would wax sentimental about these years before the collapse, when he was young and the country made sense, and during these times his eyes never left the river.

He'd been there from the beginning and watched it all fall apart; his life alone was like a window into the decline. He'd grown up in the eastern town of Bukavu, where his family owned a quarry and cinchona plantation on Lake Kivu. He later served in the French navy and, once discharged, returned to Bukavu looking for quick money and adventure, organizing gorilla tours in nearby Kahuzi-Biega National Park, and leading tourists up the smoldering Nyiragongo volcano near Goma in the Virunga Mountains.

But the government seized the family's plantation in the mid-seventies during Mobutu's nationalist land-grab campaign known as Zairianization. Buisine's uncle walked into his office one morning and found an African sitting in his chair, a midlevel government official from Kinshasa who'd never picked up a shovel. Cinchona (the natural source of quinine) requires meticulous pruning and cultivation, but the new owner rushed the harvest and the entire crop died. "People whose families had worked there a century committed suicide right then," said Buisine. Years later, Buisine was working as a supervisor at Kinshasa's Palace of the People when he received a phone call one morning at five A.M. It was President Mobutu, screaming over the line, "Buisine! From now on you work for me." Mobutu had been impressed by the Frenchman's military background and family history in Congo. Buisine took the job. "Despite everything that had happened," he explained, "when the president calls, you can't say no."

Buisine served as Mobutu's personal superintendent for sixteen years, organizing the dictator's daily schedule, security, and logistics. He was chained to Mobutu's shadow at all times, even living four straight years aboard his lavish, hundred-meter yacht, the *Kamanyola*, as it drifted aimlessly down the Congo River.

Aboard the *Kamanyola*, Buisine's living quarters were directly below the president's. "Each day would begin at four thirty in the morning, with Mobutu stomping his foot on the floor to wake me up," he said, laughing. "I'd shower and run up as quickly as possible, and he'd be fully dressed with a list of the day's events, sipping his morning Guinness from a coffee cup.

"Mobutu never felt comfortable on land," Buisine added. "He was most happy just floating the river and stopping for barbecues, having friends flown in to join him."

Sometimes, when the Big Man's mood was right, Buisine would mention his family's land. "He'd tell me, 'We'll fix that, we'll fix that. *C'est pas grave,*'" Buisine remembers. "Other times he'd say, 'Look at everything Europe lost during the world wars, and it's doing fine now. Don't make such an issue of this Zairianization.'"

After Laurent Kabila's rebel troops entered Kinshasa in May 1997, Buisine was arrested at his home, along with many of Mobutu's inner circle. "They had a list," said Buisine. "And they were out to get every person on it." With his family safely in France, Buisine spent nine months in jail, serving out the last portion of his sentence in Kinshasa's hideous Makala prison—a death sentence for most Congolese. But because of Buisine's political status, he was able to negotiate with the guards for better food and a nightly ration of beer and whiskey. He was in jail when he received the news that Mobutu, then exiled in Morocco, had died from prostate cancer.

"I didn't cry," he added. "I'm a soldier."

On August 2, 1998, someone came to Makala prison and ordered Buisine released. It was Kabila himself, who'd just learned that Rwandan and Ugandan troops—his old allies against Mobutu—had just invaded Congo. The following day, the Rwandans managed to load hundreds of soldiers and rebels onto hijacked planes and get within striking distance of the capital. The rebels would eventually reach the city's eastern suburbs before Zimbabwean, Namibian, and Angolan soldiers, summoned by Kabila, finally halted the full-on assault. So as the five-year war began, Buisine retreated to his home in the capital. There, he waited out the war as it ravaged everything Mobutu hadn't already destroyed.

Buisine's way of life for the past two decades soon vanished for good, and most people were happy to see it go. ("I don't miss it, either," he said, "especially hearing Mobutu shout, *'Buisine! Buisine!'* a thousand times a day.") In those initial years after Mobutu, he took long vacations with his family, navigating the rivers around France, Poland, and Russia, weaving through the interiors and out to seas. But after years of this, he returned home to the river he loved so well.

Buisine now led the simple life of a river rat who ran the stretch six or seven times a year. Each trip was spent in the company of his commander, Abraham Bukasa, a tall, slender man with pepper-gray hair, whose own military career had also been destroyed by the Big Man's many whims. In 1978, gendarmes arrested the young navy sergeant after suspecting him of aiding a failed coup. He spent months in a dank, underground prison in the port town of Boma, where rats chewed on inmates' flesh at night and lice infested their clothing and pubic hair. Many of his friends were executed or died from abuse.

Bound by military experience and their own place in Congo's tragic history, the two friends now spent their days in quiet comfort along the river, one place in Congo that had never cast judgment against them. "The river was created by God," said Bukasa. "It won't change. Only men change."

By the third afternoon, we'd reached the Ngobila stretch, exactly 171 kilometers upriver from Kinshasa. Five kilometers long, Ngobila was the most dangerous region of our journey, where the river was faster (8 kmh as opposed to the average 5 kmh) and over sixty meters deep, and where deadly whirlpools stalked the waters during the rainy season when the river was high.

"Sometimes smaller boats can even see the whirlpools coming," said Buisine, pointing toward the shores, where they were most often found, "and they can't do anything about it until it's too late. There are many boats on the bottom." But the *Ma'ungano* was loaded down and heavy and pushed through Ngobila without incident.

Shortly afterward we began noticing streaks of orange and brown in the river, clay-colored, silty and thick. An hour later we reached Kwamouth, at the mouth of the great Kasai River. Here the Kasai and the Congo meet in a clash of speed and color. The village of Kwamouth looked lovely along the banks: no cars, only pristine huts and homes, groves of mango and avocado trees, large gardens and courtyards, pirogues tied up and bobbing on the shore, and children playing along the banks. And just as Stanley must have done before me, I peered at this native village for signs of God or civilization, and *lo and behold*, there was a cellular tower! It would be the last traces of the modern world we'd see for the next four days.

When peacekeepers arrived in 2001 to help maintain an early cease-fire, Buisine volunteered to help pilot the first UN boats upriver to assess the damage; in recent years as river traffic slowly increased, he's helped the UN draft the first modern navigational maps of the Congo River. Many of the earth's navigable bodies of water have been mapped using satellite images, which can be downloaded into onboard computer systems on discs. The resulting charts, now used by most captains in the world, reflect new construction of levees or bridges and account for bank erosion and shifts in sandbars.

As Buisine explained this, he picked up a thick, spineless book of weather-beaten pages and slapped it down on a nearby stool. It was a set of hand-drawn charts issued by the old Belgian-run river authority, meticulously drafted in black and white, and last updated in 1936. "This is all we have in Congo," he said.

But Buisine said the UN had recently provided him with military satellite images of the river, which he ran through a global-positioning program. On a large monitor inside the wheel-house, a red-boat icon chugged up the bend. Buisine updated the digital map with each trip, recording changes in current speeds, shifts in sandbars, and average depth in rainy and dry seasons. Village names and coordinates appeared in pop-up windows, along with tribal affiliations, and logistical data in the event of UN intervention. The information would someday combine to form a massive data-base of the river, which he hoped to make available to the public.

Each morning I ducked into the wheelhouse to check the progress of the tiny red boat, and each morning the jungle squeezed a little closer in. Outside, the uniform brick settlements of the old colony disappeared and gave way to moldered huts, set high above the river on stilts of bamboo. Smoke from breakfast fires crept through their porous roofs, giving the huts the appear-ance of giant animals steaming in the mist.

But the solitude along the river was alleviated by the local traders who flocked the *Ma'ungano* day and night as she passed. They'd strike out from shore in long dugout canoes filled with fish and vegetables, four or five people in each one, stabbing the current with hand-carved paddles the shape of raindrops. We'd watch them from a kilometer out, standing upright as they pumped their arms in perfect unison to make the interception.

The river traders supplied the crew with their meals, and it was also how we supplemented ours. We'd buy huge, ten-pound tilapia and give them to the chef, along with spinach, roasted peanuts, green onion, plantains, papaya, and exotic white apples. I bought wild honey so fresh that bees still clung to the arm of the old man who poured it. And we bought mangoes to store in the ship's deep freeze, taking them out on hot afternoons and peeling them with pocketknives. It was like eating ice cream.

When the river people came aboard, Riccardo became absorbed in a world of lighting and angles, rushing down the steps to capture their dramatic approach to the boat, or the way the shadows fell on a pile of tomatoes. Other times I'd find him on the barge snapping sunset portraits of some ragged fisherman whose clothes were half rotting off, both their faces as serious as stone. *"You see his eyes, man? Did you see his eyes?"*

In my old guidebook, the "natives" were dressed in rows of beads and colorful loincloths, their bodies covered with sprawling mutilation tattoos, their lips and ears adorned with brass hooks and trinkets. It was as if nothing had changed from the days of the old monarchies, when the Kongo and Bakuba kingdoms of this region were among the strongest and most advanced in all of Africa before the surge of European interference and slavery forced them into decline.

Alongside a photo of a group of Gombe tribal dancers, the guidebook explains, "The Negro has a rugged constitution. His torso is broad and well proportioned, his hips rather narrow, his limbs well developed, but his legs are sometimes too thin . . . the Negro in his youth has a very quick intelligence. He learns easily, but this facility quickly degenerates because of sexual excess and the abuse of fermented beverages . . . The traveler must see to it that his Negro staff does not drink beer or alcohol during the hours when its services will be needed . . . The Negro is called lazy because he is a firm believer in the policy of as little effort as possible. However, when he is well trained and judiciously employed, his output is good."

While many sections of the river I was seeing seemed bountiful with food, and the people healthy, others areas appeared destitute and starving. No grass skirts or ornamentation like in the guidebook, just secondhand rags that barely hid their nakedness. The children would rush out of thatched huts and wave when they saw white faces, their bellies bloated from malnutrition. Their mothers often stood behind them, rubbing their stomachs and asking for money. The farther we went, the worse off they appeared. Buisine explained how villages along the river and in the forest specialized in different trades. Some were farmers, while others were known for fishing or hunting bush meat. The latter villages, he said, were generally worse off because of their meager, unbalanced diets.

The captain joined me on the deck one afternoon as we passed a group of people living on one of the large middle islands. They looked particularly thin and rangy. The war really leveled these people, I offered. He shrugged and said, "They had nothing even before the war. This is the new generation you're seeing. All the old ones are either dead or fled to the city. These ones, they have no education, and their diet—nothing but fish and alcohol from cradle to the grave. Nothing has changed for hundreds of years. I mean, they still make fires by rubbing sticks together."

I'd often tease Séverin about moving out to the "country" and settling down, living the simple life with the river people, but the joke would fall flat. "To think we had one of the greatest civilizations in Africa," he said once, shaking his head the way he did. "Ah, but now . . ." Séverin had grown up with some of the world's nastiest poverty just outside his door in Kinshasa, and like me I think he was hoping to find something better in the vast, green interior. "Now these people can't even read, only count," he'd say, echoing Buisine. "No school, no prospects for the future. What will become of their children?"

Unlike the workers on the barge, Séverin was hungry to know his own history, and anything he could read, any conversation with Buisine or the commander, with the crew, or the river people themselves, was like adding a missing piece to a puzzle he was slowly putting together in his head. Every morning he'd pull out his copy of *King Leopold's Ghost*, Adam Hochschild's definitive chronicle of the Belgian atrocities, and make copious notes, while using the text to also practice his English. Other times I'd find him alone on the terrace, hunched over Buisine's old river charts, studying the maps and symbols with unshakable concentration.

My past translators, Johnny and the pastor, had been products of the war, rugged and scarred individuals who'd seen immeasurable horror and became deft survivors. Johnny had buried his murdered father with his own hands, and the pastor had risked his life to save his congregants and heaped the suffering of thousands onto his shoulders. For me, their lives had redefined what it meant to be brave.

Then there was Séverin: middle-class city boy, egghead and academic, president and founder of the Kinshasa English Club, content with spending his time lying in bed studying maps or poring over his *Kid's Life Application Bible*. He was indeed the strangest Congolese I'd ever met, and it was the very reason I was so drawn to him. You got the sense that Séverin had a future outside Congo and this war. Some path would lead him somewhere great, and each missing piece to that puzzle allowed him to see it more clearly. You could tell he sensed some mission within himself, but didn't know how to define it, not yet anyway. One morning, to my surprise, he told me he was considering running for local office, perhaps a place in the new legislature.

"Be a *politician*?" I said.

"The people in my neighborhood are always encouraging me," he said. "I tell them it's too crazy, but seeing these people here on the river, perhaps one day that will be in my future." After that, he never mentioned it again, though Lionel and I began to refer to him as *Monsieur Président*.

On the morning of the fourth day we entered Sandy Beach Pool, a wide section where the current was slow compared to the channel we'd just left, and the *Ma'ungano* could punch through it at the breakneck speed of seven kilometers per hour. But we had to beware; as its name suggested, sandbars filled the Sandy Beach Pool like waiting land mines, ready to beach a rig that wasn't careful. Fortunately for us, a scout named Freddy from the local river authority—La Régie des Voies Fluviales, or RVF—paddled out in a pirogue, climbed aboard, and helped steer the ship around the sandbars, which shift with every rainy season. "The river is like a book and you must learn to read it," said Freddy, who wore no shoes and smelled of wet leaves. He spun the wheel with gentle precision, staring down the pool with the focus of a fighter pilot. "The dangers are always shifting. It's like a temperamental woman, always changing with the rain and wind." About fifty kilometers later, a new scout jumped aboard and relieved Freddy, who left to meet boats coming from the opposite direction.

Sandy Beach Pool had some of the most beautiful scenery so far: marshy finger islands with fisher birds swooping down to snatch small fish off the topwater. A silver mist hung over the islands, themselves like patches of wayward jungle, and each island was dotted with a few small huts and thatched canopies. Buisine and the commander told us about the trees that lined the shore, how many of them could be either medicinal or deadly, depending on their use. One tree he pointed out was popular with women who wished to shrink their vagina after giving birth. They boiled the ground bark of the tree into a soup, poured it into a basin, and sat in the brew for hours at a time. When Buisine was with Mobutu once in Gbadolite, an old woman noticed Buisine was walking with a grimace. "Do you suffer hemorrhoids?" the woman asked. "Why, yes," he answered, blushing. The old woman mixed this same brew and made the Frenchman sit in it for an hour. "Voilà, the hemorrhoids disappeared."

Speaking about the trees and islands, Buisine became animated. He began to explain an elaborate plan he'd been pondering for years, a plan to turn the Congo River into a national park for tourists. I laughed at first, since anything tourist-related in Congo was a fantasy. But he was serious. "I used to speak with Mobutu about this for hours," he said. "Mobutu was very passionate about the land and environment."

The plan, even if it existed only as an old man's dream, was indeed wonderful. The river would be transformed into a sprawling nature preserve that stretched from Kisangani to the sea. The vast chain of hundreds of river islands would be stocked with wild game, which would be imported from South Africa, where private game parks were becoming overpopulated. Rather than kill the animals, Buisine said, the businessmen who owned the reserves were eager to partner with people in Congo, where the wildlife had greatly been reduced by war.

"The islands on this river represent all the ecosystems of central Africa," said Buisine. "You have primary and secondary forests, swamps, savanna, everything."

There'd be antelope and zebra, leopards and lions, elephant and hyena. Villagers living along the river would be appointed game wardens and rangers to maintain the park and guard the animals from poachers and harm. Tourists would spend days cruising the park by riverboat, stopping at rustic lodges along the way to camp, barbecue, and sip cocktails while overlooking the river. Villagers would visit the boats during the day for "cultural lessons," teaching people how to fish, weave casting nets, or carve masks, which this section of Congo was famous for.

"It would be the greatest, most unique national park in all the world," Buisine mused. "And every person who lives on this river would be part of its glory."

He explained how he'd been pitching the plan for the past decade, first to Mobutu, then various environmental groups. The South African business partners were already lined up. Everyone agreed it was a good idea, but nothing was ever done. It would cost billions to implement, but it was necessary for the river to maintain its virgin ecosystem before democracy and peace brought development and ruin.

"The Congo River is the great lungs of the world," he said. "We must preserve and maintain this living thing. It's the only good thing we have left."

★ ★ ★

That evening we docked in Bolobo, 323 kilometers upriver from Kinshasa, and stayed the night. A lightning storm engulfed both sides of the river, kicking up monsoonlike winds to announce the coming rain. When we arrived in Bolobo, we'd planned to hop off and see the village. Buisine said it was beautiful and the people were friendly to strangers. But where we docked was two kilometers from town, on the opposite side of a long point. There was also no electricity, which meant that for us, Bolobo was just another black mass along our night passage we'd never see.

The port turned out to be an ominous little way station, with no lights except those of an oil tanker that had also moored for the night. A powerful spotlight illuminated the steel platform, where several workers in grease-slicked overalls sat on steel drums and listened to the storm roll in. Lights flickered through the cabin windows of the tugboat, dancing different shades of dirty yellow from a sputtering generator within. A few pirogues were pulled up onshore, some fires twinkled far up a hill, and that was all. The only sound was the low rumble of diesel engines competing against the wind.

We were docked maybe a full minute before a gaggle of government officials raced up the iron stairwell of the *Ma'ungano* and shouted for us to come out. There were eight of them, like a pack of wide-eyed mice who'd come to feed. "Show us all your papers right this moment!" one of them shouted. We politely obliged and went to retrieve our papers. When we got back, Buisine had booted half the group off the boat and was screaming at the only man who seemed to have a badge. "I only deal with actual officials," he shouted, "not your cronies looking for a beer! What do you really want?"

They insisted on switching on the fluorescent light of the deck to study our documents, which they did for over an hour. And the light brought bugs, millions and millions of bugs, as if the forest had emptied her arms to let her children play on the deck of the *Ma'ungano*. We stood there answering their questions, battling the insects flying into our mouths, down our shirts, squirming in our ears, dive-bombing into our eyes, ducking, swatting, and cursing while the officials bellowed, "What airport did you land? Where is your entry stamp? Where is your vaccination card?" They pored over our *ordre de mission* statements from our employers and copied every word into their notebooks, even from mine, which was written in English. They accused me of being in Congo illegally, fingering several of the old visas in my passport (I had six), and refusing to flip to the visa that was current. *"Attend! Attend!"* they shouted every time I attempted to validate myself. "I can see your visa! And I can see this is a problem!"

It went on and on, until they finally satisfied themselves and left. We gave them no money, and surprisingly they didn't ask. In the end, they turned out to be pretty nice guys. But we'd have more encounters like this one in Bolobo, not all so benign.

By the fifth day I began to notice subtle changes in the land and people. The daily storms became heavier and swept in with little notice, and people along the bank seemed cagey and suspicious, replacing the friendly waves we'd come to expect with a steel-eyed gaze. That night, the captain commanded the crew to tie off along the bank and wait for the moon, as the stars weren't bright enough to illuminate the rocks and drifts. As the boat edged slowly toward shore, small fires glimmered behind the jungle fronds, only to disappear once the high beam raked the trees. The engines sputtered to a halt, and I lay in bed listening to the sound of monkeys howling like deranged children from the dark. The next morning a pirogue full of women jumped aboard carrying a plastic bucket of charred monkey meat. The monkey had been quartered and its parts stuffed tightly inside. A rib cage hooked around the lip of the bucket, and next to it, a long, disfigured arm reached out from the top, its fingers curled and blackened from fire.

A while later we heard Buisine screaming from the deck at a

group of traders below. A yellow jerrican sat in the bottom of their pirogue, full of fermented palm wine. They were selling booze to the crew and the boss had caught them. "No alcohol on this boat, you hear me?!" the captain screamed. He pointed to the tall man with a grizzled beard and tattered pants who'd paddled the boat. *"Keba na yo!"* Buisine told him in Lingala, which meant "Watch yourself!" Shamed in public by the white captain, the men didn't get mad. Instead, they hung their heads in silence, carefully untied their pirogue, and drifted off.

The following morning, our sixth day on the river, the *Ma'ungano* was intercepted by two motorboats carrying men with guns. They'd set off from shore as we passed Gombe, a small village with a few rows of huts peppered along the shore. Once the boats were attached, several muscled men with AK-47s and aviator sunglasses jumped aboard and ran toward the captain's room. I was sitting on the terrace when they ran past; my first thought was we were getting hijacked by pirates, or simply robbed by the army.

They turned out to be soldiers loyal to Vice President Bemba, whose rebel army had controlled the forests during the war. The soldiers told Buisine they had a prisoner that needed transporting to Mbandaka, another soldier who'd been arrested for stealing guns. They needed a ride, a free ride. Buisine cringed and agreed, and one of the soldiers signaled for the prisoner to come aboard. He was barefoot and dressed in fatigues, his arms flexi-cuffed behind his back. His face was swollen and red from a heavy beating. The jackbooted soldiers pushed him into a metal shed on the barge and sat guard out front, eating bananas and tossing the peels into the river. With guns now aboard the *Ma'ungano*, the mood quickly darkened throughout the ship and everyone became tense and agitated. No matter how far you ran, I thought, the war would always find you.

A major dressed in a crisp uniform was aboard the prisoner's boat, and after instructing his men, he walked up the stairs and toward the captain's room, where Buisine sat at the wheel. The major was short with a round belly that hung over his belt, and medals decorated his uniform. He stood in the doorway and said nothing. Buisine looked up, expecting to see another jackbooted soldier, but instantly beamed. He jumped up and grabbed the major's hand. *"Mbote,"* the captain said warmly—"hello" in Lingala. The two men clasped shoulders and exchanged a local greeting, touching heads three times as if cheek-kissing with skulls. "How the hell are you?" Buisine said. "I wondered if you were still alive."

The major, it turned out, had once been a Mobutu bodyguard during the heyday of pink champagne and Concorde flights. When Kabila's rebels stormed the interior in 1997 to oust Mobutu, the major's position was overrun, and he was forced to join or be killed. He joined and proved his loyalty by attacking his own troops as rebels took Kinshasa. He later deserted and joined Bemba's thriving rebel army in the jungles in their fight against President Kabila's government troops. Despite being national army himself now, the major still considered himself a rebel officer.

Buisine hadn't seen him for years, and for the next few hours the two old dinosaurs did some catching up. Have you seen so-and-so? No, he's dead. What about so-and-so? Dead, too. And so-and-so? He's in Europe, couldn't find a place in the new government. They talked about the upcoming runoff, how a Kabila victory could spell disaster for these soldiers sympathizing with Bemba. The major's men were scared of their fate. "Do yourself a favor," Buisine told the major. "Keep a low profile. In six months, this whole place could be fucked."

Buisine instructed the chef to prepare a meal and a bed for the major, and once the captain was alone, I asked him if the army had a satellite phone in Gombe. It was just a small fishing village with no cellular network for hundreds of miles. No, he said, I don't think they have a sat phone.

"Then how did the major know you were coming?" I asked.

"The neighboring village told them," he said. "With drums."

II

We reached Mbandaka on the next evening, seven days and seven hundred kilometers from where we began. There was no electricity in the town, and dozens of oil lamps flickered ashore in the inky darkness. As we pulled into port, we saw what appeared to be a floating refugee camp with hundreds piled aboard, living under tents made from tattered plastic sheeting labeled UNICEF. Plumes of smoke from charcoal burners shrouded the steel surface, and somewhere a radio blared a wobbly tune as its batteries slowly died. Men danced drunk in the shadows, and toddlers rolled naked in the coal dust. She was called the *Ndobo* and her barges pointed upriver, toward Kisangani. We immediately knew: *That's our boat.*

The three of us leaned over the rail when the *Ma'ungano* touched its barge against the *Ndobo* to tie together. And when the crowds of people camped below saw our white faces, they roared and chanted, "*Mundele! Mundele!* You've arrived!"

Séverin sighed. "These people are waiting for us," he said, his face pinched with dread. I asked him what *ndobo* meant in Lingala. "The hook," he answered, and walked back into his room.

The boat would travel to Ndobo, its namesake town, located 578 kilometers upriver from Mbandaka. It was operated by a Lebanese-owned logging company called Trans-M, which was logging over one million acres of forest between Mbandaka and Kisangani. The *Ndobo* had come from Kinshasa with passengers loaded on its three barges and, after reaching its destination, would return to the capital loaded with timber bound for Europe.

Logging was now the boom business of the forests, with exotic wood such as mahogany, afrormosia, and tola fetching hundreds of thousands of dollars per barge-load in European markets. During the war years, Congo's government doled out logging titles to dozens of multinational firms, signing away over 107 million acres of rain forest, an area larger than California. Before 2003, companies were buying half-million-acre contracts for only $286 a year in taxes, never mind what was handed under the table. Zimbabwe received over eighty-four million acres in exchange for sending troops to assist Kabila's army during the war.

Environmental groups such as Greenpeace estimate that by 2050 over 40 percent of Congo's forests will be gone. And while the government had recently frozen new logging contracts and reviewed existing ones, the companies operated entirely without environmental standards. To appease the natives, they would sign "social responsibility" contracts that promised schools and clinics, but these were often meaningless and unenforceable. Like many of the companies, Trans-M had promised a lot in the forest and delivered little. But I didn't know any of this as I stood looking at the barge that would take us upriver. A couple hundred more passengers were expected to board that day, and they'd already started arriving. The fare was ten dollars each.

We needed to stake out a location on the barge, so the next morning we hurried down the market road, looking for a vendor who specialized in the long wooden poles used for barge shelters. Mbandaka was a river town, and everything bought, sold, and traded in the market somehow catered to the steel that drifted by. It was also one of the most haunted cities in all of Congo, and I'd felt it since we'd arrived.

I'd heard stories about Mbandaka, none of them very good: boat sinkings, mutinies, cholera. It floated on the map like some lost outpost adrift from the constraints of the world; the last exit before things turn wild for good.

Mbandaka straddled the equator at the junction of the Congo and Ruki rivers and was founded by Stanley in 1883 as one of the colony's first stations. First called simply Equator, then Coquilhatville, the city was a thriving port and military post during the days of the colony, with hundreds of Europeans living in rows of brick villas along bamboo-paved streets shaded by groves of coconut palms. The old steamers bound for Kisangani (then Stanleyville) would stop for the day in the Equator station, allowing passengers time to visit the Eala Botanical Gardens, a sanctuary of over four thousand species of local flora, including sections devoted to experimental strains of rubber vine. Large colonial plantations and farms surrounded the town center and in turn gave way to the "native quarters" in the trees. After independence, most of the whites fled the town, leaving their farms and plantations to rejoin the surrounding jungle.

When Rwandan soldiers and rebels seized eastern Congo in late 1996, they targeted the sprawling refugee camps along the Rwanda-Zaire border packed with hundreds of thousands of Hutu refugees. Many of these people had participated in the ethnic slaughter, and others were innocent civilians who'd fled Rwanda fearing retribution from the country's new Tutsi government. When rebels and soldiers attacked the camps, thousands of the refugees, innocent and guilty alike, fled west into the dense jungle of Congo as rebels pursued them. They were chased for seven months through the forest, dying along the way from malaria, cholera, and starvation, until finally they reached the Congo River near Mbandaka. From there, they hoped to cross over to neighboring Congo-Brazzaville, where they'd seek immunity.

But the river was too swift and wide to cross over. Dozens tried to swim and vanished in the current. The rest simply collapsed along the banks and awaited their fate. When rebels arrived soon after, missionaries working nearby stood helpless while hundreds were shot and hacked to death with machetes and bayonets, their bodies then flung into the river. Residents downstream in Kinshasa say the bloated corpses floated past for days.

I found no memorials for the dead in Mbandaka, but their

ghosts seemed to riot on the streets to agitate the living. As we walked in search of materials for our shelter, crowds along the market road soon pressed all around. Several plump, red-cheeked women pushed their way to the front. They held carcasses of smoked monkeys, hog-tied with bellies flayed open and fangs exposed in horrific death mask. A small crocodile was flung at our feet, its jaws bound with vines, its eyes like dark, smoky windows. Children ran forward and beat it with sticks, while others tormented the beast with stones. *"Mundele! Mundele!"* they shouted. The croc thrashed wildly, beating its powerful tail against the mud in its final stand. Then it was snatched away and tossed into the grass, where a group of reptiles were slowly dying in the sun.

"Ah, the Mbandaka people are *crazy*," Séverin said as we walked away. "They're Bangala tribe, very tough and confrontational, and they enjoy fighting." A famous story in Kinshasa explained everything about the Mbandaka mentality, Séverin said, and perhaps the river people in general. In the 1980s, Mobutu made one of his grand, infrequent tours of the forest and stopped in Mbandaka. "A very big crowd came to hear Mobutu," said Séverin. "Mobutu asked them, 'What do you need from me? What can I get for you? A school, a hospital perhaps?' The people shouted, 'Beer! Beer! Beer!' So Mbandaka got a brewery."

At the end of the market road we turned into the narrow maze of wooden stalls. Like any grocery or department store, African markets are divided into sections, and we were headed toward the section that sold poles. But along the way, several women selling raw peanut butter screamed for us to stop. "*Mundele*, buy some peanut butter," one said. "No, *mundele*," screamed another, just across the aisle. "Buy *my* peanut butter. My peanut butter tastes the best!" I bought some from both women, smeared it on several fried beignets, and drowned it with wild honey.

We found the wooden poles near the river's edge. Hundreds were arranged in pens according to height, some stretching ten feet. After sketching the kind of shelter we needed in my notebook, we bought eight poles for forty-five hundred Congolese francs, about nine dollars. Back at the barge, we claimed a small, empty space near the tug and set to work building our house. Riccardo had served a year in the Italian army and was proficient in knots. Under his supervision (and a nattering gang of busybodies crowded around giving advice), we lashed the poles together with nylon rope to form a reinforced A-frame, which we secured to railway ties along the barge. Our roof was constructed from the orange tarp and woven grass mats we'd bought in the market. It was sturdy and every bit cozy. Inside, there was barely room for three of us to sit, much less sleep.

We celebrated that night with cold beer and steaks at the one good restaurant in town. The dim fluorescent lights of the Métropole drew swarms of insects so large they cast slow-moving shadows across the empty tables. A dance floor sat in the middle of the outdoor patio, where a fat woman waltzed with a man too drunk to keep time. Slow soukous ballads played from an old cassette deck that ebbed and flowed with surges in the generator and sometimes blew static so loud everyone shielded their heads from some unseen attack.

The waitress sat drinking at a dark corner table with a large white man who spoke fluent Lingala—Belgian, I guessed, an importer, or one of the last romantic holdouts—dressed in a starched oxford with several empty bottles in front of him. His skin was the color of ash, with pasty liver spots creeping up his neck and cheeks. There was something already dead about him, the way his face moved in and out of the shadow but never really took shape. Watching him was like staring at a scarecrow from a fast-moving car. Like the town, he seemed to float in some restless space, cut off long ago and unable to find his way back. He put the chill on me. I ordered a beer and shifted my chair, keeping my back to the colonial ghost in the corner.

★ ★ ★

The next morning, around four hundred people crowded the barges of the *Ndobo* as we pulled out of port and waved good-bye to Mbandaka, and us, the luxury of the *Ma'ungano*. Our little shelter offered a wide-open view of the left bank, but as the hours slowly passed, the sunlight and calm disappeared, never to return. Plastic sheeting and threadbare tarps were pulled from the heaping bundles, poles materialized from nowhere, pots and pans rattled on the deck, and radios thundered to life. In a matter of hours, a small village had risen up around us.

These were the river traders, the men and women who moved Congo's jungle economy like a great army of ants. Every journey was a toss of the dice, a chance to double down or wash up in the backwater. But they took the risk because life in the city was far more unforgiving. Traveling the river was the good life, and they basked in its pleasures, an extended business trip aboard a floating disco that never closed.

"Ay, mundele," my neighbor yelled. "Put away your notebook and come drink some wine!" It was eleven A.M., an hour after we left port, and the party aboard the *Ndobo* was going full throttle. Our neighbors to the right, Lucy and Toni, were pouring milky palm wine into plastic mugs. A new camp began every four feet, and in every camp a different radio blasted its buoyant rumba. The sun radiated through our orange tarp like a heat lamp, sucking our energy. Small chores, such as filtering water or washing dishes, stole our breath and left us wilted. I finally put away my notebook and focused on not passing out.

The three barges were so crowded that corridors soon formed through the floating village. One walkway barreled past our tent, and most people passing by stopped to stare at the two *mundele* who'd come aboard. *"Bonjour,"* we'd offer, like freaks in a cage, until the people laughed and sauntered off.

The barges were like giant floating supermarkets, and one could buy almost anything in the great bazaar that spread itself along the deck. Walking through the narrow corridors you found essential items such as lye soap in blue and pink blocks, Angola-brand tooth-brushes sold in packs of six, safety razors, plastic mirrors, lead spoons, needle and thread, travel-size bags of raw sugar, beads and necklaces, women's panties with LOVE embroidered on the crotch, rubber sandals, nylon fishing nets, Betasol lotion, Tiger Head bat-teries that lasted exactly four hours in the cheap cassette players sold and used on the barge.

In its aisles you could find quinine and chloroquine for malaria, hydration salts for diarrhea, and pills for intestinal worms and pain. There were nurses and midwives, witch doctors and preachers, and a man for just about every trade. Our neighbor Lucy sold the sec-ondhand clothing worn by most everyone on the barge and along the river, the ubiquitous American T-shirts donated to charities and dumped on the African market. Everywhere I looked was a strange remnant of home, the old grandmother who advertised the strip club in Kentucky, or the stoic fisherman whose shirt read, I'M THE BIG SISTER.

Lucy was from Kinshasa, with pretty green eyes and short dread-locks wove with decorative blue thread. For hours each day, despite the brutal sun, Lucy would sit on a little stool outside her camp with her used T-shirts, shorts, and jeans spread on a blanket in neatly folded piles. Whenever a buyer with cash would come around, usually one of the other traders or passengers, Lucy would make change from a thick wad of francs she pulled from under the folds of her dress. With the river people themselves, Lucy would trade for dried fish, which were smoked black and secured between handwoven racks, like tennis racquets bound together with vine. Each rack cost three dollars on the river and would fetch five times the price back in Kinshasa.

Lucy had traded along the river for the past decade, through war and peace and all the trouble in between. During the war, when the river was closed, she often walked nearly eight hundred kilometers through the jungle from Kinshasa to Basankusu territory in the north. Soldiers and rebels prowled the skinny trails. Soldiers raped her friends in front of their children, and everyone was taxed and robbed for the "war effort." Lucy had already lost everything twice to storms and thieves. "When you lose your stuff, there's nothing for you," she said. "They don't sell insurance on the river."

With every trip, Lucy would sink her savings into merchandise in Kinshasa and hope to double her investment along the river. Everything on the barge was part of her hustle, including the plastic chairs she rented to us for a dollar a day, and the small money she made each morning selling cups of coffee boiled with gingerroot. Other traders supplemented their income by selling fried beignets smeared with peanut butter, or bowls of fresh catfish soup. Even in the dead of night, someone was always cooking.

I could tell the river traders made an impression on Séverin, who'd warmed up to our neighbors considerably. Their brassy resilience and resourcefulness impressed him, and soon he counted many friends on the barge, joking and debating politics and religion. He later discovered Lucy even lived on his street in Kinshasa and was friends with his mother.

"They are loud and uneducated, but the river people are teaching me many things," he said one night. "How to make money from nothing and survive. In many ways, their life is better than Kinshasa. Notice they eat five meals a day! Only the rich can eat like this in the city."

The second day on the barge, we passed the small village of Malela, another uniform cluster of thatched huts wrapped in a dense wall of trees. One of the *Ndobo*'s crewmen, Albert, came by our tent and pointed to the banks. "This was the front line during the war," he said, "the 810-kilometer mark. From here to Kinshasa was Kabila's men, and from Malela to Kisangani was rebels."

The 810-kilometer mark had divided the river and run like an electric fence through the forest. Traders such as Lucy who'd braved the water during the war knew the 810 mark as if it blinked bright yellow on the current. Albert had sat at home in Kisangani until 2001, he said, when many small-time traders attempted to return to work. "Soldiers would be standing along the banks in every village," he said. "They'd call out for you to come, and if you refused, they'd open fire. Neither side was better, but you'd better know who you were dealing with."

Later that day, I met an army lieutenant who was traveling back to Kisangani after reuniting with his family after eight years. In 1998, Pierre Kitebo had joined the Rwandan-backed rebels who pushed their way west toward Kinshasa, only to get knocked back by government-allied troops. When Rwanda pulled out of Congo in 2002, Kitebo was sent to Kisangani and put through the army integration process, where he remained as an instructor. His wages were never enough to travel to Basankusu, where his family waited, and few barges or trains were operating to take him. But a few months before, the army had granted Kitebo his leave, and with some money he'd saved, he set out to find his family, carrying only an old photo of his wife to keep him warm and a vague idea of where they now lived. He spent three weeks on a barge from Kisangani to Basankusu, where he finally found his family in a small hut deep in the jungle. When Pierre had left eight years before, his youngest daughter, Benedite, was still in her mother's stomach. She didn't recognize the tall, beaming man in army fatigues when he walked out of the trees.

"They all ran out and hugged me," he said. "They were happy to see their daddy."

He now sat in a cramped, ragged lean-to surrounded by his wife, two sons, and daughter, who were finally going to Kisangani to live with him at the army camp. He pulled the little girl close to his chest and kissed her head. "They were naked when I found them," he said, "but there'll be no more suffering now."

Here, I thought, I was finally seeing some hopeful signs. I'd also glimpsed it in people such as Lucy and Solange Kobo, another neighbor, who was making her first journey on the river with her husband. They were from Kinshasa, and both had university de-grees in teaching and literature, but had been unable to find jobs. Solange instead worked as a hairdresser, and her husband was an occasional mechanic, but there was hardly enough money to sup-port their two kids and still live in the city. So they decided to roll their dice on the river. After six months they'd saved four hundred dollars and bought a new bicycle, bags of sugar and salt, along with batteries, soup mix, spices, and biscuits. When I met them after my third day on the barge, the only thing left was the bike, which they hoped to sell in Ndobo. "But even without the bike," Solange said, "we've already doubled our money."

I recognized this emerging confidence in such guys as Jean Kalokula, whose last river journey was with a convoy of pirogues during the war. Despite the soldiers patrolling the banks, Jean and a few other traders would risk voyages to villages upriver, where he'd bring essential items like salt and flour that didn't otherwise get through, then trade them for smoked meats and fish. They'd set out for weeks at a time, traveling at night to avoid checkpoints, and sleeping in the jungle during the day, until malaria and cholera fi-nally killed many of his party. Their bodies were buried on the lonely middle islands, and Jean limped back to Kinshasa to wait for the war to end. He was now traveling the river again for the first time, a man who was proud to be going back to work.

I was delighted to hear some good news on the river, and the traders all seemed elated to be running their old routes and having a party. And I was grateful they'd embraced us like one of their group. I couldn't walk the length of the barge without someone holding up a ladle of palm wine with a warm, drunken grin, or one of the fat, white caterpillars that were such a popular staple in the forest, looking at my reaction while the grub squirmed between their fingers. And every time I stood up, it seemed, I was hailed with a chorus of *"Mundele!"* (or at night, *"Mundele moto!"*— which meant "turn off your light!")

An order seemed be revealed as we floated east. The racks of oily smoked fish, the charred monkeys and bushes of manioc, the palm wine, and the way the traders squatted by their wares and haggled so intensely over a sale I thought they would fight—all of this had remained the same through the cataclysmic horrors of the past century, and I wondered if perhaps that was a good thing.

Watching the river traders strike out from shore in their long pirogues, five people exactly aligned and pumping against the current, racing five hundred horsepowers of engine, and catching it nearly every time, was as primal and graceful as the fisher birds that skimmed the middle current and arched back into the trees. Even their wipeouts seemed like ancient, well-rehearsed rituals. The pirogue might catch a bad wake after releasing from the barge and spin like an oil drum, spilling everyone into the river, vegetables and racks of smoked fish slowly vanishing beneath the water. But no one ever seemed worried. Instead, crowds would gather along the side of the barge and cheer. The dumped passengers would give an embarrassed wave and swim ashore, leg strokes so powerful they sent their bodies bouncing chest-high through the current. Often the pirogue would drift aimlessly downstream, where someone would pick it up and safeguard its return.

And after a few days, we began to adapt. We'd wake up in the morning, always right at dawn, and join the dozens of others quietly brushing their teeth over the side, leaning to spit into the mist that hung on the water. I'd head to the back of the barge near the toilet and stand in line with the other men, using my plastic bucket to collect the steaming water that poured off the engines and out the side spout, then strip to my underwear and lather up. At any given time, a dozen men would be bathing off the back, their black bodies covered head to toe in white suds.

After breakfast and a stiff cup of ginger coffee, Séverin and I would make the rounds and talk to people before the sun became too hot. As we walked along the usual rows of toothbrushes, medicines, sandals, and razor blades, the river people would climb aboard carrying ten-foot pythons in bamboo cages to sell as food, or rare, prized Congo African Gray parrots they'd trapped in the forest with rubber gum and sold to traders for ten dollars apiece. There were catfish as big as bathtubs, monkeys and wild pigs tethered with vine and thrashing against the deck, and the random severed hog leg just lying in the path.

But after only two days, the novelty of the good times began to wear thin and I just craved some quiet. I wanted to sleep without music blasting from ten directions around my head, without people dancing into my sleeping bag or the pastor who waited until four A.M. before pulling out his megaphone and starting his sermon. ("One cannot know the hour of the Lord," the preacher said, while the sleepy, drunken voices chanted, *"Aha."*) It would be days, maybe even weeks, before we reached Kisangani. It suddenly dawned on me that everything I'd wished for had come true: I had passed the point of no return. The river now owned me, and the sound of its chains was a hundred radios dying in the night.

It was so hot during the day that I'd sit in my tent for hours just stoned on the humidity, watching the molecules behind my eyes ignite like tiny starbursts, until something came along to distract me. The third afternoon on the barge, a particularly wicked aroma straightened me in my seat. I swore someone's head was on fire. The heat made the smell come alive and dance, gave it a flavor in the back of my throat. I followed a pale cloud of smoke to where a woman sat flipping a giant dead monkey over a charcoal stove, scorching the fur and scraping the char with a broad cutlass. Its innards were still intact and boiling out of its mouth. The woman sensed me staring and stopped, looked up from her work, and gave me a big, toothy grin.

The next morning, while rolling up my mattress, I discovered tiny, pea-shaped objects writhing beneath my bed. *Maggots*, I thought, the words flashing like a JumboTron in my mind: *Maggots on my pillow. Maggots on my pillow.* They'd dropped from the racks of rancid smoked fish that Lucy had stored right above my head. The previous night, I swore I'd heard the popping sounds of them feeding. But how could I make a scene? I'd asked to be there, had come a long way to get up that river, and now was *definitely* up that river. I simply kicked the maggots away with my boots and went in search of breakfast. That same afternoon, while eating a stick of beef jerky, I looked down to find a matted wad of pubic hair resting on my arm. I shrugged, blew it back into the wind, and finished my lunch.

After dinner on our fourth night, I sat on the tie post near the water's edge and watched the river. The sun was sinking fast the way it does along the equator, sending cascades of orange and reds shooting from behind the green wall like a bright solar bomb. And with the darkness came the first cool breezes of the day. For some reason the radios were quiet, and for once I could hear every sound of the forest, every chirp and whistle and shrill monkey scream, as if every tree were full of beans and rattling off its roots. Despite the loud music at night, little sleep, and even the maggots, I was feeling pretty good that night, feeling positive about the rest of the journey, however it would unfold. I'd even pulled out my notebook and written these words: *Watching the river moving past—this is what keeps the spirit strong when you get low. This is when I love this place the most.*

Just as I finished writing, the engines faded and I felt the barge veer to the bank, where it eventually stopped. I then watched aghast as the tugboat *Ndobo* disembarked from the barges, turned around, and disappeared downriver, stranding us on the riverbank in jet-black darkness. The vanishing taillights seemed to hold my optimism by a thread. And when they were gone, I panicked.

Riccardo stood nearby, aiming his flashlight into the black vacuum of the jungle's edge. He smiled. "What do you call it?" he said. "The white man's grave? Well, man, they left us in the white man's grave."

I walked back to our tent, where Séverin had just returned from his nightly rounds, talking to friends and trying to negotiate a price for some fish to sell in Kinshasa. "It's the captain's son," he said. "He was burned very badly. They had to find a hospital."

"The nearest hospital is two days away," I said. I looked for panic in his eyes but found none, not even the slightest hint of irritation. He was maddeningly calm. "No one seems to care," he said, shrugging. "This is their life."

It was true. Instead of panicking, the Congolese only amped up the party. The saucy soukous of Werrason now roared behind an arsenal of fresh batteries, and jugs of palm wine sloshed from camp to camp. Stranded on a remote stretch of river in the middle of Congo, they reacted by dancing as if it were the last night on earth.

I shone my light down the barge and saw several men pissing in the river. This was normal; with only one toilet for all four hundred people, the guys usually did their minor business over the side. But now, near the bank, the current was stagnant, and just a few feet downstream, half a dozen women were scooping the same water and drinking it.

The year before, a barge had been hit with cholera in the same remote stretch east of Mbandaka. By the time it reached the next town, dozens were dead on the deck. Yes, I thought, it would happen like that, here and now. And by the time we were discovered, it would be too late.

Riccardo was standing next to me, and I turned to him with panic in my eyes. "We've gotta get off this boat," I said. "We've gotta get off this boat or we'll all die of cholera."

He shoved a handful of whiskey packets into my hand, the kind that were sold all over the barge. "Relax, man," he said. "You are just paranoid. These people, they do like this for hundreds of years."

And after a few whiskeys, I began to feel better. I still wanted to get off, and I could tell Riccardo agreed, if only for the sake of progress. We decided our only prayer was flagging down a passing boat, but we hadn't seen one in two days. "What about Buisine?" I said. "He can't be more than twelve hours behind." Yes, we decided, Buisine would save us! We began to fantasize about the *Ma'ungano* chugging past and sending its dugout to rescue us. "So long, suckers!" we'd yell, using our boots to beat away the doomed crowds who tried to tag along, tried to weasel in on our air-conditioning and hot showers. These soothing thoughts calmed my panic, and all night I lay awake listening for the sound of diesel engines passing by.

The next morning, some fishermen informed us the *Ndobo* was only a few kilometers downriver in Mankanza, which had a small clinic. Riccardo, Séverin, and I hired a passing canoe to take us there and, upon arriving, found the captain's three-year-old son, Gus, sprawled on a thin mattress and his worried father kneeling beside him. Gus had been running through the crowded barge and accidentally tipped a pot of boiling cooking oil all over his body, scorching his chest, arms, and back. The pain was so great he couldn't even cry.

"His wounds are already infected," the doctor whispered. There was no medicine in Mankanza, he added, and the best option was to return to the barge and rush him to the hospital in Bumba, sixty kilometers from Ndobo. For now, the best the doctor had to offer was talcum powder.

For the next three days, as we chugged toward Ndobo, Riccardo and I occupied ourselves by stopping in to visit Gus and treat his wounds. Both of us carried antibiotic ointment in our medical kits, and we gently applied it to the boy's blistered skin, which began to appear like the scales of a dead fish. We gave his mother ibuprofen to give Gus for the pain, but like the doctor in Mankanza, we could do little else.

On our sixth night we pulled into Ndobo and docked there until morning. When the sun rose, we saw the gargantuan stacks of felled lumber lying like dead giants in the red mud. We were at the Trans-M logging camp, just outside the village, where the trees would be loaded and sold in Europe, and the logging would likely continue until the forest no longer went on forever.

By dawn the traders had disassembled and packed up their floating city as quickly as they'd built it. And when it became light enough to see, they flocked off the barge and into the village to trade the remainder of their merchandise in the market. I was glad to leave the barge, and after packing all our gear, we watched with indifference as the traders picked apart our shelter down to the very last rope. They could have it.

III

We hitched a ride with the timber company to Bumba, where we'd cover the runoff elections, due in three days. Since the *Ndobo* was returning to Kinshasa, we hoped to find another boat to Kisangani once we arrived in Bumba—a motorized pirogue, anything but a barge. We'd now traveled 1,337 kilometers in fifteen days, with only four hundred kilometers of river left to go. Surely, we thought, the worst was over.

Bumba is the origin for one of the first roads ever built in Congo, the Route Royal Congo-Nil, which spanned over thirteen hundred kilometers and connected the Congo River with the Nile in Juba, Sudan. The road cut through the northeastern corner of Congo near present-day Garamba National Park and was once a transport route for European goods shipped down the Nile and into the colony. It also accessed the Lado Enclave, one of the major elephant-poaching grounds for the Free State's trade of ivory, allowing poachers to bring their haul to the sea. In later years, ships would unload at

Bumba, where merchandise would be taken into the northern stretches of the colony via the Juba road or Vicinaux railway, which the Belgians built in the mid-1920s.

Once the colonial masters pulled out, Bumba was left to fade like the rest. Many of the white-stone shops along the riverfront boulevard stood shuttered and empty, with market women now selling pineapples and cigarettes on the ground out front. There were two bars, where the beer was cool and plentiful, but no restaurants or cafés to kill the time. We took our meals in the Hotel Mozulua, where the heat and mosquitoes kept us awake at night and only encouraged us to press forward.

At Bumba, the Congo stretched twenty kilometers across at its widest point, but this majestic view was blocked by chains of wooded islands that only seemed to throttle the great river. Shortly after we arrived, despite Séverin's earlier deftness at finding a boat, we discovered nothing in town to carry us to Kisangani. There were no pirogues with working engines, and even if there had been, the fuel alone—so rare in the jungle— would've cost us hundreds. One barge was docked at port, but the captain was waiting long after the runoff elections to decide his departure. After the gunfights in Kinshasa following the first round of voting, the threat of sudden violence was heavy on everyone's mind. Caution prevailed, and for the moment the river would be empty. If we wanted to advance soon, it would have to be through the trees.

We weighed our options carefully. If we stayed and chose to go by river, we could easily be stuck in Bumba for two weeks. The only other option was to cross through the jungle, and the only way to do that was on bicycles. Riccardo had found himself in a similar spot on his journey six months before. He'd rented bikes in Bumba and gone three days through the jungle. On the bike he'd become sick with malaria, plus gotten the fly bites that eventually became infected. It seemed like a grueling journey, and I knew I wasn't in good enough physical shape to pedal a bike over four hundred kilometers through the forest. But Riccardo was persistent.

"Come on, man, you think the river is wild? Wait until you see the *jongle*. The people there, they never saw a white man before me. You are like some kind of UFO."

If anything, he was right about getting off the river. Between Buisine and the *Ndobo*, I felt I'd seen as much as I could. Another barge journey, I feared, would feel redundant at best and tip me toward madness at worst. And if the forest was as isolated as Riccardo described, it would be the perfect place to see how the war had truly affected the country. I'd seen the ruin in the cities, but nothing like the remote forests, which covered over half the country. Thinking about that isolation brought to mind the naked people Buisine had described, frightened and hiding behind the trees. As I did with many things, I turned to Séverin and asked him what we should do.

"Yeah, the bikes will be a good experience," he said. "The most important thing is forward progress. Bumba is no place to hang around."

So with that decision made, we spent the days before the election looking for a convoy of men to move us on bikes through the world's second-largest rain forest.

Bicycles were certainly not hard to come across in Bumba. They'd long replaced vehicles as the sole means of transporting people and product through the jungle and town. Many of these bikes were driven by a well-organized group of taximen called *tolekas*, who comprised the Association de Cyclistes Transporteurs de Bumba, the biker's union.

When the river was closed during the war, the *tolekas* had routinely braved the rebel-infested forest to bring back essential goods such as salt block, sugar, and used clothing from Kisangani. Many left and never returned. For years, they single-handedly kept the town from starving and for good reason were still considered local angels.

The union headquarters was in a small concrete building near the busy central market. There we met with the president, Dominique Lisobe, and made our requests: we needed six bicycles, two for Riccardo and me to pedal, and the rest to porter Séverin and our burden of gear. For this we needed four of his strongest men who were familiar with the trails to Kisangani. And the bikes, we insisted, had to be in top condition and have spare parts for the trip.

Lisobe adjusted his thick-framed glasses and scribbled careful notes. He warned us first about the extreme hardship of riding through the forest; the trails were now flooded from heavy seasonal rains, and given the fragile political climate, the entire region could quickly become a death trap for foreigners.

"Nonetheless, my boys are well prepared for this sort of journey," he said finally. "My only concern is you will slow them down. Perhaps hire two more riders just in case."

"No, no," Riccardo said, "we pedal the bikes."

"Right," I said, completely ignorant. "How hard can it be?"

"You will see," Riccardo said to me. "To ride in the forest, it feels *great*, man. None of these *focking* barges to delay us. Just you and the forest!"

We agreed on a price of fifty dollars per bike. We'd depart immediately following the next morning's vote. In four days, we estimated, we'd be eating steaks at the finish line.

The runoff election was the most significant step toward peace and stability in the country's history. But we'd become so impatient to keep moving that it became little more than a distraction. The vote was no mystery, either, not in that part of the country. All along the river we'd been hearing nothing but praise for Bemba and scorn for Kabila. Even though Bemba's soldiers had terrorized these people all throughout the war, the fat man was regarded as the patriot son. Kabila was just a puppet crook hired by white men. And with no real newspaper or radios for hundreds of miles, rumor was king.

The morning polls went smoothly enough, with people lining up at schoolhouses that had been converted to voting stations. Riccardo and I toured the various stations and interviewed people, and I found myself having the same conversations I'd had in every African election I'd covered.

"What kinds of changes will you demand from the winner?" Silence. "Hmmm."

"So you're demanding peace, electricity, and better schools for your kids?"

"Oh, yes, yes . . . peace. Peace and schools."

It was afterward, when we were riding bike taxis back to the hotel, that everything went wrong. The crowded streets were now empty, void of dogs and children and women ferrying to the market. Looking around, I saw people staring out windows and sheepishly standing in doorways, all the bad signs. A government lorry rumbled past loaded with soldiers with readied guns. And when we turned a corner toward the hotel, it was like being dropped into the madness of Kinshasa all over again.

A mob of about a hundred young men rumbled down the street carrying machetes, sticks, and jagged stones. Earlier that morning, a Kabila supporter had been caught stuffing a ballot box in one of the stations. The mob then burned the ballots in the streets and set fire to several buildings. They now rioted through the empty town, spewing venom against Kabila and thieving foreigners. When they saw us, it was as if we'd walked right into their trap. *"Ay, étranger!"* they shouted, and quickened their pace. Riccardo raced toward them with cameras held high. And whereas I'd usually follow, this time I froze.

It was everything I'd been running from since that night at the Grand Hotel. And here it was again, kicking up a cloud of dust straight toward me. The mobs terrified me the most. I'd been through some bad ones in Togo and Kinshasa, but that morning in Bumba, I suddenly felt my luck had run its course. A voice, diamond sharp in my mind, told me to turn back immediately. There were no lives left. If I stayed, only bad things would happen.

"*Allez! Allez!*" I screamed at my driver, just a small boy whose body had gone rigid. "Séverin, tell this kid to go!"

We turned onto a backstreet and moved parallel with the crowd, struggling for speed on the sandy streets. Some of the mob caught up and held rocks near our heads, leering and shouting threats. But we finally found our turn, and luckily no one followed us. We raced down empty streets where voting ballots still smoldered in the road. After a short while, we arrived safe within the high walls of the Hotel Mozulua.

The rioting had scared away the taximen who'd agreed to take us to Kisangani, and after several hours of waiting, we received a visit from Lisobe, the union president. Soldiers had stormed the mobs with guns and tear gas, he told us, and three people had been killed. One of the dead was his fifteen-year-old nephew. "He was only throwing rocks," the president said, "and they shot him in the head. His brains aren't even there anymore." Despite his tragedy, he'd come down to reassure us the drivers would be ready the next morning.

Depressed and frustrated, caught again by the shadow of the war, we spent our last night in Bumba getting stone drunk in the dark courtyard of the Mozulua, blasting the Stooges from my portable speakers. We drank liter bottles of beer and sent out for more, ending the evening with highway songs and Riccardo standing on the table singing "Smoke on the Water" to the Congolese watchman laughing in the shadows.

The shrill sound of bells stirred me from my poisoned sleep at six the next morning. I drew back the curtains and saw, one by one, a line of taximen pull up to the outer wall. After the previous day's violence, the president had sent word out to all *toleka*, hoping at least a few would heed the call. By the time I was dressed and downstairs, a dozen bikes were waiting.

Like most bikes found in African villages where motor vehicles had vanished along with paved roads, these were all steel, double-framed machines built for hauling passengers and cargo. They'd come off boats from India and China with brand names such as Avon Country Bike and Hobo Champion. Each weighed about forty pounds, and in *toleka* tradition, they were tricked with pink and yellow roses that bloomed from the spokes and rear reflectors.

But as we lined them up for inspection, we noticed that all were in terrible shape. The wide tires were bald and cracked, brake pads replaced by scrap rubber, and chains fastened by bits of wire and greased with bright-red palm oil. None of the bikes seemed capable of carrying us across town, much less through the unforgiving forest. But with little alternative, we chose six bikes and hoped for the best. We also picked four of the tallest and fittest-looking riders, men who knew the route and seemed capable and trustworthy, four strangers whom we'd follow like children into the unknown.

And with our gear strapped and covered, we said good-bye to Bumba and headed east toward the boiling sun. As we rolled past the final remnants of civilization, shouts arose from the sandy yards.

"To where?!"

"Kisangani!"

They smiled and waved their arms. *"Courage, camarade, courage!"* Five minutes later, we had our first flat tire.

From Bumba, Kisangani lay just four hundred kilometers by river, at the end of the line where navigation ends as the river dissolves into rapids and hooks south. According to villagers, the journey by forest trail was over a hundred kilometers farther, though the trails didn't even appear on my map. I'd only reached Kisangani by air, and flying in, it looks like there isn't enough space in that thick carpet of trees to squeeze in a human being, much less land a plane. Then something in those trees pulls you against the window. There below is the Congo River, snaking through the tangle, catching the sun like a coil of glass and lighting up the dark, murky blood of the forest. It zigzags through the green until the vegetation opens into rows of tin-roofed shacks and white-stone relics of the old colony. This civilization appears almost temporary against the jungle, as if the river itself had licked a clean place against the shore before slowly taking it back. Stepping out, the air is heavy and wet and attacks all vigor and zeal like a parasite to a cell, leaving only torpor and a thirst for beer.

You've now reached the fabled Inner Station in Joseph Conrad's *Heart of Darkness*, where Kurtz, the star agent at the ivory-trading company, is sending more ivory downriver than anyone at headquarters has ever seen. When the narrator, Marlow, journeys upriver to the Inner Station, he discovers Kurtz has become the overlord of a savage kingdom, where natives bow at his feet and rows of shrunken heads are spiked on the fence posts.

The image of Kisangani as a way station of madness was hardly a fiction. In 1890, Conrad himself made the four-week voyage upriver to Kisangani as a ship captain's apprentice in Leopold's Congo. There he witnessed the barbarous greed that would later poison agent Kurtz, as ivory hunters enslaved and murdered countless people in their binge for white gold. Conrad would arrive in Kisangani (then Stanley Falls station) five years before Captain Leon Rom of the colonial army, who, while stationed there, kept twenty-one severed heads as decorations around his flower garden. Rom, it's believed, was agent Kurtz.

Afro-Arab slave traders had also used the area as a base for their village raids, capturing millions who were sent to slave markets in the Middle East. Following Congo's independence, the city was the setting for a string of bloody uprisings and massacres. In 1964, hordes of cannibal anticolonialist rebels sacked the city and slaughtered thousands of civilians while taking two thousand American and European hostages. The uprising was put down only after a dramatic rescue operation by Belgian paratroopers and hired white mercenaries.

Rebels captured Kisangani in August 1998 and effectively divided the nation in two from the government-held west. Rwanda and Uganda supplied their allied troops in Congo from bases in Kisangani, and the two armies finally parted allegiance here in three separate battles that left the city in ruins. The last fight, in June 2000, ended when Rwanda finally pushed Uganda out of town. The six-day battle, the UN estimated, sent over six thousand mortar and artillery shells raining down on the city, killing more than five hundred people.

We raced toward the battered city along a red-clay trail that first morning, muscles pumping, lungs wheezing for breath, shouting greetings of *"Mbote!"* to the traders who passed on foot. This was the low forest, where the undergrowth slammed against the trail like a wall of sheet metal, yet offered no shade or shoulder to rest. Just a winding chute through the scrub, so we took the blind curves with a chorus of handlebar bells, craving speed and fifty kilometers a day if we could get it.

In the convoy, Séverin rode passenger in the lead with Nzimbe, the strongest of the crew and the most familiar with the trail. Riccardo rode second, a nest of camera gear strapped like the Hope diamond on the back. I was third, followed by Simon and Raifin, tall and swanlike, who pedaled entire days standing straight up. Last was Thomas, the shy and able mechanic. They humped our gear and carried nothing of their own, just an ancient set of wrenches wrapped in a plastic bag. I could hear them singing softly as we rode, and in those moments when the trail was smooth and quiet, I realized they were singing the same song in chorus.

We'd shot out of Bumba like hell's raiders, but after a few hours in the topless forest, the rays of the sun sapped our will. The trail narrowed to one winding lane, pockmarked by pits of deep sand that erased all momentum. The handlebars were also too short for my arms, causing the front wheel to pitch in the sand and send the entire bike careening into the bush.

By midafternoon we'd pushed our bikes half the distance, each man dragging sixty pounds of steel and gear through sand so deep the wheels no longer turned. Here the low Congo Basin began its gradual rise toward the western mountains of the Rift Valley, meaning most of the journey would be uphill. When we finally stopped for lunch, I laid my head against a shade tree and fell into comalike sleep, waking up fifteen minutes later. Once we were back on the road, lightning split the heavy sky and rain poured down like daggers. We pushed the remainder of the day through rivers of silt and mud.

By nightfall we'd reached a small village called Yalingemba, a few kilometers shy of the Itimbiri River. We pushed our bikes to the home of the chief, where we were given chairs under a thatched canopy. The rain and fatigue had stripped our social graces, and we insisted they build a fire since our clothes were wet and the temperature was dropping. After Nzimbe, our lead rider, screamed at some men standing in the dark, a few boys dug a pit and struck a fire. We stripped off our shirts and draped them over our knees to dry, then Riccardo prepared a pot of canned beef and sauce.

Word of our visit had spread throughout the region, and within an hour crowds of people were circled around our chairs watching us eat. Most were children, who mimicked our movements like mimes and scattered when we approached. The strobe light on my headlamp sent them all screaming into the trees.

"Please forgive them," said the chief. "This is their first time to see a white man."

The next morning, feeling rested, we entered the old-growth forest, where teak and umbrella trees now towered overhead and snaking tangles of vine smothered the sun. When we reached the banks of the Itimbiri, we loaded our bikes into two canoes operated by four young traders, who paddled us several miles through dense mangroves.

The boats glided into an oval-shaped door in the brambles, and inside the dark theater the air turned cool and every sound exploded as if piped through amplified stacks. The teardrop paddles beat against the canoe with the rhythm of timpanis, and the warbling birdsong of the boatmen was so hauntingly beautiful it nearly peeled me out of my skin. There were no posted signs or visible landmarks. We zigzagged through the thorny brush and tangle, guided by the boatmens' internal compasses. I looked across the mangrove and saw no land, only the shine of black water. I had the curious urge to jump, then wondered how long it would take for the forest to kill me. The scenarios played on a reel.

The second day on the trail was much like the first, yet the forest now shielded us from the direct rays of the sun. But without sun there was only mud, and much of our ride was spent pushing through ankle-deep channels along the trail. After two days of this torture, the enthusiasm of the great reporter-explorer had given way to simple survivalism, and the intrigue and very pursuit of knowledge in such a place just seemed like hubris. *What was I thinking?* I thought. *How did I ever get roped into this?* As I pushed the pedals through another pit of sand, gasping for breath, trying to see through the stinging haze of sweat pouring into my eyes, I looked back to see Riccardo, shirtless, bouncing along the trail like some Juicy Fruit commercial, and smiling.

"Hey, man!" he yelled. "Take my picture! Take my picture on the bike!"

That evening we arrived in Yalimbongo, six bicycles rattling down the trail near dusk and yelling, *"Where's the chief?"* As in the first village and every one after, crowds quickly gathered around our bicycles to point, laugh, and gawk. Others stood studying us in wide-eyed wonderment, not laughing, not smiling, just watching. "I told you," said Riccardo. "They think you are from Mars or something."

The chief was away from the village, but his wife built a fire in the yard and cleared a room for us to sleep. As in many of the villages, the forest trail acted as Main Street, with square mud homes with thatch roofs scattered on both sides. Each home had a large dirt courtyard that was neatly swept. Some villages even had brick chapels, weathered but sturdy, most likely built by missionaries decades ago.

The chief's house in Yalimbongo, like most of the homes where we stayed in the forest, was a four-walled hut made of mud and thatch with several enclaves shooting off a large central room. The floors were dirt and the delicate mud walls crumbled to the touch. Like other huts belonging to chiefs, this one had handmade wooden beds and tables. Cooking was done in a covered patio out back, with hand-carved wooden loungers set up in the yard for guests. A thatched outhouse and separate hut for bathing sat farther in the trees. Lots of people were around, cooking and weaving hair, talking and smoking. It didn't seem like a bad way to live, except they were all extremely poor, more destitute than the river people.

In fact, the river people seemed almost wealthy now compared to those in the forest, simply because there were fish and the proximity to fruits and vegetables. But here, despite the blossoming jungle all around, there was nothing. Most families, like the ones in Yalimbongo, survived mainly on bush meat and *chikwangue*—cassava flour cooked to a doughy mass, fermented in the sun, and wrapped in banana leaves. It was an ideal traveler's food, portable and filling, but contained no nutrients. So the children quietly suffered from malnourishment, their bellies bloated and hair tinged a golden bronze. Every family we encountered spoke of dead children. "No one is here to help us," one mother said. "The world doesn't look into the forest."

We rolled through villages every few hours on the trail, stopping at many to repair a flat tire, a broken pedal, or to look for food and refill our water jugs. And as we stopped, people would run out to greet us. Some were thrilled to have visitors or intrigued by the rarity of white skin, but many clearly expected us to help them, to pull some magic from a pouch that would end their suffering. Women would run out and hold up babies and outstretched palms, and one old man cried out in Lingala, *"Mundele, salisa ngai!"* ("Help me!"), clutching his foot that was dripping with sores.

I supposed it was something leftover from the missionaries, but one old man in a village told me they'd left over a decade ago. "A white man walked through in 1995," he said, "but he was with a logging company, and he didn't really stop to talk." None of these people had voted in the election, and UN observers hadn't penetrated these parts. Yet when we rolled through, they shouted, *"Mundele,* you've arrived!"

But we had nothing to give these people. We were running out of food ourselves. After finding no fruits and vegetables that night in Yalimbongo, we ate one of our last cans of beef and filed off to bed just after sunset. We slept on tarps on the dirt floor, and at one point in the night a rat darted across my chest. We awoke exhausted and covered in fleabites. Riccardo had even developed a rash, his arms and chest covered in tiny sores. We sat in the courtyard at first light eating our leftover dinner. As the riders were maintaining the bikes and preparing to leave, we heard them grumbling and asked Séverin what they were saying.

"They're saying you guys are slow," he said. "They want you to hire some more riders in the next village."

When we protested, Nzimbe pushed back. "Soon we'll reach the swamps," he said. "If you think this forest is hard, wait until we reach the swamps."

Later that day we pushed through rivers that rose to our knees, up incredible mud-slicked hills, and over fallen logs that had obstructed the path for hundreds of years. Instead of clearing the log with a few men and a saw, travelers had simply bored a new road into the jungle around it. By noon we'd traveled thirty kilometers and reached Yahila, where we hoped to eat lunch, refill our water jugs, and rest. But we found only pigs and naked children swimming in the same stagnant river. The villagers there offered us *chikwangue*. We were so weak from lack of food we chewed mouthfuls of raw sugar to keep us going and, when that ran out, bought stalks of sugarcane and chewed it for juice.

We finally stopped for the night in Yalikambe, depleted and weary as we stumbled in. There, I was delighted to find some tomatoes, onions, and limes, which I squeezed into the cool water we dipped from the village well. The chief also sold us a chicken for two dollars, and we slaughtered and divided it among the men.

From Yalikambe, it was only seventy kilometers to Basoko, which had become in our minds the great Shangri-la of the jungle. It was a medium-size trading town much like Bumba, and while we harbored no grand expectations, we knew Basoko could at least offer a hot meal, warm bath, and soft bed to sleep in. Maybe we'd find a motorized pirogue in Basoko, maybe even Captain Buisine and the glorious *Ma'ungano*. Basoko became the light in the forest, the great savior of us all.

But before we reached Basoko, we had to cross the swamp—fifteen kilometers of shin-deep mud. It was such a nuisance the locals just called it *mayi*—"the water" in Lingala. The previous evening in Yalikambe, Riccardo and I heeded Nzimbe's advice and hired two additional men to help cross the swamp. It was a minor blow to our pride, but for the first time, we were able to walk while someone else pushed our bikes, and the extra hands sped our progress tremendously.

Despite my hunger and fatigue, I felt a sudden swell of energy as we entered the great swamp, fueled by delirium and our proximity to food and bed. My face began to tingle and my lungs opened wide, drawing deep, charged breaths. I raced ahead, jumping into trenches that swallowed my boots and singing, "I'm a rolling stone, all alone and lost . . ." The forest rippled in waves of color, sound, and smell. Spectacular clouds of butterflies exploded from the trail in plumes of blue and white. "For a life of sin, I have paid the cost . . ." The rotting earth belched under every step and smelled oddly of beef bouillion and mushrooms. Giant, horned-billed toucans cried from the treetops warning danger was on its way. "When I pass by, all the people say . . . just another guy on the lost highway . . ."

By the time we exited the swamp we were barely able to stand. Since morning, all we'd eaten were a few bananas and avocados, which we spread among ourselves. The two new men now pedaled the bikes, allowing Riccardo and I to ride on the back and rest. From there the road was smooth and straight, and by late afternoon we coasted into the cradle of Basoko.

The town, located at the confluence of the Congo and Aruwimi rivers, was established as a Belgian military garrison in 1888 during a period of epic battles with Afro-Arab slave traders, built to safeguard navigation along the river and stop slavers who were slowly pushing west. But it was Stanley who'd first arrived here in 1877 on his maiden voyage down the Congo. According to Stanley's written account of the journey (which was later proved to be exaggerated for the sake of his audience), Stanley's fleet of boats had been assaulted by hostile tribes twenty-seven times since they'd entered the forest. But one of their largest fights came at the mouth of the Aruwimi near the camp of the Basoko cannibals, who attacked with fifty-four canoes, led by an eighty-man battleship carrying warriors with crimson headdresses and broad-tipped spears. "Boys, be firm as iron," Stanley ordered his men. "Don't think of running away, for only your guns can save you."

During the deafening barrage of rifle fire, a fed-up Stanley lost his last compunction. "It is a murderous world," he wrote, "and we feel for the first time that we hate the filthy, vulturous ghouls who inhabit it." So instead of fending off the assault as usual, he ordered his men to lift anchor and chase the warriors into the village, slaughtering them as they fled into the trees. When the warriors were finally routed, Stanley's men looted everything in the village, including a holy temple made entirely of ivory. Stanley soon realized he stood in a cannibals' lair, where numerous skulls "grinned on many poles" and half-gnawed human bones lay scattered in the garbage heap.

We limped into Basoko with better hopes, needing only food and rest, and if we were lucky, a boat to end our misery. Basoko had also been where Riccardo, during his last trip upriver, had finally collapsed from fevers and malaria, before being rescued by the pirogue of diamond dealers coming off the Aruwimi. And now, as I rolled into town, I was also experiencing fever and a sore throat and was terrified it was early malaria. We arrived at the only guesthouse in town, a little cottage with six rooms operated by the local parish. We told the manager we were famished and needed to eat immediately. "Not to worry," the manager said, and sent out for fish, plantains, spinach, and cold beer. How delighted we were! We gave him ten dollars, a fortune in Basoko, and said, "Buy everything you can!"

But after three hours there was still no food, and no one around to explain. I lay in my stifling room, lapsing in and out of fevered sleep, then heard screaming from the courtyard. I ran outside and saw Riccardo had the manager pinned against the wall. Riccardo turned to me, his face twisted with hate. "There's no food! There was never any food. They stole our money and gave us *nothing!*"

Séverin stood nearby, exasperated, "The manager says there's only *chikwangue,*" he said.

I tried to find some solution, listening to the manager explain how the market had closed early and food was impossible to find. Bad luck, I concluded, but then noticed a group of other guests being served fish, our fish. They also had plantains and rice. I blacked out with rage and joined the tantrum in the courtyard, kicking chairs against the wall and screaming, since screaming was the only thing that felt any good.

Séverin tried to intervene: "Please, please, getting angry won't help anything."

For a couple days now, Séverin had been working on my nerves, the way he never bargained aggressively for our pirogues, always accepting the first offers; the way he covered the damp logs with palm leaves before sitting down in the forest; the way he peeled the skins off peanuts before eating them, separating the loose husks with a gentle puff of breath. And a couple of days before, as we'd slogged through the slime, I'd looked back and seen Nzimbe straining to push the bike with Séverin perched on back, his leather sandals held high above the muck.

They were stupid, little things, undeserving of criticism, but all the frustration from the forest suddenly welled forward. "Just whose side are you on, Séverin? Angry? Yeah, why don't you get angry . . . why don't you stand up and see this guy's walking right over you?"

"I can see everything clearly," he said, turning now to walk inside. "But I will never scream at these people for you."

That night we ended up getting fish and plantains, even eggs for an omelet. It had really been a ploy to take our money, but it didn't matter. By the time the food arrived, I felt too sick to eat anyway. I lay in bed sweating through my clothes, the mosquito net like an incubator over my fevered skin. That night we also discovered there were no boats to take us upriver. Tomorrow would be just like today, another eleven hours spent trudging through the jungle.

We awoke at dawn and crossed the Aruwimi River. There was some sort of fight at the riverbank over the price of our boats, but I couldn't quite follow it, I was still so sick. A syrupy, septic film shrouded my vision. People around me seemed to move robotically as if under strobe light, their faces vibrating in the heat waves. My head throbbed and thoughts faded before they formed. I remembered the immigration official who'd held our passports for ransom, until we jerked them from his hands and ran. And the crowd of people who'd watched us leave, their voices like a flock of cockatoos plunging off the steep, muddy bank: "*MUndeLE . . . MuNdele . . .* why you give me nothing, my bigeeeeee?"

We'd crossed the wide river against heavy wind and now paddled through the quiet mangroves. The soaring trees became the walls of a hidden, primordial cathedral. Tiny holes of sunshine pierced the high ceiling like a galaxy of stars, each one wired into the white roar of heaven, so loud it could rip the skin from bone. The sky reflected precisely onto the placid water, as if the forest had split in half and allowed us safe passage through the middle. I let the cool river glide over my hand. We must have been there for hours.

We'd hired two more bikes in Basoko and kept the two additional riders from Yalikambe, expanding our convoy to eight bikes and nine men. I rode lead with Nzimbe after crossing the river, though we ended up pushing the bike most of the morning. I soon noticed how crushing Basoko had been for the whole party. I could see Nzimbe was now weak and listless, slumped over his handlebars, and Raifin, another rider, now complained of a fever.

Around three o'clock we reached the outskirts of a large, populated village. The narrow trail opened to a wide, sandy boulevard. And in every direction, we noticed rows of banana trees spilling with fruit. A small crowd of villagers rushed out to greet us, helping push our bikes down the boulevard, which was flanked by columns of palms. The Aruwimi River sparkled through the trees in the distance, and the setting sun painted the huts and smiling faces in a warm, benevolent glow. *"Mundele,"* someone shouted. "Welcome to Baonde!"

The chief of Baonde sat weaving a fishing basket under a tree when we arrived. He greeted us quizzically and ordered his men to fetch chairs. "We're sick and desperately need to eat," we told him. I was prepared to demand food as we'd done in previous villages. But without hesitation the chief turned to the large crowd who'd gathered behind us. "Go to your homes and bring everything you have," he said. "These men have had a difficult journey, but they're willing to pay for your things." I asked his name and the location of the village, but he waved me off. "In time, son," the chief said. "First rest and get your strength."

For the next half hour, a procession of villagers passed by our chairs. They carried bowls of tomatoes, bananas, papaya, onion, eggplant, and baskets of duck eggs and salted fish. They presented goats, chickens, pigs, and a freshly killed monkey swinging by its tail. We slaughtered two chickens and prepared a bubbling stew full of vegetables. We ate and ate, and slowly the fever released its grip and returned some of my strength.

I rested well that night in Baonde, a ten-hour, narcotic death sleep courtesy of a little grass and some sleeping pills we'd bought at a clinic in Basoko. We were feeling good when we pulled out the next morning, laughing and joking once again, basking in the giddy relief that comes with having escaped something dire. We felt confident we'd take the last two hundred kilometers in three days' time.

But the forest provided no rest, and broken chains, flat tires, and snapped pedals constantly slowed our progress. For three days, we inched through the forest, nursing our bikes and bodies on short rations. Then, late on the third afternoon after leaving Baonde, the convoy pushed its way up a steep rise and stopped at the top. The trees suddenly vanished and the trail was plowed wide and flat. Three Caterpillar bulldozers sat parked on the roadside, shadowed by tangled heaps of rooted and shattered trees. It was the Trans-M logging road. A woman passing nearby said it went all the way to Kisangani, now just a day's journey on bikes. We paused to bask in this violent and open expanse, then thanked the Lord for deforestation.

After seven days in the forest, the convoy spent its last night in Yaosuka, a small settlement just eighty kilometers from Kisangani. Being so near civilization, we expected to find a great bounty when we arrived, but the villagers there refused to sell us any food. Instead of arguing, we sent Séverin and Nzimbe on a bike to another nearby settlement, where they were able to buy some rice and a chicken, which we grilled over a fire and shared among the nine of us. We were hungry when we turned to bed, but it didn't matter now. Tomorrow we'd receive our great reward in the city. As we drifted off to sleep, a steady rain began to fall.

The downpour continued through the night, with sheets of wind and rain slapping the tin roof where we slept and shooting gullies across the dirt floor. The next morning we hurriedly packed our wet gear, not even bothering to talk about the storm, so accustomed were we now to the punishing weather. We wheeled our bikes to the crude highway as a light rain fell, speaking only of beautiful things to come.

But after a few hundred feet, our bike tires began sinking into the road, slowing us to another agonizing crawl. The new logging road had yet to pack into hard shell. The all-night storm had poured inches of rain into the freshly turned soil. And while the forest mud had been a slimy soup, we now struggled through clay-like cement that caked our boots and clung to the tires, leaving us heavier with each step. Soon the fenders were so clogged the wheels ceased to turn. Behind me, the entire convoy was paralyzed and the rain was heavy once again.

"You've gotta help me push!" Riccardo said. He'd stripped off his clothes and now strained against the handlebars, his legs sinking in the mire. We'd come this far. "Stand at the back and push!" he said, but pushing only dug us deeper. The bike felt rooted like a tree. "The worst," I managed. "It must be . . . after everything . . . the worst day."

We now dragged the overturned bike like a dead animal through the mud. The drilling rain shrank our eyes into cold, vapid holes. Riccardo lost his grip when the bike caught a snag and toppled into the muck. As he sat there, he noticed the large crowds who'd gathered on the roadside to watch our exercise in misery. We called to them, *"Quelque aide, s'il vous plaît?"* But instead of helping, they only pointed and laughed.

The Italian's curses began with a slow, fuming whisper before his gut spewed them forward, *". . . porco dio porca MADONNA DIO CANE,"* curses against baby Jesus and Joseph, God the Pig and Dog, and Mary the Whore-Fucked Saint of Congo, a torrent of boiling lead aimed straight at heaven and the pissing rain, until the words themselves disintegrated into a tirade of gibberish.

The crowd roared with laughter. Children ran into the road and cheered. They spun around and swatted their asses. I tasted the warm rain on my teeth and my breathing quickened. I found a heavy stick and hurled it into the crowd of children, praying it would miss as soon as it left my fingers. *Bravo!* The crowd howled even louder. *Mundele,* you've arrived! It was indeed a rare, spectacular show. I followed the script to the letter, even bowed before picking up the bike and soldiering on, no greater a man. "You shouldn't have done that," Riccardo said. "I know," I told him. "Believe me, I know."

That afternoon we reached the banks of the Lindi River. Across its choppy waters sat Kisangani, yet it was hard to muster the expected surge of joy. Minutes after arriving at the river we had another fight with immigration officials, who seized our riders' ID cards and demanded their money. "River tax," they said, their breath heavy with wine. But their authority meant nothing. Riccardo stormed the office, yelling, collected the cards, and calmly instructed the riders to load the boats for Kisangani. "Arrest us," we said. We must've looked insane.

After experiencing the same ordeal on the other side of the river, we finally rolled into Kisangani in the late afternoon. At the hotel we toasted our riders and paid them out, clapping as each man took his first sip of something cold. "To the end," we said, raising our glasses high. "To the end!"

But the end sat cold and awkward. There was something unsettling about the end.

Riccardo grabbed my arm, saying, "We did it, man, we survived the *jongle*! Eight days on the bikes!"

All of my emotions from the past few weeks now rioted inside me, peaked and heightened by exhaustion. I wanted to punch the walls, fall down laughing, or walk into a dark room and not come out for days.

"Yeah, man," I said. "We did it. We did it."

I'd traveled upriver and crossed through jungle and come out unscathed, triumphant even, but I wondered now what it was I'd found. The traders on the river had shown a glimmer of something like hope, but the rest had been a fool's errand, and the jungle had broken me in half and given nothing. I realized I'd risked life and limb looking for something that didn't exist, some modern notion of progress that didn't even apply. Like Buisine had said, there was nothing even before the war. And there was certainly little now, except a few naïve ideas I'd left on the forest floor. All I wanted now was to close my eyes and sleep, then go home and remember what it was about this country I'd loved so much. A good part of me wanted to climb back on the bike and just keep riding.

There was something funny down the table because the riders began to laugh. Nzimbe said to Riccardo, "We loved how you screamed at the officials. You handled them like a man!" The riders would've certainly been arrested. "The people in the villages thought you were mercenaries," he added. "They were very afraid!" The riders laughed and one of them stood up and duckwalked along the table, barking orders. I forced a smile and finished my beer, then ordered another. Outside the sunset thinned the busy streets and pulled shadows over the table. We raised our glasses a few more times until the light finally faded, leaving us exhausted in the dark.

Chapter Five

"UN PETIT DÉRAILLEMENT"

I left Kisangani two days later on a UN flight to Uganda, caught my connection, and arrived home in a wicked funk. I'd spent five weeks traveling fifteen hundred miles through some of the most brutal terrain on earth, and it certainly felt good to have finished. But I'd found few signs of promise along the way, no grand harbinger of revival or reform. Instead, I spent the winter frustrated and empty-handed.

Even if there were some markings of progress along the path, I probably missed them anyway. Because once in the jungle, my own basic needs and level of comfort had stood in the way of learning anything. I didn't even know my riders' last names or anything about their families. I'd simply been too exhausted and hungry to care. It wasn't my proudest moment, and even now, those last days on the trail leave a sting of regret.

In any case, whatever enthusiasm I may have gathered would've evaporated quickly after getting home. Twice during the winter and spring, I turned on my computer and saw Kinshasa paralyzed by more fighting between Kabila's and Bemba's men. The last battle in March 2007 killed around four hundred people, many of them civilians, and sucked dry any postelection optimism that might have remained.

It was the perfect opportunity to call off this fruitless wandering and just stay home. Except there was one last place I wanted to go, one last adventure through the vast, beckoning country. The old railway network in the southern province of Katanga was finally running for the first time in a decade. The rails were connecting market towns and villages shattered by war *and long forgotten, and it was possible now to buy a ticket and ride along. Perhaps something good would emerge down that long steel road, some kind of beacon rising out of the jungle and over the plains, something to point the way forward.*

I

I'd fallen in love with the trains back in August 2003 on a reporting trip to Kalemie, a trading town on the shores of Lake Tanganyika. One day after work, I happened to pass the brick rail station of the Societe Nationale des Chemins de Fer du Congo (SNCC), the national rail company. The old station looked so regal there at the bottom of the hill, the lake shining behind it, so I walked inside to see if anyone was home. Inside, the windows were smashed and boarded, and an inch of dust covered every surface. I managed to find the director sitting alone in an empty office, nothing on his desk but a piece of bread, a few papers, and a Bible.

"There are no trains, *monsieur*," he said. "The last one was in 1998, and I believe you've missed it."

Until the war started, Kalemie—formerly called Albertville—had been a railway hub ever since the arrival, in 1915, of the Chemins de Fer du Congo Superieur aux Grands Lacs Africains, or Upper Congo-Great African Lakes Railway (CFL). The network that ran through Kalemie linked the rest of Congo to Lake Tanganyika, where ferry boats and ships closed the gap into Tanzania, East Africa, the Indian Ocean, and Asia. It also connected to lines into Kisangani and the Congo River, thus providing access to the Atlantic.

But in 1998, the province fell to the Rwandans. Since then, the director said, Congo's national rail company had mainly been used to ferry troops and rebels, depending on who controlled the region. In Kalemie, there hadn't been a passenger train since the Rwandans swept across the border. Every few months, there was an occasional freight train loaded with palm oil and salt, but only if there was enough merchandise to make it worth the effort. And since there were no passenger trains, hundreds of people would jump the roof of the freight as it passed, oftentimes to be scraped off and killed when it hit the bridges and low clearances. Derailments were catastrophic.

Worse, in March 2000, Zimbabwean MiGs had blown up a strategic rail bridge about three hundred kilometers west of Kalemie, destroying it before it could wind up in the hands of rebel forces, who were looking for any means to push toward the capital. The bombed bridge at Zofu crippled the two-thousand-kilometer north-south river and rail network that connected Katanga to the Congo River in the north and Zambia in the south. And the old CFL railway into Kalemie had been made defunct when another bridge over the Niemba River collapsed in 1998 from soil erosion, severing Congo's link to Lake Tanganyika and the Indian Ocean.

Now, every train that left Kalemie had to stop at the washed-out bridge, unload onto pirogues to cross the river, then change to another locomotive waiting on the other side. More often than not, the locomotive never appeared on the other side, stranding freight and people for days, often weeks. With just two bridges out of commission, the entire province slowly began to starve.

"And if you can imagine," the director said, "there was a time when you could catch a train all the way to South Africa from Kalemie, enjoy a nice meal and a beer. The scenery from here is breathtaking. You could actually be a tourist here in Congo."

We walked out into the sun-baked yard, now overrun by tall elephant grass that released swarms of grasshoppers as we cut a path across the rusty rails. At the back of the lot, behind a few freight cars, sat an old first-class car painted red with silver runners. Its windows were smashed and splintered. A few bullet holes decorated its broadside, but it still appeared beautiful and so completely lonely, like a washed-up racehorse collecting flies in the back stable.

I jumped inside and marveled at the old wooden bar, complete with a cracked mirror behind the shelves. There were shower rooms and deluxe sleepers, the beds and tables long ripped out by passing soldiers. The Rwandan troops had used the cars as barracks during the first months of the war, the director said. He pointed at mounds of calcified excrement in the toilets and charred holes in the floors. "They actually built fires in the corridors," he said, shaking his head.

To me it was like finding an old abandoned cabin deep in the woods, a true and proper explorer's fort and clubhouse. As the director continued explaining the larger disrepair and decay of the train company, I imagined people on the train dressed in their Sunday clothes, lighting cigarettes at the bar with a cold Tembo, *baridi sana*, sitting down to a steak as the savanna rushed past in a golden blur, imagined falling asleep to a cool breeze through the window and the gentle rock and whine of those steel wheels in the dark.

So you can imagine my excitement, nearly four years later, when I learned both bridges had been repaired and the rail system was up and running. Never mind that "up and running" meant about three trains left Lubumbashi station each month, with no certainty when they'd come back, or how far they'd get. The trains were running, so I called ahead to Kinshasa and recruited Séverin for one last mission. And this time I asked Lionel to come along as photographer.

Katanga was the largest province in all of Congo, stretching south to Zambia and east to Tanzania, which lay just across Lake Tanganyika. Here the rain forests thinned as the elevation rose, the siphoning jungle giving way to open savanna and cool breezes. Here the melodic Swahili of the east replaced the sharp Lingala of the west, and the people themselves seemed to mellow as the air became lighter. Even the beer tasted better in Katanga. But it wasn't just the high altitude that made it different, though it reached sixty-five hundred feet in places. Nor was it the crisp breezes that whipped into the lower valleys, creating a force field against the swampy jungles in the north.

It was money, almost an endless supply of it thanks to one of the largest and purest deposits of cobalt and copper in the world. So much copper was bulging under the surface in Katanga that the earth actually glowed from space.

The mining industry certainly gave the people of Katanga a sense of pride, especially when comparing themselves to their fellow countrymen. But as in Ituri, the minerals carried with them a curse locked inside the blessing. While the minerals made the province a titan in central Africa, they'd also sparked bloody secession attempts and sucked the UN into its first enterprise in Congo back in 1960. Even now, the minerals continue to drive the wholesale pillage of the province by foreigners and corrupt state officials.

And of course, it all began with Leopold. From the moment Leopold had first acquired Congo, he'd heard of the mineral wealth in Katanga, so plentiful the tribes used small crosses made from copper as currency. Securing copper, in addition to rubber, would no doubt fortify his empire. And while he'd sent Stanley in 1879 to secure agreements with local tribes in the river provinces, Katanga remained open and untamed.

The pressure to settle Katanga built suddenly in 1890, when Leopold found himself in a race for the territory with the formidable Cecil Rhodes, the British-born South African tycoon and empire builder. As prime minister of the British-held Cape Colony (now South Africa), Rhodes had already annexed and lent his name to Northern Rhodesia and Southern Rhodesia, the areas now known as Zambia and Zimbabwe. Now he was looking to claim territory farther north, part of his scheme to connect the British empire's African colonies by railroad. Intent on pushing north toward Egypt, he ignored Leopold's borders and sent his agents into Katanga to negotiate with village chiefs. Rhodes, who had already founded De Beers Mining Company and would later control 90 percent of the world's diamonds, was as hell-bent as Leopold on claiming Katanga's copper. "I would annex the planets if I could," he once famously said.

At the time, Leopold was broke. Building a railroad along the Congo River had left him deep in debt, and the project was only in its first year of construction. And half the Free State's funds were tied up in the Force Publique, which was staging its murderous sorties into the jungles to extract the colony's quotas of rubber. And farther east, other Free State troops were becoming mired in battles with Afro-Arab slavers along the Congo River south of Kisangani.

And there was another obstacle: Msiri, chief and supreme ruler of Katanga. A savvy and cunning chief, Msiri had used the region's minerals to build a sizable army of warriors and arm them with guns purchased from Portuguese traders. With these weapons, he'd launched a series of tribal wars in which he'd seized surrounding chiefdoms and incorporated the armies of his enemies, many of them taken as slaves, building an empire that was feared and respected throughout central Africa. Msiri was known as a cold-blooded sadist, who enjoyed locking his estimated hundreds of wives in huts full of starving ravenous dogs, and executing prisoners—but not before feeding them a meal of their own ears.

Rhodes approached him first, sending a delegation to bargain with Msiri, offering the chief bolts of cloth, beads, and a few cases of gin for all of Katanga. Insulted, Msiri refused and sent the delegation away. Hearing this, Leopold saw his chance. Despite being strapped for men and cash, he sent his own teams to negotiate with Msiri before the Brits could rally another attempt. Leopold would not be as diplomatic.

The Belgian king sent three military expeditions into Katanga and built a garrison near Msiri's village. With a small army in place, he then dispatched William Stairs—one of Stanley's former men—to win an agreement by force, if necessary. Stairs's method was direct: he simply marched into Msiri's village with a hundred men and planted a Free State flag in the ground. Msiri fled to a nearby settlement, so Stairs sent one of his officers to drag him back. When the chief resisted, the officer shot him three times with a revolver before being gunned down himself by the chief's bodyguards. With Msiri dead, Belgium imposed its own handpicked chief over Katanga, thus sealing their stake in the region, and for that matter, in Congo as a whole. Because once Belgium organized itself around the mines, they never stopped producing.

The red dirt, it turned out, was also filled with cobalt, tin, diamonds, coal, silver, magnesium, uranium, and other minerals in huge demand as nations built themselves for the industrial age. Even more than rubber, the mines brought wealth to the colony, built the European-style cities that sprouted along the southern savanna, with the largest and proudest of them being Elizabethville, or modern Lubumbashi. The mines financed the hospitals and roads that set the Belgian Congo apart from other colonies and gave jobs and pensions to thousands of Congolese. As a result, Katangese were healthier and better educated and also more worldly, as the mines also attracted Africans from elsewhere in the continent, in addition to one of the largest populations of Europeans in central Africa.

All that would change on June 30, 1960, when Congo was granted her emancipation from Belgium. The mutiny and rioting of the Force Publique that followed independence spread rapidly across the country in days, with Belgian paratroopers helping evacuate the thousands of foreigners who fled in panic as soldiers raped and looted in the cities. In Katanga, the Congolese governor, Moise Tshombe, vowed to keep business operating and safeguard European residents, who were largely employed by the mines. When the mutiny finally reached Katanga on July 9, Tshombe called in additional Belgian paratroopers to restore order, a move bitterly opposed by the freshly appointed premier, Patrice Lumumba, who wanted no more association with the former colonialists.

Worse, in Lumumba's eyes, Tshombe allowed Belgian officers in the Force Publique to remain in command of their Katangan troops. Tshombe even hired hundreds of white mercenaries, who poured in all summer long from Europe, Rhodesia, and South Africa, thus creating a separate standing army for the territory.

Perhaps no one in Katanga was more grateful to the paratroopers than officials at Union Minière du Haut Katanga, the Belgian-British-owned mining company that had essentially built and owned all of Katanga, who were desperate to protect their holdings from the raving mobs. Two days later, these men got an especially pleasing announcement: Katanga was seceding from Congo.

The announcement came as Lumumba and Joseph Kasavubu, Congo's president, were involved in heavy damage control, traveling around the country trying to reel in their troops and impose their authority. Lumumba appealed to Dag Hammarskjöld, then secretary-general of the UN, to send troops to invade Katanga and crush the secession and remove the foreign invaders by force. The UN cannot invade Katanga, the secretary told him. But with anarchy threatening to destroy the Congo government, Hammarskjöld sent several thousand peacekeepers on July 15 to replace Belgian troops in other parts of the country, hoping to maintain some semblance of order.

Determined to outflank Tshmobe, Lumumba traveled to Washington to request American tactical support, but was rebuffed. The Canadians also balked, so Lumumba appealed to the Soviets, who obligingly sent dozens of Ilyushin transport planes and trucks and about a thousand technicians to Leopoldville. Washington, fearing a Soviet foothold in Africa, ordered the Soviets out and parked an aircraft carrier at the mouth of the Congo. The CIA went as far as hatching a plot to slip poison in Lumumba's food or toothpaste, but the agent, Larry Devlin, had a change of heart and wound up pouring the poison into the river.

The CIA then went to work on Mobutu and Kasavubu, pressuring them to rid themselves of the erratic Lumumba, who they saw as a Fidel Castro in the making. In September 1960, Mobutu went further and declared martial law, neutralizing Kasavubu. He gave the Soviets forty-eight hours to leave Congo, then placed Lumumba under arrest. After the former premier was caught trying to escape, Mobutu put him on a plane and sent him to Katanga, dishing him right onto Tshombe's plate.

Mobutu's soldiers reportedly beat Lumumba so badly on the plane ride into Elizabethville that the Belgian pilots closed the cockpit so they wouldn't be ill. Several versions exist of what happened next, but the most likely is that Lumumba was executed on arrival by a Belgian-led firing squad while Tshombe stood witness. It's believed his body was then chopped into pieces and dissolved in a barrel of acid.

Meanwhile, talks between the government and Tshombe had gone nowhere. Eventually Hammarskjöld decided the white mercenaries were in violation of Congo's new sovereignty, and an unacceptable threat to security. In August 1961, thousands of Indian, Swedish, and Irish UN soldiers launched Operation Rum Punch, fanning into Katanga and arresting several hundred white military officers and mercenaries. The UN followed the next month with Operation Morthor, where UN troops battled Katangan forces. It was a rout: Katangan fighter jets destroyed UN planes and military camps, and 130 Irish peacekeepers surrendered and were taken prisoner.

Tshombe fled over the border into Zambia during the attack, so Hammarskjöld flew to meet the governor with hopes of persuading him to allow peacekeepers to replace his Belgian troops. But before he could reach the meeting, Hammarskjöld's plane crashed into the hills just across the Zambian border, killing everyone aboard. A cease-fire reached in the wake of Hammarskjöld's death quickly fell apart.

Over the next year, the UN continued to hammer Katanga, and after successive battles late in 1962, the Katangese resistance broke. The central government assumed control again on January 14, 1963, and two years later, Mobutu staged a coup and took Congo for himself. When Laurent Kabila's forces reached the capital in 1997, the rebel leader announced his presidency from a stage in Lubumbashi—just a few hundred kilometers south of his ancestral home in Manono.

So much of the country's history had played out in Katanga, collected in that bottom crevice and pushed into the heart by all the money buried in the dirt. William Stairs's murderous expedition into Msiri's kingdom undoubtedly secured the vast mineral fields for the cause of Western civilization. But the droves of fever-driven men couldn't have moved an ounce of copper until another crucial milestone was passed: September 27, 1910—the day the Chemin de Fer du Katanga, or Katanga Railway, finally rolled into Lubumbashi. If the copper gave birth to the cities along the plains, the railroads fed them and kept them growing. As Stanley once said, "Without a railway . . . Congo isn't worth a penny."

When Leopold sent Stanley up the river to negotiate treaties in 1879, one of the explorer's first tasks was to build a service road around the 350 kilometers of rapids to Stanley Pool, then portage two disassembled steamships to take him upriver. A railway would then follow, allowing unhindered access from the jungles to the sea. Traveling with him were a crew of porters and laborers from Zanzibar, along with a handful of British, American, French, Danish, Belgian, and Italian volunteers who would help maintain the stations. They established a camp at a village called Vivi along Congo's estuary with the sea, then began chipping away through the Crystal Mountains toward the Pool.

After five years, which included a brief stint back home due to illness, Stanley completed the road and established a series of stations along the river—including Kinshasa, Mbandaka, and Kisangani—luckily experiencing none of the tribal hostility that had plagued his maiden journey in 1877. But due to a lack of cash, Leopold couldn't begin the promised railroad until 1890. The great railway project took about sixty thousand men, mainly slaves from Congo, Zanzibar, Senegal, and Sierra Leone shackled and dragged into service. Leopold also brought in five hundred Chinese laborers, many of whom died from disease or deserted. Several who managed to escape were later found five hundred miles in the jungles, trying to walk home to China by following the eastern sun.

The railroad followed along Stanley's rugged wagon trail through the jagged cliffs of the Crystal Mountains. Without the aid of heavy equipment or steel cables, workers hauled materials on their backs up the steep cliffs, which climbed as high as six hundred feet in just a few miles. In all, ninety-nine bridges and over twelve hundred aqueduct canals were required. After the first two years, crews had completed only five miles of rail. The punishing terrain, tropical heat, disease, starvation, and beatings from colonial guards took scores of lives each week and littered the service road with hundreds of corpses. In 1890, Joseph Conrad spent nearly two months walking this road around the rapids en route to the steamer that would carry him upriver. Along the way, he described in his diaries seeing "at a camp[in]g place the dead body of a Backongo. Shot? Horrid smell"; further along, he encountered "a skeleton tied up to a post." The railway from the Atlantic to Stanley Pool stands as one of the shining benchmarks of Belgian atrocity in Congo. But after its completion, what had been a twenty-day hike along Stanley's road now only took two days by train and allowed the ivory and rubber to flow as if from a spigot.

Cecil Rhodes had died in 1902 without ever having acquired Katanga or his Cape-to-Cairo railroad, but his deputy Sir Robert Williams managed to find his way inside Katanga. Desperate for funding to begin mining, Leopold partnered with Williams's company Tanganyika Concessions Ltd., granting them a stake in mineral rights in exchange for helping finance a railroad to the mines (this merger would later become Union Minière).

To build the railway, Williams brought in British-owned contracting firm Pauling & Company, who'd built railways in South Africa and Rhodesia. The nearest rail station to Katanga was 212 kilometers south of Lubumbashi at Broken Hill mine in Northern Rhodesia. The station was the northern terminus of a railroad that extended east to the Indian Ocean port city of Beira, Mozambique. The objective was to extend this railroad into Katanga, thus connecting Katanga to the ocean.

The work was fast and efficient, with crews of 15 white foremen and 350 Africans laying track in assembly-line fashion, while locomotives followed behind loaded with material. The Greek, Italian, and British contractors drank heavily, packed pistols, and often wagered their pay on how many kilometers they'd push the following day, as bonuses were given to quick teams. In December 1909, the tracks crossed the Congo border, and nine months later, reached Lubumbashi. (Once inspectors closely examined the tracks, however, they discovered only half the bolts had been fastened to the rails.)

Belgium's priority of connecting the mines to the Beira seaport had been realized. But Katanga's main mineral markets were in Europe, which meant boats leaving Beira's Indian Ocean port had to travel north, around the Horn of Africa, and pass through the Suez Canal, where heavy taxes were levied. The route quickly became a financial drain.

What Congo needed was a river and rail route completely within its own borders that could reduce the overhead. So the Belgians immediately began building the Great Lakes Railway to extend the line north from Lubumbashi, connecting it with the Congo River at Stanleyville, where goods could flow downstream to the Atlantic. The network also connected the Congo River with Kalemie and Lake Tanganyika. But this internal route wasn't ideal: freight leaving Katanga and out the Congo River went through seven transshipments through the thick forest and river and often took months to reach its destination.

The ultimate goal was the National Route, finally opened in 1928, an all-Congo rail and river network from Katanga to the Atlantic, which extended the line from the town of Bukama (the railhead along the Congo River) westward to Ilebo, which sits along the muddy Kasai River, 820 kilometers east of Kinshasa by river. From Ilebo, steamers shipped goods down the Kasai, linked with the Congo River, then headed toward the Atlantic.

The National Route would be Congo's principal network until the Second World War, when demands for copper and minerals tripled for the Allied effort (even as Belgium itself was occupied by the Nazis). During the war, Katanga provided British and American troops with the bulk of their copper, cobalt, industrial diamonds, tin, gold, silver, and uranium. In fact, the mines in Shinkolobwe supplied the uranium for the U.S. atomic bombs dropped on Hiroshima and Nagasaki. By the 1950s, Katanga was the fourth-largest copper producer in the world, and minerals constituted nearly 70 percent of Congo's export revenue (aided by gold fields in Ituri and more diamonds in central Kasai).

By that time, Sir Robert Williams had achieved a dream of his own, the 1,348-kilometer Benguela Railway across the barren landscape of Angola, Congo's southern neighbor, which provided Katanga with an even shorter route to the Atlantic. Congo had built a link with the Benguela line in 1931, so by the time of the war, the colony divided a large chunk of its export between the Benguela's all-rail network and Congo's own National Route.

However, the Benguela Railway was lost in the 1970s during the opening salvos of Angola's civil war, which lasted until 2002. And much of Congo's network slowly crumbled under the weight

of neglect and unremitting conflict. Two separate secession attempts in Katanga during the late 1970s caused severe damage. And
when the great war settled over the copper belt in 1998, it emptied
the railroad towns of the men who kept the machine alive, scattering them over the borders into squalid camps and across the plains
where those big giants once rolled. But now with peace, elections,
and the resulting flood of foreign investment, the old network was
struggling to return, and I had plans to meet it.

In late April 2007, I caught an SN Brussels flight straight into Kinshasa, met up with Séverin and Lionel, and began looking for a
train. Since I'd ended my previous journey in Kisangani, I was
hoping to follow the Great Lakes line that ran from nearby
Ubundu down to Lubumbashi, with a river-barge ride in between
where the trains didn't operate.

With this plan, Séverin and I visited the Kinshasa bureau of the
SNCC, the national rail company. As we entered its musty office just
off the boulevard, we began to get our first glimpse of the company's
decline. Here the gold wallpaper peeled off the Sheetrock and
drooped to the floor, and threadbare carpet revealed the cement underneath. Light fixtures had been ripped from the ceiling during the
last *pillage*, and an absence of electricity explained why the secretary's
computer wasn't plugged into the wall. On further notice, I realized
she didn't even have a monitor.

The bureau's director was a polite, well-spoken man named
Mulapu, who wore a pink silk tie and French cuffs. The train
schedules were so erratic it was impossible to plan for them, he
said, and usually his office was never even informed of trains on the
other side of the country. In fact, the route from Ubundu through
the forest that had looked so pretty on the map wasn't possible now
because the train was broken, and Mulapu didn't know when it
would be repaired.

Mulapu offered to call the other bureaus in Lubumbashi and

Kalemie and get some answers. But since the government owed him many months' salary and didn't pay his bills, his phone had no credit. I loaned him mine. Mulapu called several people for short conversations in rapid French and Lingala then handed the phone back. "It will be difficult," he said, "but I think we have something in terms of a freight train."

A World Food Programme train was leaving Lubumbashi early the next week, hauling food aid to Kindu in the north. The year before, fighting between Mai Mai rebels and government troops had left two hundred thousand displaced in northeastern Katanga, and since then the WFP humanitarian trains had made regular runs to ferry food to the isolated reaches. Mulapu said there wasn't a passenger carriage attached, but maybe we could ride in the loco-motive with the engineer.

"That's perfect," I said.

"But along the way, many people will pile on top and force their way inside."

I nodded. "Okay."

He laughed, resting his hands on his round belly. "This is a dan-gerous way to travel. The people have destroyed these trains. Sometimes you wonder if they're meant for humans or animals."

I looked at Séverin. Horror shot from his eyes like sparks on a broken rail.

"That's exactly what we're looking for," I said.

The river and bike journey through the forest had been punishing on my body and I'd lost nearly fifteen pounds. I was determined to never run out of food again while on the trail, so this time I came extra-prepared. I'd gone shopping in the States and stuffed a nylon sack full of canned milk, potted meat, tuna, powdered cheese, and enough beef jerky to survive for weeks. I'd also brought along two backpacks full of every piece of gear I could ever need, and some I would not, including three hundred yards of nylon rope and a gadget that heated buckets of cold bathwater (this last one I never even took out of my pack). And I'd also stopped by the REI outfitter store and bought Bug Huts for Lionel and myself, which were simple, pop-up mesh cocoons the length of a man's body, and quite possibly the greatest Africa gear ever invented besides the headlamp. No more torturous, sleepless nights with faulty mosquito nets. And given their compact size, we were certain we could use them on the trains. "We'll just toss our racks on the roof and sleep in the open," said Lionel. "Mate, the Congolese will be so jealous of our Bug Huts."

Two days later, Lionel and I were thoroughly prepared, packed and repacked and reduced to sitting in his apartment, whiling away the four days before we caught our freight train. On a whim, Lionel decided to call the station director in Lubumbashi just to check in. Mulapu had given us the director's number, and Lionel had called the day before, just to introduce himself and make it known we were serious. Everything had been sorted. But when Lionel called back, the director had startling news: the WFP train had just left without us.

"But we had an agreement," Lionel told him.

"I would've called you," said the director, "but my phone had no credit."

After the river journey, I'd grown indifferent to these kinds of delays and disruptions, expected them even. So I'd returned to Congo with a new attitude, a new way of facing down stress by simply tuning out. And now as we careened into the first barricade of our journey, I didn't mind at all, actually felt relieved to have it out of the way.

"There isn't another train for seven days," Lionel said, hanging up. "A passenger train going to Kalemie. He said something about it being express."

Express, I thought, and the memory of that abandoned dining car in Kalemie came knocking by. We immediately decided to travel to Lubumbashi and wait there before another train slipped past. We would go to Katanga and try to literally catch a train.

II

I'd always wanted to visit Lubumbashi. The very name bounced off the tongue like fingers on a drum. The copper mines, the history, the arrogant swagger from having something the others didn't. Even while supporting Mobutu's ravenous hunger for decades, Lubumbashi had played second only to Kinshasa. But in the 1980s, the state-owned mines known as Gécamines (the former Union Minière) collapsed from neglect, causing the city to finally fall on hard times like the rest of the struggling country.

But all of that changed once China came along.

With its economy growing faster than milkweed, China had swooped into Katanga and begun hauling out commodities at enormous rates, pushing the price of copper to three dollars a pound and cobalt to thirty—the highest in a decade. China's demand for cobalt—used to manufacture rechargeable batteries in cell phones— rose tenfold from 1997 to 2005, when up to 90 percent of China's imported concentrates and ores were coming from Congo. And with the demand set high, over 150,000 local informal miners answered the call, squatting on the old government-owned Gécamines mines that had collapsed or others that were abandoned during the war. The peaceful elections also brought other companies that had anxiously been waiting in the wings. Phelps Dodge, the American mining firm, began developing a sixteen-hundred-square-kilometer, $900 million concession that encompassed two villages, Tenke and Fungurume, and sat on one of the largest copper and cobalt deposits in the world. Other companies such as Anvil Mining, from Australia, and Forrest Group, a Belgian firm, had concessions worth hundreds of millions more.

The big multinationals had to operate on the up-and-up since many eyes were scanning their affairs, especially Anvil, which had been busted several years earlier for letting government troops use their vehicles to assault a local rebel group, a battle in which many civilians were killed. These companies met regularly with aid groups and consultants about how to better serve the community. They built schools and publicized their numbers, which only accounted for about 20 percent of all mining in Katanga, a mere sliver of the money being pumped out of the ground.

The rest of the mining was illegally done by local men with pickaxes and shovels, many of them digging atop the concessions recently acquired by the big multinationals such as Phelps Dodge, which now faced the dilemma of removing them. The local miners were scattered across the province, working shirtless in their broken flip-flops and living off manioc in the sun, earning five dollars a week selling to Congolese middlemen who often disappeared on payday. The middlemen then sold the minerals to the foreign trading houses and Chinese businessmen who lined the mining roads, and they in turn set the market price and made a fortune off these holes that never ran dry.

So where did all that money go? In Katanga, the ore was smuggled out in the dark of night, across the border in beds of covered trucks and railcars, past the eyes of police who hadn't been paid in months and so were hard-pressed to refuse the hush money. It went down through Zambia, Tanzania, and South Africa, where it was processed, then put into giant containers and shipped east into Asia. By the end of 2005, an estimated three quarters of Katanga's minerals were shipped out illegally, greasing the palms of government officials and police on many levels before finally hitting the sea.

The bulk of profits from informal mining never saw the sunlight in Congo, but an estimated $37 million still trickled into Lubumbashi each month, and as a result the city became a boomtown—for some. You felt that money as soon as your plane hit the tarmac, saw it at the customs desk where the official demanded to see the *ordre de mission* of the portly South African, who instead slipped a crisp bill under the window and boarded the mining-company van. It was in the baggage claim, where white men in safari vests stood smoking in rows, their faces like old leather gloves stiffened by sun and whiskey. You felt it on the ride into town, the blacktop smooth as a sheet of marble, with first-world rail guards and streetlights that actually worked at night. It was in the giant billboards advertising Caterpillar tractors and extractors, in the neon signs that blinked from the commercial façades, and in the smell of hot grease that wafted from the chain of KFCs, Lubumbashi's famous Katanga Fried Chiken.

If there was one thing you couldn't find in Lubumbashi, it was a hotel room. The once-stately Leopold II Hotel, now called the Park, was full of miners and Belgian investors, and if you did cadge a room, it would cost you two hundred dollars a night. A soda in the bar was three dollars, served on trays by black waiters in white coats and gloves. With every hotel booked or too expensive, we threw ourselves at the mercy of the Catholic Church, which operated a procure near the grand cathedral. The priest had informed us there were no rooms there, either, until Lionel practically dropped to his knees and begged, explaining how we "were good practicing Catholics and servants of the Lord," until the priest felt sorry for us and offered the floor of his own apartment. When he heard our plan to ride the trains to Kalemie, he laughed so hard he had to brace himself against the wall. "Oh, we shall see!" he howled.

We waited a full week at the procure but I was never bored or sorry to be there. The place was a catchall for the new players in town because the room rates were cheap and included two hots a day. It was a clean way station for foreigners looking for middle-man deals, men who left in the early morning and returned well past dark, putting in their time in hopes of leaving on a first-class upgrade with a full wad of cash and never looking back.

The local diggers operated there, too, trolling the long, shaded corridor like trench-coated pushers at the junior high. One morning after breakfast, I walked out of the dining room and was approached by a guy in a tank top and Kangol cap. His eyes pointed down to his pants pocket, from which he produced a small film canister. He popped open the lid, and inside I saw something that looked like a blob of silver.

"What is it?" I said.

"Liquid mercury."

"Huh?"

"I can get four tons by tonight. Interested?"

That same afternoon while we were walking through town, two men approached us wanting to sell us three tons of coltan. They'd dug it out of a mine eight hundred kilometers north of town and were looking for a buyer to load it onto trucks to Tanzania, then by boat to South Africa. The price was seventy-five thousand dollars.

"It's an open mine," the guy said, "and there's lots more where that came from."

"What about taxes to the government?" I asked.

"Maybe a few hundred dollars to the local chief," he said. "The government doesn't even know it exists. And we have people who can get it across the border, no problem. So are you interested?"

I told them no, and after talking to them a while longer, I learned they were both medical and law students at the local university, trying to sell black-market coltan just to pay their tuition. As they said, "Everyone there does it."

At breakfast the next morning at the procure, I explained the coltan deal to Leo, a Chinese miner who worked for a Canadian firm, or who lived in Canada and worked for a Chinese firm; he was never very clear, and I liked that about him.

"Seventy-five thousand dollars?" he said, tipping the jar of instant coffee into his cup, then drowning it in steaming milk. *"Oh man."*

I'd first seen Leo the day we arrived, walking into the procure with a group of local men, hired translators dressed in starched shirts with threadbare collars and holding clipboards. They'd disappeared into a conference room, where I could hear their conversation as I sat reading in the courtyard outside. Leo was loud and arrogant with the Congolese, bragging in his strangled accent about how much money he was making in Katanga. "We buy twenty thousand tons of copper and ship it to warehouse in China," he'd said. "Twenty thousand tons. Tons! Tons! Then we sell, sell, sell! My friends, we work three months out of year, and rest of time—drive cars and lots of girls! Ha! Ha! Ha!"

So at breakfast, I was anxious to hear his opinion on the coltan deal, more as just a conversation piece. He dumped six spoonfuls of sugar into his coffee and, before he could finish what he was saying, held up his palm. "I explain everything after prayer." He bowed his head and his lips moved in rapid silence. He finished his prayer and looked up. "Seventy-five thousand dollars?" he said. "You get ripped off, man. I get for you much cheaper. Ha! Ha! Ha!"

An Indian named Sibu also usually ate with us. He'd been in Lubumbashi for five months but hadn't been so lucky. The day I met him, Sibu was wearing a bandage over his eye, blood still seeping through the gauze, and his cheek was purple and swollen. He'd been badly beaten by the mayor's soldiers two days before, he said, after a mining deal gone sour. He'd gotten mixed up with some Chinese newcomer looking for easy contacts and, with nothing of his own cooking at the moment, agreed to accompany the Chinese guy to a cobalt mine outside town. Soldiers stopped them on the road and asked for their mining certificates. They only had tourist visas, and an hour later they found themselves in the police station facing the commander. "We can make all of this go away for two thousand dollars," the commander said.

"It's worth it," Sibu told the Chinese guy, but he refused and demanded to see the mayor.

The soldiers brought the two men to the mayor and separated them. Sibu was a citizen of Tanzania, an African. So instead of risking trouble with the Chinese embassy, the mayor ordered his men to beat Sibu instead. Sibu eventually paid them four hundred dollars of his own money just for them to stop. The Chinese miner was released and now ignored Sibu on the streets. This was a small and not unusual price to pay for doing business in Lubumbashi, and for small-time guys, these risks were part of the gamble.

A few days later, Sibu got a job with a Canadian looking to land a contract with Gécamines, the government-mining agent. The Canadian needed someone to shepherd the process, someone on the ground who would smooth things along for a cool 10 percent. The contract was for one hundred tons of copper.

"The price on the London market is nearly eight grand a ton," the Indian said. "Multiply that by a hundred, then factor my cut." He smiled and bobbed his bloodied, bandaged eyebrows. "Not bad. *Not bad at all*." The contract was still tied up with the government by the time I left, and I never heard whether Sibu ever landed the big score.

The passenger train wasn't arriving for several more days so we used the time to explore the station and the yard. The SNCC had carefully maintained the colonial architecture of the station, everything from the cobblestone on the platforms, to the giant station clock that still kept the time, and the café with bonewood chandeliers draped with silver garland. In a way, the café itself resembled an old dining-car saloon, so cool that Lionel and I found ourselves returning there every day for beers, tall bottles of Simba that we drank slowly as the crisp Katanga breeze called down the night. Once the waiter even dragged a couple of beer crates onto the platform itself and let us drink there, right atop the giant copper arrow pointing north, toward where we hoped to go.

The station sat at the end of a wide cobblestone square, where three old locomotives sat high on earthen platforms like sentinels, proud trophies of the glory days. The steam, diesel, and electric engines—progressive touchstones along the time line—were painted blue and yellow, shimmering in the sun, and looking mighty. They were the first things you saw when rounding the corner from the Park Hotel, and the sight of such beautiful machines made me want to run toward them, made me want to hear the locomotive blow its high, brassy whistle, made me thirsty for a cold beer in the old café.

Many of those same proud machines now sat idle and rusting on the rails, and the sight of them boiled the blood of Fabien Mutomb, whose office overlooked the central yard. Fabien was the director of logistics at SNCC, a company man who kept the president's stoic portrait above the calendar on his wall, but over the years he had become a dispirited patriot. He now chaired the local chapter of the opposition party, and during our regular visits that week to his office, we'd be audience to his venom-fueled soliloquies against the plague of corruption.

"How can we redevelop this country when all of its people are looking to steal?" he said one afternoon. "We have one of the biggest mining industries in the world, but no real contracts to feed back into the country. We send men to check the validity of these contracts, to weed out the fake ones, but the people we send can't even afford a bicycle ride to work. You show these men one hundred dollars and they bend like everyone else. We're talking billions of dollars in contracts. Even the mayor of Lubumbashi has a concession."

Fabien pointed out the window, where nothing had moved all morning. "I can show you what leaves this station in the middle of the night, all that cargo on its way to Zambia, and it's a scandal. I can show you what the average Congolese eats in one day, and your dog probably eats more. Years ago you could get a well-paying job here at the mines, benefits and everything. Now the dream of young people here is to make it to South Africa and wash the streets. People are now saying, 'Let's bring back the white man.' Can you believe that? 'Bring back the white man because we can't do it ourselves.' There is no more dream in this country, no more ambition. The dream here is dead."

The railroad employed thousands of people in company towns all along the line, but still owed these workers two years of back pay, and most hadn't seen a cent in months. As a result, they'd clustered in the SNCC company camps and slowly gone down with the ship. That afternoon, Fabien wanted us to see these people, for no other reason, I guess, than to remind himself they were still around.

We climbed into Fabien's pickup and crossed the wide railyards that once served as the final bulwark between the city's whites and blacks. Across the tracks was the *cité indigène*—the colored town of old Elizabethville, where black colonial police ensured no one left unless to work, or unless they held the card of the *évolué*, the badge that certified an extra effort to adapt had been made.

We tore down a straight dirt road, kicking up red dust behind our wheels, until we arrived at the workers' camp. The road divided two sections of trim brick cottages, once prim and efficient, now derelict and crumbling in the sun. Manioc gardens grew in plots inside the maze of homes, and down the road a young boy ran dragging behind him a tattered kite made of black plastic bags.

As we sat in the truck with Fabien, a frail old man emerged from the warren of houses and walked over. He carried a bundle of documents under his arm, and I thought of all the men you saw in every town and city across Congo, men who put on their one good suit or collared shirt each morning, briefcase in hand or a bundle of documents under their arm, and set out to search for a job that didn't exist, until the act of searching, of walking around the same blocks with that same look of purpose on their faces, became the vocation itself.

As the old man approached the truck with his documents, I hoped that's what he'd been doing that day, out looking for a better job in the boom, getting his piece of that gleaming $37 million a month. But as the old man stepped forward and Fabien rolled down the window, he reached his wrinkled hand inside the cab and said, "Boss, we're starving." Fabien looked at him and said nothing.

"Boss, please, we need—"

"I know," Fabien snapped, and took the man's hand off the wheel. He clasped it for a second, then said, "We'll take care of you. Just be patient."

It must have been all the old man needed to hear; he withdrew his arm from the cab, turned, and walked away. Then Fabien rolled up the window and the truck moved forward. "Like I was telling you," he said, his eyes nailed to the road, "those are the camps."

As the sun continued to rise every morning over Katanga, the rail workers left the squalor of those company camps and returned to work, out of duty and a dog-blind faith in the boss who told them, "Just be patient," and from a knowledge deep in their marrow that if they ever quit, death wouldn't be far behind.

So the morning we were scheduled to depart, the rail workers awoke before dawn as usual, ate their meager breakfast of manioc and tea, and filed down the long dirt road and across the tracks, hoping perhaps today the payroll boss would be there smiling. But the payroll boss wasn't there, so they slipped into their green coveralls anyway and prepared for the morning train to Kalemie.

We'd arrived there at six thirty, just as the workers were trickling in and the first soft light was creeping across the iron tracks. I sat on a pile of luggage against the station wall and watched four women begin their daily chore of sweeping the platform. They bent their backs toward the ground and slashed their short straw brooms against the concrete like scythes, flinging the dust in every direction. Just as one woman scoured a patch clean, another would come alongside and cover it back with dirt. Down a ways, another woman swept a pile of gravel for an hour. There seemed to be no end to their work other than the work itself, since the cloud of dust would no doubt settle again and guarantee more work tomorrow.

I was thinking long and hard about what Charles Diamba had told us the previous day when we'd visited his office to inquire about our trip. Diamba was the station manager of Lubumbashi, the same man who'd sent the World Food Programme train on without telling us. He'd called the day before to say there was good news about our train to Kalemie. After stewing in Lubumbashi for days, and after visiting the workers' camp, I was ready for some good news. We'd walked into Diamba's office and exchanged the standard Congolese greeting.

"*Ça va?*" we'd said. How's it going?

"*Ça va un peu,*" he replied. It's going a little.

Then, also in standard Congolese form, Diamba began by telling us the bad news first. He sat behind his desk and read out a list of things gone wrong. How the SNCC had only thirty working locomotives to serve over three thousand kilometers of track, how the newest engine dated back to 1975, the year of my birth, how they only kept the trains running by cannibalizing one to fix another. The state of the tracks was deplorable, he said, with just about every kilometer of rail needing to be replaced. "North of Kamina," he said, "part of the track is actually missing, so the engineer just hits the gas and prays."

Over the past year, residents along the 750 kilometers of electric track between Lubumbashi and Dilolo had ripped down twenty-five hundred tons of cable, using tree branches as tools, and sold it to foreigners for scrap, causing the entire system to shut down for weeks for repairs. And if that wasn't enough—"If the traders feel they haven't sold enough product during our station stops," he said, "they'll rip out the brake systems. It may take days to fix. And our workers haven't been paid in months, so how do you expect them to keep an eye on things and enforce the rules?"

He paused and leaned forward. "Once you get outside Lubumbashi, it's the Wild West. *Vous comprendez le Wild West, monsieur?*"

I'm afraid so, I said. But wasn't there some good news?

"The good news," he said, "is you won't have to deal with much
of that. You'll be traveling aboard the *Rénové*, our luxury express.
If all goes well, you could be in Kalemie in three days. *But that's if
all goes well.*"

We'd been hearing about the *Rénové* for days, but weren't harbor-
ing any expectations. We'd seen another passenger train leave a couple of days before going to Dilolo, just off the Angolan border, with
hundreds of bodies crushed inside, arms and faces pressed against the
glass and dangling out windows. The whole caravan had the whiff of
smoked fish and warm urine. I asked one of the workers what kind
of train that was considered, and he'd replied, "Second class."

We'd also heard nightmare stories about the *Kambelembele*, a passenger train that had recently left and taken three months to reach
Kindu. There'd been twenty carriages and two thousand people
crammed inside. The day the train left, two children had been
crushed on the platform as people rushed the doors. That was in
Lubumbashi. No telling how many had died along the way.

So in Diamba's office, I didn't know how to interpret what he
meant by "luxury." And I certainly wasn't comforted to hear him
say, as he rushed out to catch a meeting, "It's true. This company
should've shut down years ago."

As I sat on the platform that morning amid the cloud of broom
dust, I was wondering what kind of luxury train would roll in the
Congo, and if the *Rénové* was as much a harbinger of revival as its
name suggested. It was all speculation, of course, until I heard the
screeching feedback of an announcer on a microphone and the
faint whistle bellowing down the yard.

The several hundred people who'd arrived to board the train were
corralled inside an airless waiting room just off the main platform.

When the whistle sounded down the yard, the iron gates opened and the people spilled forward into the cool air, lugging several tons of bags and boxes atop their heads and dragged behind. They flooded onto the platform, where a fat man greeted them with a microphone and a sweep of his arms. "Ladies *a-a-a-a-nd* gentlemen," he shouted. "*Welcome* to the *Rénové!*"

The fat man, whom everyone called the *animateur*, was the showman and jester hired to keep our spirits high on the long journey ahead. He was also the company tout, the snake-oil salesman sent to promote the *Rénové* to the people along the route, to convince the frail and dispirited masses that change was finally here. Now, like a ringleader in a juggle of spotlights, the *animateur* swept his stubby arm into the air and the *Rénové* rumbled into the yard.

She was an electric locomotive pulling three sleeper cars behind, bright blue and yellow birds like the one I'd seen that day in the Kalemie yard, plus a copper-sided dining carriage straight out of *Bonanza*. As the train rolled to a stop, the powerful sun blasted through the windows on the opposite side, bending starbursts of golden light out the other.

"This is no ordinary train," cried the *animateur*. "This is the luxury express going straight to Kalemie. No, no, people, this is not the train of yesterday . . ."

"It's quite beautiful," Lionel said.

"Yeah, so it was true."

We pulled our tickets from our pockets, for which we'd paid a staggering $140 each (ticket prices started at $75), and found our assigned carriage: *565 Premiere Classe Deluxe*. Our car was the rear caboose, and the two of us jumped aboard.

Inside, I found myself back in that discovered fort deep in the woods, reliving that same dream as that day in the Kalemie yard. Was this the same car? No, it was better. Open the wood-panel doors and there was the restroom with a stainless-steel toilet with a step-flush contraption and sink. I ran down the long corridor, bathed in brassy light by a wall of windows, and found cabin B, our home for the journey. The eight-by-eight-foot room had a fold-down table in the center, flanked by bunk beds on either side, with soft leather mattresses dressed in pink sheets and blankets, all monogrammed with the SNCC logo.

We threw our bags onto the beds and walked two carriages down to the restaurant car, still holding out the dream of cold beers at sunset watching the savanna. And upon reaching the corridor, I saw a man loading crates of Simba into the train, hoisting the black plastic boxes onto his knees and stacking them in the pantry. He was skinny as sugarcane and wore a white apron.

It was our chef, Andre, who shook our hands and welcomed us aboard. He told us he'd spent fifteen years cooking for a big-shot Belgian brewery executive and his family. When that job ended, he was picked up by the SNCC, which, judging by his expression, had been like moving back home to care for his parents, who'd turned senile and diaper-bound.

"But be assured," he said, "I can prepare recipes for every na-tionality." He smiled and gave a dignified bow. "Please request any-thing you wish, it will be a pleasure."

On the way back to our room, we caught a glimpse of the dark kitchen and looked at one another in wide-eyed amazement. "Look, he cooks on coals!" Lionel said.

Séverin was standing in the room when we entered, still holding his bags. What do you think? I asked him. It certainly beats riding a bike through the jungle.

"It's good," he said, and surveyed the room. "But I still don't be-lieve it."

"What's not to believe?" I said. "Look at these beds. And we just met the chef, Andre, who's gonna cook big dinners for us."

"I'll believe it when we move," Séverin said. "If you notice, we're already two hours and twenty minutes behind schedule."

Lionel smiled and popped him on the shoulder. "Welcome to Congo, bro."

Séverin cringed. We'd tried that joke on him all week, much to our own amusement, but it never seemed to land. He'd just grit his teeth and smile. Sometimes we suspected he hated us.

All week in Lubumbashi we'd teased Séverin about a girl named Nanu, a strong-headed waitress we'd met in the Versailles bar. Lionel and I had gone there one afternoon and she'd chatted us up, told us how she was from Kinshasa but had come to Lubumbashi after high school to work in her aunt's bar. "I miss Kin," she said, breathless. "Lubumbashi is . . . *uh, so boring.*" She was cocky and kind of obnoxious, so naturally we thought she was perfect for Séverin.

We brought him there the next afternoon and introduced him. "He's a really sweet guy," we said, pointing at Séverin, whose face was as close to beet red as possible, all smiles and teeth, and probably cursing our cold graves under his breath.

A few weeks before, Séverin had been accepted to the University of Liège in Belgium to study education and computer science that fall, an accomplishment we'd been celebrating all week. So of course we laid it on thick to Nanu. "He's going to Belgium on a scholarship," we said. "He's very intelligent, wants to learn Chinese so he can make a lot of money. He's very industrious like that. He'll be a big-shot banker one day, maybe even president."

Nanu stepped back and studied him for a long beat, then made small talk in Lingala: where are you from, what's your last name, and so on. When she walked back into the kitchen, we prodded him to make his move: "Get her number, man." And when she returned, he pulled a pen and notebook from his back pocket and, as cool as peppermint ice cream, said, "Give me your number. I'm going to call you." She took a breath and cocked her head, beaten at her own game, then dished out the digits.

Every day after that we'd teased him about marrying Nanu,

insisted he was stealing away in secret after work to the Versailles bar to see his new girlfriend. He'd just grit his teeth and smile. Until one day he said flatly, "I don't see her. Her phone is turned off." It turned out he'd been calling every day and stopping by the bar, only to be told she was home sick.

We started giving Séverin tips about wooing Nanu, making him listen to Fela Kuti late at night, Lionel saying, "Mate, to get the girls you need good music."

He nodded. "Like Phil Collins—"

"*No, man*, not Phil Collins. Play Fela, and turn the lights down."

He'd finally gotten through to Nanu after a week of calling her phone. But minutes into their conversation, she'd mentioned she needed to go, then asked for Lionel's phone number. Séverin had even called Lionel at the bar and asked permission to give out his number. Lionel never picked up when Nanu called, but the damage had been done.

From then on, we were always trying to get a rise out of Séverin. What usually worked was my reenactment of our hellish day in the mud near Kisangani, where I'd tie a Rambo bandanna around my head, fists knotted toward heaven, and scream, *"Porco Dio PORCA MADONNA DIO CANE!"* until he snorted from laughter.

Séverin was right about being late. After adding four additional carriages, the train sat there in the sun all morning and afternoon, while we sweated in our room and paced the crowded platform. Then a whistle would blow and send us running, just to be told to wait some more. Finally around five o'clock, the whistle gave one long whine. The station agents scudded people into the carriages and we lurched forward. We'd just about cleared the platform when the baggage car snapped loose from the locomotive and stranded us again.

An old mechanic standing near the locomotive said the first day of our journey would be along the electric lines, the best section of track on the network. If we punched it through the night, we could keep up over fifty kilometers per hour and make some time. After that, the track was old, so old it had busted loose from the ballasts. For this stretch we'd switch to the diesel and crawl down the line on our hands and knees. As he spoke, I watched the tracks in the station bounce up and down as the locomotive pushed the new baggage car into place. Even here at home base, the rails weren't bolted to the ground.

But before I could register that fear, the long whistle sounded and it was time for us to board. Hanging out the window, I saw how the setting sun struck the station and illuminated the darkened letters of ELIZABETHVILLE, still visible where decades of dust and bleaching African sun had yet to blot out the colonial name. And as the *Rénové* rolled away from old Elizabethville, the agents and family members left standing on the platform cheered and waved good-bye and sent us into the falling night, knowing they might never see anyone on that train again.

I remained in the window as the train rumbled out of the yard, feeling the cool wind whip through my clothes and hair, and marveled at how even ten seconds of true forward progress was enough to clear away the fog of a week's wait. I stood there breathing in all those charged, electric molecules that swim in the air of virgin darkness and couldn't seem to remember anything that had happened before then. The adventure had begun, and I sucked the moment down into the very floor of my being, and as I did, I felt a slight stab of sadness in my guts, for I knew this was my last adventure across the great country.

We sat on our bunks and kept the windows open, rocking back and forth as the train collected speed, spinning on electric tracks in a land where most had never owned a lightbulb. As Séverin snored from the upper bunk, Lionel and I brought cold beers from the dining car, rolled a joint, and passed it in the dark, zoning out to the way the steel wheels sounded like swords clashing underneath.

About thirty kilometers outside town we stopped at a small station platform, and in the stillness I heard the hum of wilderness in the trees, not the biblical swarms of insects like on the river, but the shrill whistle of nothingness, that white noise that fills truly empty expanses of space. A single fluorescent bulb flickered on the platform, casting silhouettes of the power lines above. We heard the sounds of the crew, men shouting in Swahili, "*Wanakuita!* They're calling you," their flashlights darting along the tracks like lightning bugs. The whistle sounded twice, a short and friendly tap on the shoulder that said, "Look out, a train is coming." And sure enough, a whistle screamed on the opposite track and a train rumbled past, gliding by slow like a black, sparkling beast breathing through our open window. All I could see were white T-shirts emerging in the dark, the rest concealed by night.

"*Tika, tika*, Dilolo, Dilolo!" they shouted from the passing train. Séverin stirred from his sleep long enough to hear their shouts and explained they were former child soldiers who'd recently disarmed. But instead of joining the army, they'd gone to work in the maize fields of Dilolo in service of the government, migrant field hands now rolling across the vast country at night.

"*Tika, tika*, Dilolo Dilolo," they shouted in Lingala ("Losers stay put, we're from Dilolo"), until their taunts faded and were swallowed by the night.

The whistle blew a labored wheeze as we cut the darkness toward Kamina. As the train gained speed over the open tracks, we lay on our backs and stared up through the open windows, where the heavens froze and pulsed with the flush of my lungs.

"The sky is unbelievable."

"Yes, you can see everything, every single one of them."

Lying there, it dawned on me we weren't alone inside this little box, where beer bottles clanged in the dark and the Specials played quietly from small speakers on the table—but were attached to a living chain of hundreds of souls, all silent now from the chilly wind and lullaby of forward motion, that great regulator of the road. It was one of those rare unspoken moments, I thought, when all of us people came a little closer to being one and the same.

But who were all these people? I told myself I'd find out tomorrow.

I awoke the next morning with the sting of warm sun on my face, forgetting where I was for a moment, until I felt the rumble of wheels and the groan of the old caboose as it reckoned with another day. Rising in my bed, I saw the door slid open and Séverin standing in the corridor by the wall of windows. We'd reached Tenke, he said. Looking out, I saw the brown hills surging from the savanna like camel humps and remembered reading how they indicated the cobalt deposits below.

Tenke, 237 kilometers northwest of Lubumbashi, was a smattering of brick mining homes with tin roofs surrounded by hills and brown scrub. The area had been developed around the 1920s after the mine was discovered, and where studies would later reveal contained ore ten times as rich in copper than most similar ores found around the world. Phelps Dodge estimated the site would produce around four hundred thousand metric tons of copper over the next decade.

Tenke was also the junction for trains heading west to Dilolo, where they once linked with Angola's majestic Benguela Railway, which after the war only had about thirty miles of functional track, near the Atlantic port of Lobito. But a new $30 million project, funded by Hong Kong–based China International Fund Ltd., had begun to rehabilitate the entire network, reconnecting Congo's quick link to the Atlantic. Repairing the railway also guaranteed the Chinese financiers lucrative concessions in oil fields off the coast of Angola, which was being prepped to become a major world producer.

As we rolled through Tenke, I heard a clanging sound somewhere in the next compartment. A few seconds later, an old man stumbled down the corridor ringing a large yellow bell, bracing himself against the windows as the train jerked around the turns. He rattled it like a Salvation Army Santa, shouting, *"Karibu, karibu."* Everyone was welcome to the dining car, breakfast was ready.

And what a breakfast! It was almost too good to believe, riding that decrepit rail network through a country as broken as it was, and here I was being seated at a table dressed with clean, red cloth and white china, each table situated near windows that opened to the sweeping, aurelian plain. The rising sun was on the right and warmed our faces after the brisk and chilly night, and the breeze pulled in soft notes of wild eucalyptus and jasmine blooming on the prairie.

The waiter burst out of the kitchen balancing ten plates of omelets in his arms, each dish wobbling to the jerks and jolts as if spinning on pencils, and set them down on tables with a clatter. Another man followed with hot milk and packs of Nescafé, and while he poured the frothy milk, we steadied our cups and watched it steam in our hands. That morning, as dishes rattled off tables and most of my coffee ended up in my lap, the two dozen war-weary passengers in that dining car ate quietly in a sheen of sublime content—so normal, it was almost boring. Looking back, I regard that first morning aboard the *Rénové* as one of my happiest moments. Because it was the first time out on the road where, for a brief moment, I felt I could've been anywhere in the world.

So again, who were these people?

In Congo, war and peace acted like the mighty arms of a hurricane. One arm would be wrapped with gunboys and death and send thousands into the bush, and meanwhile, across the country, another arm carried providence and relief and guided the lost ones home. Tens of thousands in, tens of thousands out. War and peace always seemed to sync. At that particular moment to pick out one instance, fighting in North Kivu between Rwandan Hutu rebels and the army was pushing droves into the mountains, while here in Katanga, hundreds of thousands who'd fled the great war were finally looking homeward.

When the second war began in August 1998, the fighting had emptied villages and towns between Kalemie and Kabalo and pushed people south toward Lubumbashi, while countless others fled over the borders into Zambia and Tanzania, where the refugee camps became permanent little cities. Those who'd fled to Kamina and Lubumbashi also remained in camps, where conditions had improved little.

All throughout that spring, UNHCR (UN High Commissioner for Refugees) was repatriating thousands from Zambia on ferryboats and trucks across the border. I'd wanted to meet some of those people, but could never align my own trip with their convoys. But at the same time, that benevolent arm of the storm was returning all those who'd fled Kalemie and villages in the north. My best option, I thought, was to meet them once I arrived in Kalemie.

That morning after breakfast, Séverin and I walked eight cars to the front of the train, where I began meeting everyone aboard. And by the time I'd made it halfway through the first carriage, I realized my search for the homeward-bound had in fact found me.

Almost everyone aboard the *Rénové* had fled the war and was returning home for the first time, going home to reunite with family, going home to check on friends and property, to reclaim jobs, to start again.

They'd all left in similar ways when the gunfire had sounded on the shores of Lake Tanganyika, signaling the Rwandans had arrived and the country was at war. They'd scattered south in blind pandemonium, coming together in small groups on nameless dirt roads, and started walking. They walked for days and weeks, across the barren scrub and over the hills, into battlefields shifting and destroying, and like the countless others I'd asked to relive that horror, they watched their children, husbands, and wives murdered by soldiers, starve to death in the tall grass, or simply vanish from sight. The dead were laid to rest without ceremony in hand-dug graves along the trail, and the dead who are buried this way do not glow like the fields of copper.

For nearly a decade they'd lived in the squalid camps of Lubumbashi and Zambia, or with relatives if they were lucky, scattered across the windswept plain with one eye always on the road back home. So when the trains finally started running, they jumped aboard the first ones to leave, knowing there might not be another train again. Many had been saving money for years for the ticket in case the opportunity arose.

Inside the *Rénové*, the company had packed them ten deep in the second-class compartments. They sat buried in children and luggage and took turns sleeping on the two sheetless beds. The carriages were hot and already smelled of moldered vegetables, the way humans tend to smell when they sleep and sweat too close together.

"They told us three days to Kalemie," one man said. "And what's three days when you've already waited this long?"

Séverin and I spent the afternoons going from compartment to compartment, making friends while standing in the doorways taking down notes. In compartment 3211C, Jeanne Mbuyi was going to Kalemie to see her five kids for the first time since that day in August. She'd been selling salt and soaps in Moba, near the Zambian border, when the Rwandans crossed the lake. Her husband fled with the children without her, catching a boat across to Tanzania, where they lived five years in the camps. Jeanne herself had ended up in the camps of Zambia. For years they didn't even know one another was still alive, until a family member heard the kids were still in Tanzania, somewhere near Kigoma. So Jeanne was setting out to find them. "I don't even have an address," she said. "Just an idea, a feeling where they might be."

In 3211C, a man named Floribert Tumbwe was going home to see his wife and two children. They'd lived outside Kalemie and waited out the initial invasion, until one early morning, when Tumbwe awoke and stepped outside to relieve himself. While in the outhouse, government soldiers appeared at his door, shouting, "Where is your husband?" It was a sweep of suspected rebels, he said, and many men were being killed. "So I decided to run," he said. "I didn't even say good-bye." Through friends, he later learned soldiers had returned two days later and killed his two oldest sons.

Overcome by shame and guilt, he remained in Lubumbashi where he'd fled and was only now attempting to contact his wife and two other children. "I need to see what's become of them," he said. "If they're even there at all."

All down the line the stories were similar, the same stories I'd heard in Bunia, Drodro, Bukavu, Aveba, and every place where people had awoken one morning unaware that at some point during the day their livelihood would crumble to dust, everything they owned would be lost, and they'd be force-marched into a years-long struggle to survive where every day was a new blade on the heels.

The train was full of those people, from the woman in 3214A who said to me, "You ask me if I'm happy to be going home? My family will never be the same after what happened, how can I be happy?" to the man so filled with anticipation at going home to see his mother, he worried she might not recognize him. "I'm fatter now and lost all my hair," he said. When he finally got home, he said, "I will ask her to make my favorite dish. Peas. My mother makes really good peas."

★ ★ ★

In the late afternoon we arrived at Bukama, where the Congo River met the rails. If you depended on news searches to tell you anything about Bukama, you'd know that eleven people had been killed by a recent outbreak of cholera, the scourge that crawled out of the ground every few years to take its fill. You'd know about the displaced camp nearby that had been attacked by Mai Mai rebels the year before, forcing tens of thousands to pick up and run, losing step with their lives all over again. And how a train had derailed around that same time, flipping over and crushing eighteen *clandestins* who'd been riding on top.

So of course I thought of these things when Séverin shouted, "Bukama!" and we rolled to a stop. But when I stepped off the train, bracing for a newfound patch of misery, all I heard was music. Haunting, ethereal music that grabbed hold and spun me around. A children's choir was standing on the platform, no doubt pulled together when they'd heard the whistle down the track. They'd struck into song as soon as the wheels stopped rolling, sang through the chaos of passengers coming and going, and the mobs of sellers who swarmed the platform hawking *chikwangue* and dried fish and shouting *"Mayi hapa!"* waving bags of chilled, boiled water for sale. Passengers who remained inside hung their bodies out the windows and listened to the chilling music, carried in full by a young girl soprano whose bright voice gave the songs great, razor-tipped wings. I even watched as the *animateur* readied his microphone and bullhorn, only to sit down near the young girl and shut his eyes to the sound.

We rolled out of Bukama with the setting sun and crossed the great river, where orange light bounced off the top and brought back memories of the *Ma'ungano*, standing in the captain's room with Buisine watching the river silver-plate at dusk, hoping the night sky would be clear enough for us to keep moving on.

Construction on the Bukama-Ilebo route, known as the Chemin de Fer du Bas-Congo au Katanga, or Bas-Congo to Katanga Railway

(BCK), began in 1923 with separate teams beginning in the north and the south and slowly working their way toward the middle. Southern crews began in Bukama and were blessed with flat, arid terrain, while teams working from Ilebo slogged their way through thick equatorial jungle and heavy seasonal rain. The construction of the line drew many of the same Greeks and Italians who'd built the Katanga line into Lubumbashi years before, and also attracted a large number of young Europeans looking for adventure in dark, untamed Africa. For those who were hired, the journey to Congo was probably as surreal as anything they'd ever done.

From Europe, workers embarked on a three-week journey by ship to the port of Matadi, then boarded a train on Leopold's railway over the rapids and arrived in Kinshasa two days later. This was followed by a two-week boat ride up the Congo and Kasai rivers, with stops each night to load tons of lumber cut from the dense forests to use on the railroad's construction. At night they slept under mosquito nets in airless cabins, losing the first of many nights' rest to the sucking tropical humidity, listening to the chatter of Congolese crewmen below in the holds and the jungle vibrating outside. Once in Ilebo, the new recruits were put into *tipoyes*, small, basketlike chairs, which porters carried on their shoulders through the jungles to the camps.

Tools and building materials bound for Ilebo followed a similar route through jungle and river, usually taking months to arrive, sometimes an entire year. And when they did finally arrive, workers would amuse themselves by watching the Congolese try to adapt to the foreign equipment. In one account, white contractors arrived at a work site to the spectacle of natives scooping dirt with their hands and placing it into shovels, which they hoisted on their heads to unload. Full wheelbarrows of dirt were unloaded the same way.

Food and medical supplies arrived on average once per month. The Congolese crews were given six kilograms of manioc and maize, along with pieces of dried fish and beef taken from the colony's herds near the mouth of the Congo. Whites, by contrast, received monthly "medical comfort" boxes from Belgium, loaded with canned meats and vegetables, along with many luxuries shipped in from the modern world. One such medical-comfort inventory listed four boxes of pâté, two cartons of Camembert cheese, chocolate, whiskey, cognac, and two full cases of Bordeaux.

The construction through the jungle was exhausting and slow, food supplies ran low, and heavy rains often destroyed several days' progress, forcing crews to begin all over again. White foremen also found themselves in tricky negotiations with local chiefs for permission to proceed through tribal land. In one account, a local chief forced a young Belgian foreman into nightly drinking marathons, where the chief would agree to allow the railroad, then withdraw his approval the following morning. This went on for weeks before the chief finally gave in, but not before seriously depleting the "medical boxes" the foreigners so dearly cherished.

The north and south lines finally converged on February 13, 1928, in a stretch of jungle 762 kilometers northwest of Bukama and 359 kilometers southeast of Ilebo. A small ceremony was attended by the European workers, dressed in pith helmets and starched white shirts, and native laborers, in their bare feet staring stoically into the camera. A white-stone pillar was erected at the site, indicating the time and date of the union, and the chief of the BCK Railway was present to drive the last bolt. As the first train crossed the junction at 2:40 P.M., a priest popped a bottle of champagne. The entire ceremony took place under a driving equatorial rain.

On our second night on the train, just after dark, we arrived at a village called Mulundu, where another choir of children gathered at the base of our window shouting for *"Copo! Copo!"*—wanting bottles or cans they could use for toys. We tossed some empty water bottles out the window and the kids danced at the wheels, then tore away in fright when the *Rénové* blew three short whistles, a call of distress. It was a sound I'd grow accustomed to in the days ahead. For here in Mulundu, we experienced our first breakdown.

The cable that supplied power to the electric engine had snapped. And after several hours of waiting, the engineer came by and said, "If we can't fix the power line, we'll have to switch to the diesel." The diesel locomotive was being pulled behind the electric for later use. "But that will mean we'll run out of fuel before Kalemie."

We waited at Mulundu for eight hours and tried to sleep, despite the gang of children who returned outside our window to demonstrate their gangly kung fu moves and sing goofy songs like, "Mzungu likes chicken and eggs, mzungu likes chicken and eggs. Ooh ooh ooh, mzungu . . ." Around two in the morning, the broken cable was fixed and we continued with the electric locomotive pulling us toward Kamina. It was a good thing we weren't forced to switch to the diesel engine, because the following day we discovered it had a busted alternator. If we had switched, we would've broken down minutes later, stranded with two dead engines. And while waiting in Mulundu, we'd stepped out into the dark to get some air and found out the tracks were still stamped with the signature of the BCK Railway and hadn't been touched since their construction in 1925.

But the true condition of the railway didn't register until the next morning when we pulled into Kamina. There, lined up for half a mile, sat boxcar after boxcar loaded with freight that hadn't moved in months, some even a year, simply because there weren't enough locomotives to haul them.

Just like on the river, the war had stopped the movement of essential goods and merchandise along the railway, severing market towns one from the other and isolating them on the plain. Farmers and traders were displaced and removed from their fields and stalls, and even if there were goods to ship, rebels and soldiers had commandeered locomotives for moving troops and supplies. All of this created a massive hunger crisis, and basic goods such as salt, soap, oil, and used clothing were in extreme demand. Like the folks I'd met on the river, the traders in Katanga braved countless obstacles just to get flour, sugar, and medicines into the villages, risked soldiers and rebels, bad weather and bandits, and the myriad other traps that lie hidden during war.

Now peace had returned to Katanga and people were going home. The traders were back in their stalls, and farmers in the mostly barren province were enjoying a bumper crop of maize. But amid all these hopeful things, the economy remained stalled because the railroad was in shambles. As we rolled into Kamina, it became clear that peace and goodwill alone could not revive Congo's economy, not without the infrastructure to move it along.

Back when I'd visited in 2003, everyone was saying how the problem was structural: just repair the two blown-out bridges at Niemba and Zofu and all those cars would ride again with prosperity in their hulls. "Fix those bridges," an American aid worker had told me, "and the markets will blossom."

So the American government and the Belgians fixed those bridges for a million dollars apiece, nothing compared to how much it cost to fly in C-130s loaded with food aid. (It cost one thousand dollars per ton to send a UN cargo plane nearly a thousand kilometers from Lubumbashi to Kindu, while a train would cost one fifth that much. The WFP estimated transport ate 60 percent of its budget.) And just like with the elections, once those bridges were finished, we all stood back and waited for greatness.

But what we forgot (or I did) was that decades of neglect and corruption had killed most of the locomotives needed to pull freight over those beautiful bridges. And so the freight backed up and the economy backed up, just as the debt and loss of wages backed up, until the entire network was backed up and filled with stranded boxcars in every station. After all the hungry and barren years of war, the fruit had finally blossomed on the vine, only to hang there and rot in the sun.

III

At Kamina, the lines of stranded boxcars didn't deter the *animateur*. For him, every station was a stage. The fat man waddled off the train in his crisp khaki suit, microphone in hand. An eager assistant followed close behind clutching a remote speaker under his arm like a pet chicken. *"Ladies and gentlemen, this is the* Rénové," he cried. "This is an express train to Kalemie, made for our clients who need to get to their destination quickly. *This is no ordinary train.* This is one seat, one person. We don't stack people and merchandise inside or on the roof. Don't embarrass yourselves, people, this is a special train and she's pulling out soon . . ."

As I jumped off the train and walked under the shadows of the stranded boxcars, a man walked up and stopped. "So this is an express train to Kalemie?" he asked.

"Yes," I said. "The *Rénové.*"

He slapped the steel broadside of one of the cars. "You mean my maize has been sitting here for three months and the *Rénové* just rolls on through? *Incredible!*"

The trail of boxcars wasn't a promising sign for the many traders who also rode the *Rénové*. As the *animateur* had stated, this was a luxury express train—which meant that the *only* train to Kalemie had no room for the mountains of cargo afforded on the river barges, or the rat-infested third-class trains, or the rooftops of freights that so many rode. So instead of taking their cargo with them, the traders had loaded it into separate freight cars in Lubumbashi with hopes of meeting it down the line.

"That's how precarious this life is," said one woman, who'd left boxes of used clothing in a freight car in Lubumbashi, which she prayed would meet her in Kabongo, some 750 kilometers north.

"It could take two months to get there, but then again, it used to take one year. So I'll wait again. It all depends on the goodwill of the SNCC."

Down the tracks in the mechanics' depot, where our locomotives were taken for repairs, goodwill was about the only thing left to spare, and even that was full of cracks. The depot sat half a kilometer down the yard, so Séverin and I walked along the rails, through oil slicks and thornbushes and ancient rusted steamers like dinosaur bones in the tall grass, past the young soldier who clicked his tongue and told me in Swahili, "*Mzungu*, here you go enjoying all our money when we have nothing." We continued down the tracks until we arrived at a giant aluminum hangar opened on both ends, where locomotives sat on rails while men tinkered with them from service pits below.

The depot was like stepping into my great-grandfather's old farm shed, a museum of midcentury, American-made heavy machines, still being maintained and used. The four mechanics stared up into the bellies of the engines, their coveralls jet-black from grease, just like every other surface left exposed in the old garage. Even the men's lockers were coated with an inch of gunk. The depot was loud and smelled like work, and after five minutes you realized that within those walls, greater decisions were being made regarding the nation's future than inside the president's chamber itself.

As I stood watching the workers service the *Rénové*'s locomotive, Joseph Tshibangu, the chief mechanic, walked up beside me. "That's a 1972 General Electric V-eight," he said. "American-made. We used to have fifty like these all along the line, now we're lucky to have ten. They're so old we can't even get parts anymore, so we build the parts ourselves."

It was like a trauma ward for the old network, and it had been that way for years. During the war, the government troops controlled Kamina and kept the depot open to carry soldiers and equipment to the front. But fighting the rebels—who'd seized most of the east, including the Kalemie station—took its toll on the haggard troops, and in turn on the beleaguered railroad employees. "They would hit us with their guns if things didn't work," he said. "They even stabbed one of my mechanics. They were so messed up from the front lines."

Tshibangu's mechanics were now harassed by traders whose goods were stranded at the station. But some of that stranded cargo, mostly boxcars of maize, would be leaving shortly for up north, Tshibangu said. He pointed to a second locomotive being serviced near ours. "We'll send that one soon. But it's the only train from Kamina all month.

"If I had ten strong diesel engines and four electric engines," he added, "I could turn this country around. If these trains were fixed, it would improve everything, everything, especially the conditions in these villages you'll see along the line. If these rails were working, Congo could be a powerful nation."

After a while, the mechanics signaled they were finished with our diesel, then carefully began rolling it into the yard. I watched as the harsh sunlight fell on the engine and exposed its ugly sores as if it were an infirm patient being wheeled out for some air. As I turned to say good-bye to Tshibangu, he shook my hand and said wistfully, "We grew up in better conditions than this. We had a lot of dreams about the future. Back then it was okay to dream big things."

"I'm hearing that a lot," I said, then hesitated. "Maybe things will get better."

He smiled and released my hand. "Maybe so."

We waved good-bye to the mechanics and climbed aboard the diesel, which belched a column of inky smoke and crawled toward the station. But a few hundred feet from the platform, we reversed direction and returned to the depot. After fidgeting with the engine, a mechanic determined we had a busted plug.

"What do we do?" asked one. The others sighed and shook

their heads, then pointed to the second locomotive in the garage, the one scheduled to pull the maize. "Take it from there and we'll fix it later," said Tshibangu. Everyone nodded and agreed, and within minutes we were moving again.

Around noon we finally rolled out of the Kamina yard, leaving the marooned boxcars behind, along with a long trail of peanut shells, empty plastic bags, and mounds of toilet paper and shit where the toilets dropped their loads. Once out of Kamina, the plains stretched far until the earth bent south like the fields of West Texas where I grew up, punctuated now and then with tall, bright flowers, Popsicle red, that stood regal and alone on the expanse. We crawled at ten kilometers an hour over rails that were buried and concealed in the sand, traveling so slowly that a man on a bicycle hugged our tail for an hour, complaining because there wasn't room for him to pass.

That night in the dining car, Andre served us a heaping dinner of fresh *capitain* with vegetables and rice, which he'd artfully sculpted into two rising towers on the plate. *"C'est bon!"* we shouted into the kitchen. *"C'est super, magnifique!"* Andre poked his head around the corner and gave a little bow. "I manage with what I have," he said.

The electricity had disappeared somewhere past Kamina, so we ate by the light of a candle melted to an overturned saucer. And with the orange, dancing light, the creak and moan of the wooden car, and the smell of coal smoke wafting from the kitchen, I expected the Duke himself to swagger by at any moment.

Just after dinner, the wheels screeched to a halt in a station called Lusenji. The diesel's whistle gave three short distress blasts, and we knew the rest. After a few moments, Pancha, the *chef du train*, stopped by our room to say there was bad news. Some workers in the next town had just radioed to say a section of track was missing up ahead. We'd have to send the locomotive back to fetch some technicians. "We'll be here for the night," the chief said, his voice quivering with frustration. "In the meantime, I present to you lovely Lusenji."

In the meantime, the villagers of lovely Lusenji—industrious and on their toes—were seizing an opportunity, bursting out from the bush carrying bowls of *chikwangue*, roasted peanuts, and fresh-water, crying *"Mayi hapa!"* through the darkness. Fires flickered through the trees, as snaking lines of sardine-can torches bobbed along the trail toward the *Rénové*, not an ordinary train, but one that stammered and suffered *à la Congolais*, never sure when the rail would be missing for good and the bottom would fall away.

So the diesel disconnected and left us there. And as it disappeared down the black rail, the mechanics and engineers waved good-bye from the tail. "Be back in a few hours," they shouted. *Ça va,* the crowd answered, *ça va un peu,* we'll be waiting here as always, playing music softly through the window for when you return.

We awoke at first light the next morning, our fourth day on the train, and jumped down to explore Lusenji. Like many of the small rail towns along the way, Lusenji had a small brick station that was the center of everything, with a few grass-topped huts in the distance and not much else. A few village women were selling peanuts and food outside, so I paid a woman one thousand francs (about two dollars) to wash some of my clothes, which had gotten a bit gamy on the trail. She also returned with fresh buckets of water. Since there were no showers on the *Rénové*, we used them to take quick bandanna baths on the back of the caboose.

The railyard was empty and quiet, and a warm, stiff wind whipped the dust into my teeth. At Lusenji, the stranded sacks of maize were stacked as high as my head. A group of men sat atop the bags drinking cups of maize beer (it was good for something), and as I walked passed, they shouted the usual greeting: "Ay *le blanc*, give me money!" They were ragged and filthy, with a layer of dust and grass tangled in their hair. Looking around, I realized they belonged to the long freight train parked next to ours, which I hadn't noticed in the night. It was a freight hauling some of the maize west to Kananga, someone said, and a small city had formed on its flat roof. Amid heaps of bags and bundles sat scores of tired and rangy-looking people, wind-beaten and gaunt. It was a true river barge of the open rails.

Around ten that morning the locomotive rumbled back into the station and rejoined the train. The broken track was fixed, they said, but we'd have to go slow. The engine gave a long, farewell whistle and jerked to life. And as we left the station, everyone ran to the windows to feel the cool breeze drive away the vapor of last night's sewage that rose from the tracks below. It was always good to be moving, for moving was an instant pill that cured everything.

We basked in that liberating breeze for about half an hour. Then the train derailed.

At first there was a screech and guttural sound of grinding steel, then the train lurched to a halt, slinging all the cups and bottles from our table onto the floor.

"Something bad just happened," Lionel said, then we heard someone down the carriage yell, *"DÉRAILLEMENT!"* Everyone poured out of the train into the sun. Sure enough, carriage 32110 had jumped the tracks and been dragged about five hundred feet, plowing a trail about six inches deep. The tracks below the train were completely buried in the sand. The carriage had simply lost traction and skidded off.

One by one, the train passengers made an obligatory pass of the damage like mourners at a wake. Each stooped low to get a good look, then shook their heads to the side. But instead of throwing a fit, cursing, or even giving it a second thought, they simply grabbed their charcoal stoves and moved under the trees to make lunch.

Pancha, the train chief, strolled up behind us and stared at the wayward carriage, its wheels sunk in the sand. *"C'est un petit déraillement,"* he said, waving his hand. "Not a big deal." He said the locomotive would soon leave for Kabongo, fifty kilometers away, to fetch a derailment crew. "We'll be out of here soon. Trust me, it could be worse."

All throughout the trip, I'd been waiting for the derailment. I'd waited for it in the dining car, while doing interviews in the door-ways of second class, and especially while sitting on the toilet. I'd obsessed about it those nights lying in bed as the train pounded the turns and tipped the caboose, worrying if I was lying in the right position on the bed, on the right side of the cabin, trying my best to anticipate the physics of a crash, the jagged path of flight for a six-foot breakable object in a tiny metal box. And now that it had happened, almost without my noticing, I felt a giant sense of relief.

But I knew my level of patience, for it had been field-tested the hard way along the Congo River. So after leaving the chief, I set out to occupy my time. A small village was down the road, where I found a girl selling ripe green oranges and bought a few for the cabin. The prairie had now given way to forest, so the three of us ventured into the trees and found a stream to refill our water jugs, guided by a young boy named Idrissa, who strummed a homemade reed guitar as he walked.

Three hours passed, then six. We finally went to find Pancha. Maybe he had a radio, maybe he had some answers. He'd pulled his mattress out into the shade of the carriage and now lay there with his wife, staring up at the clouds. We asked him how long this would take.

"Ten minutes if we had a crew on board," he said. "But we don't."

Everyone got along with the chief. He was a straight shooter like Fabien, a company man from back in the good ol' days whose loyalty had earned him a bellyful of vinegar.

"You want to know why we're taking so long?" he said, and propped himself up on his elbows, still looking away. "The workers in Kabongo haven't been paid in twenty-five months. They probably started running as soon as they heard our train.

They ran because they knew they had to work. Our crew is probably somewhere in the village now trying to convince them to help one last time. Or they can pretend to be working in the fields and not hear the whistle. And how can we blame them for working in the fields, how else are they going to survive?"

It had gotten so bad, Pancha said, that in places like Lubumbashi, the authorities even threatened to arrest the crews if they didn't come back to work.

"Back when things were good," he said, and I watched his eyes shrink, for we'd reached that storied green pasture of history, never as lush as everyone remembered (how could it be?), but good enough to now make their tired feet throb a little harder, the empty stomach growl a little louder, the marrow in their bones grow a little stiffer. Everyone had his own version of history, and how he'd fit inside it. And everyone had his own reasons why things had gone so bad.

"Back in the good days," Pancha said, "well—it was when the white man ran things."

I'd been hearing it all week, starting with Fabien. I'd heard it again from a pastor going to Kongolo, standing outside during the long Lusenji breakdown, asking me, "When is the white man coming to fix this train? When is he coming back to fix this mess?" Then again from the old man who rang the breakfast bell, who told me with those same pinched eyes, "The black man can't run this company because he lacks compassion. The black man lacks love."

"Whites have the same problem," I said. "Believe me."

"No, no," he shot back. "A black man laughs at his countryman who's suffering. White men would never do that. If a black man continues to run this company, the end is certainly near."

Everyone had his own history. Ask an old man in Kinshasa what he thought of the white man, and he'd spin you a picture of Stanley snapping a whip and taking heads, ol' Bula Matari, the rock breaker, or show you the statue of Leopold now facedown in the city dump. The white man was the UN, the fleshy figure behind the tinted glass with a weakness for Tintin and tight, young girls. And on the river he was *l'étranger*, the thief and mercenary, the cloaked shadow who controlled their leaders with fingers that pulsed with war.

But in Katanga, the bejeweled trough of empire itself, where the international firms took their 80 percent on the straight, and where that strange, warm breeze at midnight was the anxious breath of hundreds more waiting to pounce—well, the people couldn't wait to bring them back.

I understood where it came from, even if I became confused when I gave it too much thought. Yes, life was tough under the colony, especially in the interior, and Africans had few rights or privileges, including in Katanga. But in Katanga there'd been real industry that had required many hands. The people had jobs and contributed to a system that functioned and turned a profit. They'd learned and utilized technologies and reaped the fruits, and as the world spun on its axis, they felt they were part of it. Their fathers and grandfathers fought and toiled during both world wars, helped protect the world from fascists and Nazis, for Belgium's future was theirs as well. They'd even been taught to drive those big locomotives and trusted to move them down the line, only to trade places with white drivers once they crossed into Rhodesia, where a black engineer was still unthinkable.

And when black men had finally taken power in Kinshasa, the whites had fought to keep the system intact in Katanga, before finally giving up and watching it all swirl down the drain—a black man in a leopard-skin hat holding the plug.

That's what Pancha was talking about, same with the pastor and the old man in the dining car, when he said that the "black man" was greedy and heartless and let them down at every turn. To them, Mobutu was just a later cast of the old tribal chiefs in Congo who'd sold their own people into slavery, and just a touch above the *genocidaires* who'd killed so many in Rwanda. That black man was always in the game for himself and couldn't be trusted. And when that black man took the reins, things just fell apart. I couldn't blame them for being bitter. In the end, a man just wants to go to work and be paid.

Pancha was also remembering a brief period, from 1995 to 1997, when South Africans and Belgians had operated the trains under a group called Sizarail. Mobutu had let the rail network grind down to absolutely nothing, until the South African rail company Spoornet brought in Belgian managers and took control of the Lubumbashi–Dilolo line, adding $50 million worth of locomotives and freight cars. It had been one of the only state-run companies under Mobutu that operated well. Freight moved on time, employees were paid quickly and in full, and there were regular, weekly trains. But Laurent Kabila's rebels seized the company in 1997 as they marched toward Kinshasa. They booted the foreigners out and nationalized Sizarail as Mobutu had done with so many foreign companies two decades before. The company quickly went under, and when the war swept through the following year, all those good times everyone remembered limped toward the green pasture and died.

"There's something about the Congolese," Pancha said. "We suffer and endure and never act like it bothers us. People can sleep here in the dirt for four or five days. They'll complain but they won't act. And because they don't act, the company and government let it go by as usual. This mentality developed during the Mobutu years when everyone was forgotten and left to survive on their own through war and everything. We're all so traumatized, yet we don't even know it."

Pancha turned his head and motioned down the tracks, where the afternoon shade was shifting, leaving the hundreds of people to wait in the hot sun.

"Don't you find it bizarre that there are pregnant women, sick people, elderly on board, and they'll sit like this without food for three days and not do anything? The normal travelers will bring three days' worth of food, but in the end it takes eight days to get to the destination. Years ago there was a medical team on board, doctors, nurses, and medicine. Now there's nothing, not even aspirin. Recently we lost one of our own employees, a ticket collector who contracted typhoid on the train. We could do nothing for him and he died. We buried him in Kabongo, just buried him without a funeral. These are the cases we know. No one knows what happens on those freight trains loaded with people. But no matter what happens, there are no demonstrations, no protests, no revolts, nothing from nobody. They just say, 'It's God's will.' That's the mentality. But with this mentality we'll never improve. We simply cannot keep going with this mentality. It's a miracle we're still even a company. How long do we have before the bottom drops? My friend, it could happen tomorrow."

And really, what could I say to that? I walked down the length of the train, where the sun was now in full, hoping the bottom wouldn't drop until we got to Kalemie, until everyone at least got that fair shot to make things better, people like Jeanne and Floribert, who only wanted to find their kids and hold them high above the floor, because we all knew the bottom would drop again.

I'd also met another woman on the same quest. Fatuma Luzingo had boarded the train in Kamina and, like Jeanne, was on a quest to find her three children. When the war swept into Kalemie, Fatuma and her husband had been washing clothes on the shore of the lake. They hurried home to check on their kids, only to discover Fatuma's father had already taken them away. As the shooting got closer, neighbors ran past saying the soldiers were killing people in the streets. With little else to do, Fatuma and her husband followed the crowds into the bush. "We left everything in the hands of God," she said. "I'd never felt so out of control."

They walked for weeks and were finally picked up by Zimbabwean soldiers, who were fighting Rwandan rebels in the area. The soldiers shared their rations and took them to Kamina, where they lived in a camp until the day they boarded the *Rénové*.

Fatuma was thirty-three years old, with long, immaculate braids, and buxom in a way that gave her a deep, throaty voice. It had only been a few months that she was able to speak to her father on the phone and learn about her kids. The children had been one, three, and four years old when she'd seen them last. Nine years will do a lot to kids at that age. "My kids are my blood," she said, undeterred. "I'll recognize them."

And now as I walked down the train, saying hello to people, walking just to walk, I saw her sitting alone on a blanket, fidgety, impatient, all that anxiety and nowhere for it to go. "What is happening?" she snapped. "How many hours can we wait?" She'd run out of money the day before and now depended on her neighbors to feed her and her husband.

Just as I stood there, I heard a long, booming whistle, looked out, and saw the *Rénové* rolling down the track. Everyone leaped up and jumped with joy and sang, *"Wanatukumbuka! Wanatukumbuka!"* SNCC remembered us!

But it wasn't so. The crew said the derailment technicians weren't in Kabongo after all, but aboard that freight train to Kananga, the one we'd passed back in Lusenji. We'd have to intercept them quickly before they got too far away. Standing there, I could almost feel the freightliner drifting farther and farther away, as if our hopes were stuck there on its windswept roof, slowly losing grip.

I went back into the cabin to try to sleep, and when I did, I noticed everything had changed. The cabin now looked small and dingy, and the table was covered with grit. My blankets were scattershot with pollen and grass from the open window, as if someone had emptied a lawn bag onto my bed. Inside the bathroom, there was no running water and had never been. The toilet was caked with hardened shit that snailed over the lid, with ten inches of piss coagulating in the bowl. It was true, we were riding on the last train in Congo, and here's where it finally stopped. Here's where the strong one finally failed to fix the broken one, where the cog in the system finally slid backward and threw us all off the tracks. I needed to sleep. I went into my bag and pulled out a bottle of Jim Beam, took three long pulls, and lay down. When I woke up, it was dark, but that's the only thing that was different.

For several hours we lay on our bunks in the dark listening to music from the battery-powered speaker on the table, the guitars fusing with a rhythm section of insects out the window. After a while, the entire carriage began to gently rock from someone having sex down the hall.

"I think it's Patrick," said Lionel. Patrick was the security guard assigned to the *luxe classe deluxe*, who had told us the day before that Congolese women were the wildest on the continent. "The way they move," he said, "you'd think they had no bones." He'd pulled out a pouch of white powder bought in a shop in Kamina and swore of its powers over women. "Just massage it into your penis forty-five minutes before action, and it's like a tree trunk," he said, clutching his forearm as if pumping a shotgun.

"The black African can last a long time with a woman. But the Congolese woman—she'll destroy a *mzungu* in under two minutes."

Around ten thirty, as I drifted in and out of a hot sleep, I heard a faint whistle and the voices of men, then realized the derailment crew had arrived to fix our train. We ran outside and saw several men jump off a single diesel engine parked behind our caboose. They'd come from Kipokwe, just north of Kamina, and traveled nine hours to get here. The crew wore greasy blue coveralls and shuffled down the rails like tired, old men, calling out in Swahili to the *Rénové* crew, "We've come to help you, so be real men and get to work. No standing around!"

The *Rénové* crew scrambled to help carry their equipment, enduring their gripes all the way down the line. "We haven't eaten since this morning. We're starving! And do you know how dangerous it was to rescue you? We risked derailing ourselves. *Then where would you be!?*"

Standing next to the derailed car, Lionel pulled a camera from his bag and started shooting. As he pressed in close, one of the derailment crew barked, "You're just here to take pictures? Why don't you do something useful," then handed him a flashlight.

With deft efficiency, the crew dug two deep holes in the sand beneath the derailed car, then filled them with wooden blocks. One man followed behind with heavy steel jacks, groaning *"Yah!"* as he swung them atop the wood. They cranked the jack and the train's belly popped and moaned as it rose. The air was thick with diesel exhaust and dust that hung like a white sheet against the engine's bright lights. When the diesel revved, fountains of fire and spark shot into the darkness.

The men cranked the jack. *"Yah! Yah!"* With each pump, the steel wheels lifted off the sand. Another man attached a winch to the undercarriage and anchored it to a thick acacia tree. The winch tightened—*"Polepole!"* they cried, easy, easy—and the train pulled left. *"Polepole."* The train jerked once, tipped off the jack, and landed perfectly on the rails. *"Yah!"*

Just like that, we were saved. The whole operation had taken just under two hours. And when it was finished, the crewmen collected their tools and walked back to their train for the long journey home. Once again, the railway inched forward into another day of life. We thanked the crew and waved good-bye, the same way we once waved at firefighters and don't anymore. And as we watched the crew disappear down the line into darkness, true heroes tonight, we could hear them calling into the windows of the *Rénové*, begging for something to eat.

As the *Rénové* lurched forward, I imagined the crew's nine-hour journey home, imagined them cold and hungry in their thin, blue coveralls as they rolled against the Katangan chill, and at every desolate station along the way, under every dim lamp in the night, having to stare at all that rotting food.

The insult would've been triple had they gone to Kabongo, where we arrived at dawn the next morning, our fifth day. There at the station was a giant pavilion stacked to the roof with fourteen thousand tons of maize. The white sacks rolled and cascaded like a snowdrift, two stories high at least.

The same farmers who'd harvested and bagged the maize now sat drinking it at the base, while others sprawled out atop the pile and slept.

"How long have you been here?" I asked one man.

"Thirteen months," he answered.

One of them scaled the heap with a pad and pencil and meticulously, almost obsessively, tried to count each sack, and I wondered how many times he did that in a day. Looking at the sacks more closely, I noticed they were all teeming with bugs.

While the farmers waited for their train, the *Rénové* dropped two carriages of passengers and picked up more. And in less than half an hour, we blew the whistle and pulled out.

(Later back in Kinshasa, I told the story of Kabongo to a friend at the U.S. embassy, about stacks of maize rotting like manna in the sun. My friend shook his head and laughed and said only this: "Forty million." That was how much the U.S. government sent Congo that year in food aid.)

Every company town we passed that day told the same story, stacks of grain bags waiting in waste. Meanwhile, someone said, Lubumbashi was experiencing a great shortage of maize. Most of it had to be imported from Zambia, causing the price to triple in the market. Nothing was connecting.

At Kitunda, angry farmers and rail workers jumped aboard the

Rénové and kept the train from leaving, not until the company paid them some back wages. A few workers even climbed aboard our carriage and stood at our door, holding their hats and saying with swallowed pride, "Please, if you can spare a little something."

At every station, whether we stopped there or not, dozens of people rushed to the platform just to watch us pass, as if to confirm the company was still alive. Despite not paying the crew and allowing their crops to spoil, the SNCC was still the mortar that bound the community, if only on promises and history.

In Kitunda, when Lionel casually repeated what a mechanic in Kamina had said, that the company was on its knees and could close within the year, one of the men in our doorway nearly jumped out of his shoes.

"*Close?*" he said, aghast. "What do you mean, *close?*"

"Nothing," Lionel said, quickly realizing his mistake. "Nothing—I was just being stupid."

By the time we got to Kabalo that night, the mountains of rot had become so common I hardly noticed, until I saw the swarm of people ready to lynch the *animateur*. A mob of farmers and traders and angry passengers now crowded around him, screaming a blue streak. I had to smile.

"I paid three thousand dollars to move this maize and it's still here," one farmer said. "And now you're asking me to pay again?!"

"The carriages are too crowded!" said one woman.

"Yeah," shouted another. "You call this an express train?"

The *animateur* just sat there doing nothing, looking exhausted and depressed. His pressed khaki suit and polished shoes had long vanished, replaced now by a stained white tank top and flip-flops. He wiped his sweaty brow with a handkerchief and panted in the heat like a tired hound. I realized he'd gone missing during the entire derailment. When the crowd finally parted, I walked over to say hello.

"The farmers are very mad," he said, wiping his neck. "They

want to know who's in charge, why won't we take their maize down to Kamina. Hey, I don't know who's in charge anymore. There are just no locomotives. Someone should fix this problem."

I asked him when he personally thought the goods would get delivered. Prompted by a serious question, he somehow summoned back a professional veneer. "The products will get delivered within the month . . . or maybe next year . . . but the SNCC . . . we're doing our utmost . . ." Finally he gave up even trying. "Look, that's just the way it is, okay?"

Kabalo was a key rail junction where the route continued north all the way to Kindu, and east to Kalemie, where barges and ferries still made regular trips across Lake Tanganyika. Kabalo itself sat on the banks of the Upper Congo River, known here as the Lualaba, but had limited use as a port. Just ninety kilometers north, near Kongolo, the broad river collapsed into a deep, narrow gorge known as the Gates of Hell, rendering navigation impossible. So from Kabalo, a small spit of track connected our route to the Great Lakes Railway, the network of rails and barges that ran all the way north to Kisangani, then downriver toward the Atlantic. It was still the main route for the informal traders riding the barges and rails.

Many traders aboard the *Rénové* were headed north to Kongolo to sell items on the river, so the officials decided to send the locomotive and two carriages on the eighty-five-kilometer journey. They would drop the passengers and return to Kabalo by dawn, then continue east to Kalemie. Pancha found us on the platform and gave us the choice of staying or riding along to Kongolo, just to kill the time.

We'd arrived at the point where the pleasant savanna finally slammed into the wall of jungle and vine. Being back on the river again, even in the dark, I could hear the familiar din of the forest. Mosquitoes now swarmed thick around my ears, and the tropical heat had smothered the crisp air of the plateau. We decided to ride along to Kongolo. At least there'd be forward motion and the breeze that came with it.

"Fine, I'll alert the crew," said Pancha. "But understand, the stretch of track is very bad. If anything happens, we'll have to call for help at Kamina, and depending on the problem, that could take weeks."

We boarded the second-class carriage they'd set aside for Kongolo and, to no one's surprise, waited two hours for the locomotive to be serviced. Our compartment was small and smelled like it had been used to breed horses. In the far corner, the floor was freshly scorched where someone had built a fire between Lubumbashi and here.

For two hours we sat there, swatting mosquitoes and sweating through our clothes, Basoko blues once again, but in another sink-hole way upriver, in the swamps where centuries ago the exploring caravans had been bogged and slain by disease, moved along by countless Africans who'd portered them and died with no name. All around I could hear the radios with their fading batteries, blasting that warbled anthem of the river that cooed like night birds for the restless presence. I could feel myself begin to recede, to tip and lose balance, slide toward the deeper darkness that had crept in from outside. It happened so quickly and took me by surprise; sometimes I just turned around and found it there—*ah, camarade*—unaware it had been waiting for me for days. And just as this was about to happen, as the twitch of despair crawled up my arm, the *Rénové* blasted her whistle down the tracks, so brash and strong it lifted the top of my skull and brought me back around. I looked out the window and saw her light tunneling down the tracks, so bright it burned away the mosquitoes and promised its own breeze.

"*On y va!*" screamed Pancha, and the train pulled away.

As those first breezes rinsed the cabin clean, Lionel and I sat on the bottom bunk taking turns with the bottle of bourbon, until finally the drink and gentle motion rocked us to sleep. I awoke two hours later when the train jolted to a stop. The cabin was now thick with the smell of deeper jungle, the tang of a million years of moist, dead earth. I felt something jerk violently next to me, then heard Lionel struggling, *"Fck-fck, get it off! Get it off!"* he shouted. He was swatting his head as if it were on fire. Clearing my eyes, I saw the walls around our bed were solid black and pulsing with flying insects. When he moved, they exploded.

Séverin leaped off the top bunk, screamed once, and ran out of the room flapping his arms. Lionel and I burst into the corridor, where the black swarms seemed to drip off the pale yellow lights. We buried our heads in our shirts and plowed through, feeling them snap between our fingers as we ran.

Outside, they swarmed even thicker around the lone fluorescent lamp of Kongolo station. A gang of fat geckos sat perched on the wall in the escaping light, snatching up the easy prey. The lamp was attached to the station pavilion, and beyond the light there was nothing—no candles, no torches, only the muffled voices of strange shadows. And somewhere in the outer darkness, the river hummed its savage music. Lionel turned to me, foreboding in his eyes, and said, "Well, mate, I believe we've arrived at the Gates of Hell."

Séverin smiled and popped him on the shoulder. "Welcome to Congo, bro."

Just then I heard a low moan, like a man crawling on his belly toward me in the dark. I spun around and heard it coming from a small building behind me. From a square hole in the wooden door, a hand came fingering the air. "Help me," the voice said. "Please help me. They've locked us up."

I shrieked a bit, then realized it was the station jail. The man inside the door said he'd been standing on the platform the day before, waiting for a freight train to arrive. But when the freight arrived, the police arrested many of the *clandestins* riding on top, and he'd been caught in the sweep. "They'll release me for fifteen hundred francs," the voice said. "Please, there are nine of us here."

Then someone emerged from the dark pavilion, another man. There'd been a terrible train accident a few kilometers away, he said. That same freight train, the one the prisoner had been waiting for, had left the station a few hours before and crashed nearby. Many people were riding on top. The station manager appeared and said it was the WFP train.

"The humanitarian train," said Lionel. "The one we were supposed to catch last week. That means—"

"Yeah," I said. "We would've been on the roof."

The carriages had disconnected from the locomotive as the train climbed a hill, sending everyone racing backward. The train was a runaway for nearly five kilometers before flipping over into the bush.

"There were people scattered all over the ground," the manager said. "We fear many are dead."

All I wanted to do was leave Kongolo. The place put the creep all over me. I then remembered I'd been there before, at that same station, back in August 2003. It was during the same trip as when I'd seen the trains in the Kalamie yard. At the time, the Rwandan-backed rebels who'd controlled the area had eased their grip following Rwanda's exit from Congo the year before. Fighting had mellowed and movement on the roads was slow, but finally possible. During that grace period, the WFP began a series of food deliveries by airplane into the region, and I'd tagged along. It was the first humanitarian mission in the region since the end of fighting, and many of the villages we visited that week were hanging to life, entire streets full of children with bowling-ball bellies and hair turned yellow from hunger. We'd flown into Kongolo our second day and I'd got out to walk around. The station, the jailhouse, all of it had been falling down then. Many families were living under the pavilion, children with ballooned bellies and peeling rashes running up and shooting me with finger pistols, holding the aim just a little too long.. *This is misery,* I'd thought. *This is what real misery looks like.*

I knew the station had been renovated since then, and the people

I now saw were healthier and not as desperate-looking. But that feeling of dread still hung on the humidity. It was one of those places like Mbandaka, where you seemed to cross through an invisible door you could never find again. Beyond Kongolo you entered the wild.

The crew finally motioned for us to reboard the train for our journey back. I felt a rush of relief to be leaving. But seconds later, the idling locomotive sputtered and stopped. "Oh, no," someone said. And when the engineer started the engine back up, it sounded as if someone had tossed a handful of screws into a clothes dryer. *No—!* Quickly we all crowded around the sick diesel, staring into its guts with horror and anticipation. *"Toujours!"* someone shouted. *"Toujours! Toujours! Toujours!"*

We peered inside the locomotive's cabin and saw the engineer with a flashlight in his teeth, jerking out wires and fuses as if he were pulling weeds. The locomotive refused to start. The engineer then came out and said flatly, "Technical problems. Who knows when we can fix this," then disappeared back inside, unaware of the weight of his words.

As we walked back toward the station, defeated once again, I heard it like a clap of thunder, like a dead fish swinging down from heaven to slap my face. Somewhere under the pavilion, barely alive on the battery's last drop, a radio was singing "Another Day in Paradise."

"Hey, guys," Séverin shouted. "It's Phil Collins!"

And I knew then, without a doubt, we would never leave Kongolo.

The three of us huddled on a bench in the dark and waited for the sun to rise, and when it did, we saw the Congo River sparkling like a glass-topped canyon in front of us. Across the river to the east, the purple outline of the Mitumba Mountains rose above the jungle. Lone fishermen rowed past one by one in long pirogues, standing tall in the stern and stabbing teardrop paddles into the still current, their black silhouettes drifting silently on the pink.

Near the water's edge lay the rusted hulls of old steamers and passenger ferries, more relics from the great industrial age, now half-sunk and dead in the mud. And up the bank near the station I found something unexpected: the remains of the legendary Ocean Pacific.

During the war when nothing moved on the rails but soldiers and guns, the Rwandan rebels had attached a single red railcar to a Caterpillar tractor engine and used it to ferry troops and supplies between the towns of Kongolo and Niemba. In 2000, two local mechanics had taken over the railcar—by now known to all as the Ocean Pacific—and used it instead to save their people. They ferried salt, soap, oil, and essential food items between these two market towns, and like the *toleka* taximen in Bumba, they risked life and limb to keep the villages alive and the economy breathing.

For years I'd heard their story like legend, but never figured out what the name meant or what had become of the men and the train. I'd even asked around a few years before, hoping to maybe catch a ride, but no one knew where it had gone. Now here it was at my feet, the words OCEAN PACIFIQUE handwritten in white paint on the corner of the car. The engine itself was missing. All that remained was the boxcar alone in the yard, with grass and weeds growing through a hole in its belly.

As I stood there, I watched a woman lead her young son by the hand toward the river. They stopped at the water's edge, where the river beyond them was covered in a frost of mist. The mother turned loose of the boy's hand to fetch some water, and when she did, the boy staggered backward and held out his arms, grasping for balance. I then noticed his eyes were badly infected and swollen shut.

"He woke up this morning like this," she said, her voice taut with panic. "We've been waiting here for days on a train to Lubumbashi, but I don't even know when it's coming."

It would be a week or longer, I thought, when ours returned.

But I didn't know for sure so I said nothing. The mother then bent down, scooped water into her hand, and let it drip over the boy's eyes. As the water rolled down his face and soaked his shirt, his head tilted skyward and arms reached for the river. And as the boy stood in his own darkness and mimicked the motions of the blind, his mother covered her mouth and cried.

Back at the station, the crew informed us the engine problems were far more severe than expected. We'll have to bring another locomotive, they said, and in my head I heard the nightmarish echo of Pancha saying, "If anything happens . . . *that could take weeks.*"

Don't worry, the engineer said, the locomotive was close and would arrive this afternoon.

"Which locomotive is it," asked Lionel.

"The one that crashed," said the engineer.

The locomotive was sitting just a few kilometers away on the tracks, where it had finally reunited with its wayward carriages, several of which were lying in the bush. Three people had been killed, two of them children, and nine others badly wounded. But that wasn't enough to keep the locomotive from working another day. In the end, we'd catch that WFP train after all.

We decided to get a few hours of sleep and found a larger cabin this time with four beds and no bugs. I slept deeply and woke up in a daze, our sixth day on the rails, soaked in sweat as the train cooked in the rising sun. The smell of sewage rose from the tracks and danced in the heat, and I knew we couldn't stay there all day.

I remembered seeing a white Land Rover at the station earlier, one of the only vehicles I'd seen in town, and knew it belonged to the Catholic procure. We could go there, I thought, and they'd have to take us in. There we'd find showers, hot food, and maybe even a beer. We'd wait in comfort until the train rode again.

But on our way to the procure, we had a spectacular realization. We remembered there was a UN base in Kongolo. And look, there it was just down the road from the station, an old colonial mansion with that powder-blue flag flapping in the wind, and two white SUVs with antenna the size of surf rods. The options now seemed immense.

Lionel gasped with joy. "Mate, if there's a Bangladeshi in there, we're laughing!"

"Oh, yes," I said. "Parathas and jam, chicken and rice. Tea, coffee, and biscuits."

There were no Bangladeshis, we discovered, but there were equally hospitable Nepalese, Peruvian, Bosnian, and Kenyan military observers who welcomed us like brothers. "What in hell are you guys doing *here*?" they asked. And we told them about the train. Well, take a rest, they said. Would you like a cold soda? *Yeah!* Shower? *Yeah!* Stay for lunch? *Definitely!*

We spent a pleasant afternoon with the UN officers, who seemed happy just to see new faces. The men had been on tour for six months and seen little action, an easy hitch compared to military observers like Juan whom I'd met in Bunia during the siege. The Kongolo officers acted mostly as town cops but without guns, settling disputes and facilitating any gunboys who wanted to surrender their weapons and join the good guys.

That morning, a few of them had visited the local hospital to check on the victims of the derailment. "It's dreadful in there," said the captain, a Bosnian with a thick, meaty face and hands like raw hams. "Their injuries are horrible, and there's not one X-ray machine in the whole town. No medicines, nothing." They discussed putting them aboard our train and sending them to Kalemie, then decided it posed a greater danger than the hospital itself.

The Peruvian had sent one of the servants into the market for some chickens for lunch, and just as we were about to feast, we heard a train whistle blow long and loud. It was our signal to leave, so we bid our UN pals good-bye and ran back to the station, where the cursed locomotive was rolling into the yard.

Pancha hurried us aboard a third-class compartment, saying,

"You guys barely made it." Then we sat another two hours. The splintered windows were missing their glass, and the tin walls and roof were covered in rust-eaten holes. I dozed in the heat and woke up to the river passing by as our train left the yard.

About ten minutes outside town, we passed the scene of the derailment. Luggage and clothing were scattered in the trees as if tossed by a cyclone. Several carriages were tipped into the high grass, while others stood upright with mountains of cargo still stacked on the roof. The three of us looked at each other in a way that said, *We would've died.*

And then, as if the ghosts themselves had appeared and winked at him from the wreckage, the driver punched the gas and the crazy train rocketed toward Kabalo atop the worst tracks in Congo. The carriage pitched and tipped as we sped faster and faster, and grown men bowed their heads and prayed. The scrub forest had grown too close to the track and now reached over both sides of the rails. As the train cut a path through the brambles, branches and tall grass snapped in the windows and sent clouds of pollen and dust swirling inside. I closed my eyes, and when I opened them again, I saw thick smoke filling the car just before we blasted through a brush fire that had jumped the tracks. *Whoosh!* And right as we exited the flames, rain started pouring through the windows.

We arrived back to Kabalo to find the station in a rage. "Where have you been?" people screamed, and I realized they knew nothing about the problems in Kongolo.

"We broke down," Pancha said.

"Toujours!"

The officials sent both locomotives to the station depot to be serviced, which took five more hours. I sat on the ground and watched the *animateur* pace the length of the platform, his eyes now cold as marble. He still wore the stained tank top and flip-flops and now held both the microphone and speaker in his arms. His assistant was nowhere to be seen. He paced the platform in the fading sun and locked his eyes on each official who passed, then at some chosen moment unleashed his torrent of rage. *"What's taking so long?"* he began, increasing his pace and breathing heavily, as if all that frustration would kill him if he didn't get it off. *"Why are we still here? Why won't SOMEONE ANSWER ME?"*

The shop boy had become a magpie for the masses, the voice of the people. The rage fit him well.

"These clients pay way too much to be treated this way! We're staying way too long in these stations. Why are we still in this station? I can't take it anymore! Hurry! Hurry!"

As I walked down the length of the train toward the engine, I saw that the passengers and cargo from the derailed WFP train had been transported to the *Rénové* for the journey to Kalemie. Luggage and cargo now spilled out the doors and was stacked against the windows. The corridor in the first-class compartment squawked with chickens tethered at the feet, and a pig stared me down from the doorway of second class. As I reached the front of the train, I saw dozens of *clandestins* perched on the roofs amid their grimy piles of luggage. I shone my light down the tracks and saw dozens more standing in the tall grass, wrapped in blankets with bundles on their heads, waiting to pounce on the train once it rolled out of the station.

The locomotive finally emerged from the depot and I understood what had taken so long. Every empty space in the diesel had been stuffed with merchandise—sacks of maize, salt, dried fish, everything that wouldn't fit inside the overstuffed carriages. Even the engineer's room was stacked to the ceiling with grain, so full the driver was pinned against his instrument panel.

Lionel yelled up to the engineer, something about the overloading, the *clandestins*, everything. The engineer shot him a look. "What do you expect us to do, *monsieur*?" he said. "Do you have a better idea? The last train to Kalemie was a month ago, and who knows when the next one will be."

I stood there taking in all that chaos—all the frayed nerves and strange energy of yesterday's crash still clinging to the clothes of those who'd survived it; the pigs and chickens; the *animateur* still screaming, *"People are shitting directly on the tracks now! Move this train before it gets any worse!"* Standing there before this scene, it was as if the *Rénové* weren't even a train anymore, but some living animal born of this very soil, now in a desperate struggle to either adapt or die.

All those dreams of the luxury express coasting atop the ashes, a harbinger of better times to come, all those dreams now seemed to fade. It had been such a tall order for the times. The *Rénové* had rolled out with such noble intentions, too, with men like Andre and Pancha trying so hard to make the experience real, all of them trying to resurrect some of that big-hearted pride and glory from days long gone. But in the end, not even the express train could outpace the avalanche of ruin. In the end, the *Rénové* became just another battered part in the vast faulty machine, a barge on wheels, just an ordinary train rolling through Congo.

But none of that seemed important now. Sure, it would've been cool to race through the old war zones eating steak with cold beer, and I might've let myself put that feather in my hat. But in the end, it didn't matter. In the end the *Rénové* still moved forward. In the end, it still took all those people home.

It rolled slowly out of Kabalo with a long, brassy whistle, then leaped into the darkness, as if to chase down all the time we'd lost. Faster on the straightaway, chewing down every second, so fast I gripped the table to keep from falling off the bed. Faster, as the driver pushed the limits of train and track, all that anxious energy tunneling under the floors and through the cars and pressing on his back like the tall stacks of maize, all the collective weight of hopes and wishes too strong a force to let him slow down.

Faster, so fast I began to lift off the bed from the sheer momentum. Faster, as we hit the curves with terror speed, tossing water buckets against the walls and sending a tidal wave down the corridor. (Somewhere inside a dark compartment, the *animateur* smiled.) Faster, listening for the dreaded snap of carriages leaving the loco, that fade of the whistle as we slid backward and down. Faster, as Nigerian psychedelic blasted loud on the speakers, Ofo the Black Company telling us, "Love is you, love is me." Faster, as the forest gave way to the dark plains of Tanganyika, the crunching guitar galloping with the blur of voices in villages racing by, or were they the screams of *clandestins* clinging to the roof? How on earth, I wondered, were they surviving this furious dash to the lake? Faster into the night we sped, hell-for-leather, the wheels grating like a kettle about to blow, until we reached that speed that would wash away all memories of ever having waited.

I woke to the same velocity churning under my bones and Séverin screaming, "Get up, look!" I shot upright, still fully clothed, the bed still made, and threw myself against the window, too dazed to understand what I was supposed to be seeing. "The Niemba Bridge!" he said. "There!" And sure enough, there it was, the little bridge that had reconnected Congo to the lake and its neighbors in the east. I stuck my head out the window just as we passed over the seemingly inconsequential span that had been repaired, nothing but a small patch of fresh tar and steel to distinguish it from the rest. That was it, that's all it took. One million dollars, and because of it, the train rumbled over the river and the route to Kalemie was open.

An hour later we hit the Mitumba hills, green as a golf course and iridescent in the morning mist. We crawled up the hills and raced down, winding along the course of the narrow Lukuga River. We passed villages buried behind the reeds, tossing *copo* bottles out the windows for the children to use as toys. In every village we passed, and in company towns the same, crowds of people rushed out to greet us as if heaven had split apart and laid down this train. The *Rénové* then let out a long-winded blast of the whistle, the longest and hardest yet, as if reaching up to punch the sky. Looking out the window I could see the blue, shimmering waters of Lake Tanganyika in the distance.

A minute later, we pulled into the Kalemie station.

Crowds were waiting to greet us on the platform. Women held up their arms as if to catch the train as it rolled to a stop, their faces igniting when they saw their loved ones in the windows. They shouted, *"Karibu Kalemie! Umeshafika!"* Welcome to Kalemie, you finally arrived! And ran to the doors.

All down the platform people were hugging their loved ones, looking around, then around again, as if to confirm they'd actually made it home. I rushed down the platform and looked for Fatuma and Jeanne, not wanting to miss them before they left to find their kids. I found them both near the customs office, where they waited to clear their belongings. Jeanne was planning to stay in town a week to gather some things, then set out across the lake, into Tanzania to search the villages for her kids. I wished her good luck and said good-bye.

Fatuma and her husband scanned the crowd outside the gates for any signs of family, and not seeing them, grabbed their things and went to find a taxi. They couldn't wait. "I'm so full of joy," she said, wiping a few tears that streamed down her cheek. "Did you know they held funerals for me and my husband? My children thought we were dead. And now here we are. I can't believe I'm standing here."

"You made it," I said, and hugged her good-bye.

As I turned away from Fatuma, two young girls raced past and threw their arms around a tall, gray-headed man behind me. The old man hadn't seen them coming, and the second those arms touched his body, his cheeks puffed once with air and he let forth a buckling sob. The girls pressed their heads against his chest, weeping and clutching him tightly, as if he were a ghost ready to spirit himself away. The whole scene almost dropped me to my knees.

The old man was named Albert Janga, a railroad employee who'd been working in Zambia when the war had started. He'd been stuck in the south ever since. His two girls, Gentille and Elena, were only babies when he left. "I haven't seen these girls in so long," he said, fighting to speak. "I could feel them here, even when I didn't see them. I could feel them near me."

The girls closed their eyes and squeezed their father. They held on and wept, and as their tears fell to the cobblestones below, they repeated over again this one thing: "You're home, you're home, you're home."

EPILOGUE

Three months later in September, in Providence, Rhode Island, where Ann Marie and I had moved the previous summer, I got an incredible piece of news. The Chinese government had announced a remarkable plan to refurbish thirty-two hundred kilometers of railway in Congo, and to construct a highway that would span the nation nearly top to bottom. In addition, they would build 31 hospitals, 145 clinics, 2 universities, and 5,000 government housing units across the country. The $5 billion loan for the project would be repaid in mining concessions, and everything, they vowed, would be completed in under three years. It was a project Leopold, Belgium, and Mobutu couldn't have imagined doing in over a century.

A new railway would connect Katanga's mines directly to the Atlantic Ocean by adding seven hundred kilometers of missing track between Ilebo and Kinshasa. That project had been part of Belgium's Ten-Year Plan, drafted in 1952 for the long-term development of the colony, but was abandoned at independence. The existing track from Lubumbashi to Ilebo—almost a century old—would be completely overhauled, and new locomotives and railcars would be purchased. The proposed thirty-four hundred kilometers of new road would include a fifteen-hundred-kilometer highway that would barrel through the jungle, connecting Kisangani to the Zambian border in the south.

The Chinese plan for Congo would rival some of the greatest public works projects in the world, and the new road and railway alone had the potential to turn the entire economy around, connect markets, reunite families, and create jobs—even while China settled in over the mines and satisfied its growing appetite. It would certainly move some of that maize, along with the countless people who were still stranded and waiting to go home.

Around this time, Séverin said good-bye to his family in Kinshasa and boarded a flight to Belgium. He arrived in Liège, where he moved into a small apartment near the university and began his degree in education and computer science. He'd never been out of Congo, and when I called him on the phone, he sounded a bit overwhelmed. "The sofa in my room," he said. "Do you know it also folds into a bed? And where I live, there are more than forty bridges! And the highways, wow. I've now seen the true world."

Seeing the true world, and looking down at Congo from its high vantage, had filled in many of those missing pieces in his mind. "I feel ashamed to see how we're so behind," he said. "And I see now how much of their wealth came from our country. The young people here don't even know what happened in Congo. All they seem concerned about is maximum pleasure." But Séverin was having no trouble adapting: soon after arriving in Liège, he'd caught the attention of a cute Italian exchange student, and as we spoke on the phone, she was on her way over.

In Ituri, Cobra Matata finally came down from Tchei and reported to Kinshasa in October. Two other Lendu leaders joined him, men who'd ordered the deaths of hundreds of civilians and reaped terror across the province for nearly a decade. One of them was Mathieu Ngudjolo, who'd led the May 2003 attack on Bunia. Like previous warlords who'd surrendered to the government, the three men were given rooms at the Grand Hotel, welcomed into the national army, and awarded the rank of colonel.

However, the surrender brought a much needed respite in Ituri, and the hills remained quiet throughout the fall. And with nothing happening between the gunboys and blue helmets, Johnny was transferred to MONUC headquarters in Bunia, where he spent much of his day sitting in an office. He'd gotten married a few months before, but his fiancée's father had insisted on a big religious wedding, so they'd eloped instead. He was lying in bed the night I called him, his wife asleep beside him. "She's putting me to work ever since I've been home," he said, laughing. "You were right, man. My fun is over."

With the hills quiet around Bunia, Pastor Marrion renewed his zeal to save the lost and broken. He set off down those roads he'd journeyed all his life, this time recruiting souls for a massive, healing revival, something he called the Ituri Gospel Crusade. "God has given me a new vision for Ituri and Congo," he said. "My chief, I was with Pygmies last weekend and God's *power* started moving *beyond* my expectations!"

In August, Lionel and Nathalie left Kinshasa and moved to Goma, where Nathalie took a new position with Save the Children. They arrived just as Congo's army launched a major offensive against rebel leader Laurent Nkunda in the hills above town, resulting in the heaviest fighting since the 1998 war. The heavy shelling emptied villages and towns across two provinces, and by early December the UN estimated nearly eight hundred thousand were displaced or living in camps across North Kivu. Doctors were treating hundreds of cases of cholera, and diarrhea and starvation were taking their usual toll. Cease-fires came and went, and the battles continued into the winter. The last I spoke with Lionel, his voice was tight and shaky and he was headed out the door. "Look, mate, got to run," he said. "It's really kicking off." I told him to take care of himself and be safe, but by then, he was already gone.

The crush and stress of working in Congo had finally chiseled away on Dave Lewis. In early November 2006, he'd gotten pinned down under heavy rocket and mortar fire between Kabila's and

Bemba's men, then found himself diving into a ditch two weeks later when it happened again. By the end of the month, he told his editors he was done. He flew out in mid-December, kicked around New Zealand for a few weeks, then resettled in Dakar. There he could regain perspective and watch Congo from afar, pop back every couple months for the longer view, but always have a ticket out. The last I heard he was trudging through Guinea-Bissau working on a documentary about cocaine smugglers, and happy for the fresh soil under his boots.

As for me, I was left with all these stories of the past four years just waiting to be sent home. I'd collected them from all those dreadful places, carried them with me over river and forest, through town and village, through a marriage and into our home. I'd memorized each one, and together they'd cut the road that now defined my life. So I gathered them up for one last hurrah, and led them down that path to the dark place at the end. And there on the trail sat the box I'd opened so long ago. I folded each story into the collective memory and placed them down inside, then closed the lid. And without looking behind me, I walked off into the trees.

AFTERWORD

In March 2008, a year after I caught my last flight out of Congo, I returned to a different Africa. I had started writing a book with a twenty-year-old Malawian kid named William Kamkwamba, who had transformed the life of his village by building windmills from old tractor and bicycle parts. He'd started his projects during one of the worst famines ever to fall upon the country, and William, then fourteen, was forced to drop out of school when his family couldn't pay the tuition—a problem that's endemic throughout the continent. Rather than sit still and wait out the famine, William visited a local U.S.-funded library, where he discovered an American science book with windmills on the cover. Over the next five months, he gathered up enough junk metal to actually build one of his own, which provided his family with electricity. He eventually built another that pumped water for irrigation.

After spending nearly five years in the great charnel house of Congo, where every dark cliché about the continent is made real, it was a relief to fly home with a good story to tell. Many guidebooks call Malawi "Africa for beginners," and it's certainly low-impact for the foreign traveler. Malawi was a poor place, one of the poorest in the world, and was ruled by an iron-fisted dictator for thirty years after gaining independence in 1964. But unlike Congo, it has no mineral wealth, and for that reason (among others), it's never been ravaged by war. There were no guns in the street, no bloodshot soldiers with beer breath and shaky fingers, no mobs waving clubs and machetes, no fearful eyes peering from the doorways. At Lilongwe's international airport, I breezed through immigration, got my bags, and walked to a taxi without losing money or even raising my voice. I took a minibus across the country and not once did it break down. People were friendly, the roads were generally smooth, and most towns even had cash machines. To me, Malawi was, well, *normal*, almost boring, and absolutely what I needed to restore my optimism in the African spirit.

I realized just how difficult Congo had been. I'd always screamed and cursed the evil logistics, but figured anything easier wouldn't be as fun. Talking to the people I met in Malawi, most of them approachable and relaxed, I realized how uncomfortable the Congolese had seemed around most strangers—always warm and welcoming, but never truly off guard. As a writer, I want to connect deeply with the people I'm profiling, but I found that in Congo, a true connection was almost impossible because of all those layers, pressed and pounded hard by lifetimes of trauma, distrust, and desperation. Maybe it was different for other writers, who spoke the language better or who didn't put much stock in personal interaction. But that didn't describe anyone I knew there. I started to understand why I had lived in a constant wide-loop swing of hope and depression the entire time. With each visit or move, I was hoping to interact on some deeper personal level, and each time I left, I just seemed to have more unanswered questions.

Working in Malawi helped me realize something more significant, too: that a current generation of resourceful and savvy young entrepreneurs—already tagged the "cheetah generation"—are the ones who can hope to deliver Africa from poverty, not the politicians and aid workers we've relied on all these years. The Internet is now filled with blogs and Web sites of Africans who are using emerging and innovative mobile phone and Web technology to improve the quality of life for their people, instead of waiting on their ineffective governments. They're finding their own positive stories, and U.S.-based conferences such as TED and POP!Tech, which pull these great minds from obscurity and allow them to share their projects with an audience of tech innovators, scientists, and idea generators, as well as corporate leaders and potential investors, are doing wonders in broadcasting them to a larger audience. The guard is changing, and as reporters and advocates for the poor we must support and celebrate these efforts. These individuals have given us a call to fundamentally transform the way the world views the "dark continent." While it's still our responsibility to report the death and brutality wherever it unfolds, it's our equal duty to grab hold these small, flickering lights and demonstrate that life does exist, then nurture this starved brilliance with diligence. The great South African physicist Neil Turok believes the next Einstein will come from Africa, and I'm not too cynical to join in his dream.

But while I worked elsewhere in Africa, encouraged by these stories from Malawi, Kenya, South Africa, and Ghana, the situation in Congo continued to deteriorate. In October 2008, Laurent Nkunda finally made his play for North Kivu, taking the town of Rutshuru and threatening to go all the way to Goma, again justifying his actions by accusing Kabila's government of supporting Rwandan Hutu rebels and persecuting the local Congolese Tutsi (true on both counts). As usual, the blue helmets scrambled to contain the offensive, but were handily outnumbered. The Congolese army was defeated at nearly every junction and took up old habits of rape and pillage in its retreat—the same old story. A November 4 battle with pro-government Mai Mai militia briefly pushed the rebels out of a village called Kiwanja, so they retaliated by slaughtering one hundred fifty of its residents. By December, over a million people were hiding in the mountains or living in camps, where cholera quickly claimed hundreds.

To my colleagues, and to the Congolese I talked with, the

fighting—aside from the Kiwanja massacre, the largest in North Kivu in years—seemed no worse than those of the previous fall, or the year before that, or the year before that. Murderous assaults and rebel troop movements had become routine cycles of nature, like Mt. Nyiragongo waking up to smoke and billow above Goma. But for whatever reason (I never could think of one that properly explained why), the recent spate of violence had received worldwide publicity like none I'd ever seen.

Beginning in October, the *New York Times* began to feature the fighting in its international section, running a handful of front page stories and lengthy updates in between. I began getting phone calls and e-mails from newspapers across America and from as far off as the United Kingdom and Venezuela. I spoke to radio stations and sat on panels, mainly just explaining to people what it was like to work there.

One event, held not long after Ann Marie and I had come back to Brooklyn, was a fundraiser for the playwright Eve Ensler's V-Day campaign, which had turned its vigorous energies toward helping raise awareness about the scourge of rape in eastern Congo. The event was held at a chic furniture store near Union Square in New York City. Inside, the ceiling dripped with crystal chandeliers, and the floor was covered with exotic, indigenous rugs and furniture. Standing at the door, I feared I'd read the address wrong. The place was packed with people, mostly wealthy-looking Manhattanites, middle-aged women who dressed modestly but wore thirty-carat stones on their fingers. They sipped wine and mingled over piped-in African music. I heard a conversation between two women about a recent safari.

Then Ensler, a severe-looking woman with short-bobbed hair and bright-red lipstick, stood up and began to describe a recent trip to the Kivus. She spoke about rape victims she'd met in Panzi clinic outside Bukavu, where I'd worked two years before. She held back nothing. The detail she used was straight out of my notes, about women being mutilated with the ends of gun barrels, machete blades, and sticks; about young girls so damaged they urinated and defecated on themselves daily.

For some odd reason, perhaps out of embarrassment, my first reaction was to laugh and cover my mouth, as if I'd just heard a raunchy joke in front of my grandmother. I'd never heard anyone really speak about these things outside Congo—certainly never in such company, and never with the detail and hurt that only comes from having been to the place and having absorbed its myriad pain. I'd given up talking about this stuff, partly because the blank stares and dismissals ("Oh, isn't that awful?") just made me angry. So sitting in the audience that night, I braced for the collective recoil, the raised eyebrows and shaking heads. But instead, I saw people crying, and when it was finished, most of them pulled out their checkbooks. Something had changed.

At the peak of this surge in press coverage, the UN Group of Experts released a report stating that Rwanda had assisted Nkunda in Congo. It found not only that Rwanda had contributed financially and allowed Nkunda's forces to recruit across the Rwandan border, but that weapons had been smuggled through Rwanda, and former Rwandan army officers had also joined ranks with the rebels. To anyone who followed this story, this was no surprise, only a welcome vindication.

About 50 percent of Rwanda's economy was floated by foreign aid. The daily news reports in American and European papers, plus the UN's report, now put that in jeopardy. Both Sweden and the Netherlands cut funding to Rwanda, and the United States and Britain—its biggest Western backers—began placing greater pressure on President Paul Kagame's government, yet never threatened to cut their financial support.

The press then began reporting an apparent split in Nkunda's rebel movement. One of Nkunda's lieutenants, Bosco Ntaganda, was quoted as saying he'd just ousted his boss and taken over as commander. But Bosco was no idealistic leader. Bosco was an opportunist, a loot-monger, a degenerate with a trail of bones behind him; he seemed to poison whatever place he went.

In 2003, he had been a lieutenant to Thomas Lubanga in the Hema militia in Bunia, working under the nickname "The Terminator." In 2005, Lubanga was arrested by UN and Congolese authorities and surrendered to the International Criminal Court in the Hague. Out of a job with the Hema, Bosco (by then also wanted by the ICC for conscripting child soldiers) had switched sides and worked with Mathieu Ngudjolo, commander of the Lendu in Bunia. In 2006 Ngudjolo was arrested in his turn and handed over to the ICC, but by this time Bosco had already moved south and linked with Nkunda. The two men had both served together under Kagame as rebel soldiers in the Rwandan Patriotic Army, helping crush the 1994 genocide. In fact, it was Bosco who'd ordered the massacre in Kiwanja, and had pressed Nkunda to push onward to Goma after taking Rutshuru. Nkunda had instead stopped at the outskirts, a move favored by his Rwandan sponsors, who were under heavy international pressure to straighten out their act in Congo.

In late January 2009, Rwandan appeased its Western friends by apprehending Nkunda and ostensibly placing him under arrest. The sudden double-cross was shocking, but it wasn't the first surprise that month. A week prior, about four thousand Rwandan troops had marched into Congo, as they'd done twice before with devastating results. But this time, the invasion was part of an apparent agreement between Kagame and Kabila to join their forces and eliminate the Hutu militia together, a kind of end-all blitz into the mountains. (The Congolese people and its parliament were told nothing of the deal until their former enemies were across the border.) After several days in country, forces intercepted Nkunda on the Rwandan side of the border. Analysts believed Nkunda's arrest was a prerequisite for Congo's allowing Rwandan forces to enter the country to hunt

Hutu rebels. As for Bosco, he agreed to integrate all of Nkunda's remaining rebel force into the Congolese army, presumably in exchange for something. Some assumed Kabila's government would help him avoid arrest by the ICC, or at least make the promise before handing him over themselves when he finally proved worthless.

On the surface, it appeared that Rwanda's sudden willingness to work with Kabila's government had all but ended thirteen years of war between the two countries, both conventional and proxy. It was certainly a major milestone, possibly one of the biggest in the history of the Great Lakes conflict. But if you'd seen the Dow Jones article earlier in the month—that one that reported Rwanda's mining sector output had grown 20 percent in 2008, and that mining for minerals such as coltan, tin, and tungsten accounted for about 40 percent of its total export revenue earnings in 2007—the "agreement" between Kagame and Kabila had a whiff of the same old, tired scam: re-ignite ethnic tensions to justify a troop surge, then appease the foreign donors with declarations of solidarity and promises to play nice. Once the heat was off, continue to rape at will—this time, with Kabila's presumed consent. Getting rid of Nkunda was just another step in the rebel-leader shuffle that Rwanda and Uganda had been doing in Congo for years (later reports indicated Nkunda wasn't even placed in custody), and will continue to do until Western leaders finally shed their genocide guilt and start poking around behind the fronds.

It reminded me of a conversation I once had with the U.S. ambassador while living in Kinshasa. I mentioned how the U.S. government, after doing nothing about the genocide, had helped beef up Kagame's army in 1996— just in time for them to invade Congo and overthrow Mobutu (slaughtering tens of thousands of Hutu civilians along the way). The ambassador had stopped the interview, apparently revolted, and indignantly denied that such a thing had ever happened. It was as if he were telling me that when I stepped outside the sky would be pink.

Whatever Rwanda's intentions were this time around (apparently two earlier invasions and a six-year occupation hadn't been enough to lick the Hutu rebels), it was all the same to the Congolese. More fighting would only cause more displacement, which would only lead to more dead children, and God knows the red soil had swallowed enough of them.

The only way a real solution can come is politically, with Rwanda agreeing to allow Hutu militia to return without fear of reprisals, since a large majority of the rebels were too young to even have participated in the genocide anyway. As I write this, a bill is on the floor of the U.S. Senate, proposed by senators Sam Brownback and Richard Durbin, that would work to certify all minerals exported from Congo, much the way "blood diamonds" from Sierra Leone had been. Certification and transparency would slow the black-market trafficking of coltan, gold, tungsten, diamonds, and tin, and in turn cut off the flow of funding to gunboy militias, most of which depend on forced slave labor to excavate the mines. Legislation would be a great start in finally addressing the mineral issue, which has been and will continue to be the core of this conflict.

Political pressure must also be placed on Kabila to take responsibility for his rogue security forces. The army must be sufficiently paid, trained, and equipped with proper boots, uniforms, and weapons. The soldiers should have better access to health care, clean water, and food on the front lines. And a better job must also be done integrating former militia into the army, because for years their only indoctrination has been to put on an official uniform. If the U.S. and British governments are as concerned about peace in Central Africa as they report, they must be willing to hinge all foreign aid on Congo meeting these requirements.

And then perhaps some healing can start.

While I was in New York working on my other book, speaking on panels and watching the old patch unfold, Lionel was also home and not the least bit happy. A few months before, he and Nathalie had returned to London when her work contract had expired. Both were burned out and in need of a break. Goma for a year had been like the inside of a pressure cooker. In August, they'd rolled through New York on their way home and stayed with me and Ann Marie, enjoying dinners and wine and long walks through the city. They spent a couple weeks in Montana with another friend, driving across the West, before returning to Europe.

By November, though, both were getting calls about working again in Congo. Nathalie had chosen to stay in the U.K., but Lionel was anxious to get back, if just for a while. The world had quickly become dull.

"Do you know what I did for work yesterday?" he said on the phone one night. "I took photos of mobile phones, then waited all afternoon outside Parliament. I'm cracking up, mate. Goma was tough, but I miss the real work."

As we spoke about where he'd live and how long he'd stay, the small details I once cherished, I found myself unable to tune in. Before we hung up the phone he asked me the same thing my wife had that morning.

"So with it kicking off, I bet you're itching to get back?"

I didn't even have to think. "Nah," I said. "I'm done."

As the stories trickled in about Nkunda's arrest and subsequent joint-offensive, I saw a photo of Congolese troops manning a checkpoint near Goma. It was pouring rain, one of those jungle storms that drill the thoughts straight out of your mind. The road was gushing like a river. You could almost hear the miserable silence. I didn't even have to close my eyes to feel it, or to smell the smoke from the wet-wood fires and the black exhaust from rattletrap trucks. The recall was always automatic and instant, like the children's music or the way sunsets seemed to explode across the river. Congo had given me all those things, and not a day went by when I didn't think of that place.

As I stared into the photo, I caught the byline at the bottom right-hand corner. It was Lionel Healing. For once, I was glad it was someone else.

January 26, 2009
New York City

ACKNOWLEDGMENTS

Special thanks goes to Kiley Lambert, the first person to read these stories and help shape them in their raw and nascent form, and Roger Hodge at *Harper's*, who first gave them a home. Anneke Van Woudenberg at Human Rights Watch, one of the foremost experts on the Congo conflict, graciously read over much of this material and offered invaluable advice, and to her I'm grateful. Thanks to Susan Linnee, Ellen Knickmeyer, and Todd Pitman of (and formerly of) the Associated Press, all great bosses and friends alike. Also, thanks to my agent Heather Schroder at International Creative Management and to my editors Colin Dickerman and Nick Trautwein at Bloomsbury, whose thoughtful and poignant insight into the work made it twice the read, and me a better writer. And most of all, thanks to the many proud people of Congo who offered their hospitality, friendship, and told me their stories, mainly with hopes that such tragedy would never be repeated again. This book is for them.

A NOTE ON SOURCES

Most of what appears in the book came from my own reporting and the countless interviews I've conducted with residents and officials over the past four years. To fill the gaps in history, I relied on a variety of sources. Some of the background material on Ituri came from several reports written by human rights groups over the past decade. The International Crisis Group's (ICG; www.crisisgroup .org) "Scramble for the Congo: Anatomy of an Ugly War," published in 2000, gives an extensive breakdown of the conflict and its players. And two reports by Human Rights Watch (HRW; www .hrw.org) are must-reads for anyone interested in the link between minerals and war: "Ituri: Covered in Blood" (2003) and "The Curse of Gold" (2005). I also took material about the pillaging of resources from *The African Stakes of the Congo War,* edited by John F. Clark (Palgrave Macmillan, 2002).

For the general history on Congo, I drew mainly on *In the Footsteps of Mr. Kurtz: Living on the Brink of Disaster in Mobutu's Congo* by Michela Wrong (Fourth Estate, 2000), a vivid, sharply written journey through the last days of Mobutu; *King Leopold's Ghost* by Adam Hochschild (Houghton Mifflin, 1998) is the definitive account of the rubber atrocities and gives a startling, even cinematic view into Leopold's lust for power; and Tim Jeal's biography *Stanley: The Impossible Life of Africa's Greatest Explorer* (Yale University Press, 2007) offers the most authoritative, reliable rendering thus far of Stanley's life and travels. Stanley's own accounts of his trans-African journey, *Through the Dark Continent: Volumes One and Two* (Harper & Brothers, 1878), were somewhat exaggerated for his readers, as Jeal demonstrates, but a spellbinding read nonetheless. I also drew from Joseph Conrad's *Congo Diary* (Doubleday, 1978); Peter Forbath's excellent *The River Congo* (Harper & Row, 1977); Robert B. Edgerton's *The Troubled Heart of Africa: A History of the Congo* (St. Martin's Press, 2002); *The Irish Army in the Congo, 1960–1964: The Far Battalions* edited by David O'Donoghue (Irish Academic Press, 2005); *Rebels, Mercenaries, and Dividends: The Katanga Story* by Smith Hempstone (Frederick A. Praeger, Ltd., 1962), and my trusty field book, *Traveler's Guide to the Belgian Congo and Ruanda-Urundi* (Tourist Bureau for the Belgian Congo and Ruanda-Urundi, 1951).

Further background on Mobutu and Kabila's government came from news reports and ICG's 2006 report "Escaping the Conflict Trap: Promoting Good Governance in Congo" and HRW's "Elections in Sight: Don't Rock the Boat?" (2005). Information about mining and logging came from interviews, news reports, and two recent studies: Greenpeace's 2007 report on the timber trade, "Carving Up the Congo" (www.greenpeace.org), and Global Witness' report on the state of the mining sector, "Digging in Corruption," published in 2006 (www.globalwitness.org).

Background on the rail networks came from interviews, news reports, and a beautiful treasure I picked up while in Lubumbashi: the two-volume *Le Rail au Congo Belge* (G. Blanchart & Cie, 1993 and 1999). Other information came from various reports: "Africa's Strategic Minerals During the Second World War" by Raymond Dumett (*The Journal of African History* 26, no. 4 [1985]) and "The Port of Lobito and the Benguela Railway" by William A. Hance and Irene S. Van Dongen (*Geographical Review* 46, no. 4 [1956]).